NEGRITUDE
AND LITERARY CRITICISM

Recent Titles in
Contributions in Afro-American and African Studies

Alice Walker and Zora Neale Hurston: The Common Bond
Lillie P. Howard, editor

A Journey into the Philosophy of Alain Locke
Johnny Washington

Time in the Black Experience
Joseph K. Adjayé

Folk Poetics: A Sociosemiotic Study of Yoruba Trickster Tales
Ropo Sekoni

Public Policy and the Black Hospital:
From Slavery to Segregation to Integration
Mitchell F. Rice and Woodrow Jones, Jr.

Aunt Jemima, Uncle Ben, and Rastus:
Blacks in Advertising, Yesterday, Today, and Tomorrow
Marilyn Kern-Foxworth

A World of Difference: An Inter-Cultural Study of Toni Morrison's Novels
Wendy Harding and Jacky Martin

African Market Women and Economic Power:
The Role of Women in African Economic Development
Bessie House-Midamba and Felix K. Ekechi, editors

African Labor Relations and Workers' Rights:
Assessing the Role of the International Labor Organization
Kwamina Panford

The Gong and the Flute: African Literary Development and Celebration
Kalu Ogbaa, editor

Masters of the Drum: Black Lit/oratures Across the Continuum
Robert Elliot Fox

Africa's Agenda: The Legacy of Liberalism and Colonialism
in the Crisis of African Values
Harvey J. Sindima

NEGRITUDE
AND LITERARY CRITICISM

The History and Theory
of "Negro-African" Literature in French

Belinda Elizabeth Jack

**Contributions in Afro-American and African Studies,
Number 178**

GREENWOOD PRESS
Westport, Connecticut • London

Library of Congress Cataloging-in-Publication Data

Jack, Belinda Elizabeth.
    Negritude and literary criticism : the history and theory of
    "Negro-African" literature in French / Belinda Elizabeth Jack.
        p.   cm. — (Contributions in Afro-American and African
    studies, ISSN 0069-9624 ; no. 178)
    Includes bibliographical references and index.
    ISBN 0-313-29511-5
    1. African literature (French)—20th century—History and
criticism.   2. African literature—Africa, Sub-Saharan—History and
criticism.   3. Negritude (Literary movement).   4. Blacks in
literature.   I. Title.   II. Series.
PQ3980.J33   1996
840.9′896—dc20   95-35714

British Library Cataloguing in Publication Data is available.

Library of Congress Catalog Card Number: 95-35714
ISBN: 0-313-29511-5
ISSN: 0069-9624

First published in 1996

Greenwood Press, 88 Post Road West, Westport, CT 06881
An imprint of Greenwood Publishing Group, Inc.

Printed in the United States of America

The paper used in this book complies with the
Permanent Paper Standard issued by the National
Information Standards Organization (Z39.48-1984).

10 9 8 7 6 5 4 3 2

For
my mother and my father

Contents

Acknowledgments

My primitive interest in Francophone African and Caribbean writing was first encouraged by Clive Wake; I remain immensely grateful to him. The doctoral thesis on which this book is based was supervised by Toby Garfitt. His careful attention to detail and scholarly rigour are examples to which I continue to aspire. I would also like to acknowledge his enormous kindness. The British Academy, and St John's College, Christ Church, and the faculty of Medieval and Modern Languages, Oxford, all provided generous support. My editor at Greenwood, Nina Pearlstein, has been exemplary. I would like to thank colleagues, friends, and family, who have helped me in all kinds of ways; and especially to thank Allan, for always believing that what I was doing mattered.

NEGRITUDE
AND LITERARY CRITICISM

Introduction

The aim of this study is threefold. First, to follow the development of secondary discourses concerned with the body of literary works known (in one instance) as "Negro-African literature in French." Secondary discourses include works of theory and criticism, literary histories, essays and articles, and, to a lesser extent, prefaces and introductions to anthologies. In tracing the emergence of a now substantial body of secondary works, emphasis is placed on the dominant phases discernible, and on the range of approaches exemplified.

Second, the book explores the relationship between the area defined by secondary discourses and the criteria of evaluation proposed by them. Frequently this relationship is an "incestuous" one (one that should be proscribed on grounds of too close relation) which gives rise to what is described as a major "critical tautology." For example, where the "area" is defined as "Negro-African literature in French," literary works falling within it are then explored, and in some cases evaluated (either implicitly or explicitly), in terms of the degree of "Negro-Africanness" which they display; "neo-Africanness" is required of significant "neo-African literature," and so on. Whereas most "autonomous" literatures are marked by national, geographic, linguistic, and racial homogeneity, the literature explored by the secondary texts under scrutiny emanates from a less stable context and is governed by more problematic characteristics. It is this instability of the literature as an obviously autonomous body of texts which invites the "critical tautology" mentioned above. For it is a literature constantly in search of its own coherence, of its own identity. It is a literature permanently under threat of "annexation" by other literatures, French literature in particular. Checking the shifting boundaries of this literature, and considering the ways in which the criteria of evaluation proposed by secondary discourses are affected by those changing boundaries, provides a focus for the account constructed here. It is for this reason that the emphasis is on works of a general and theoretical kind rather than on studies of individual authors. For it is the former that, in establishing the criteria of the literature's autonomy, coherence, specificity, and so on, provide the framework within which studies of individual authors take place.

Third, and intimately associated with the dialectic between definition and evaluation, the role of Negritude is monitored in the multifarious guises in which it appears in secondary texts. Few studies of Negro-African literature avoid the term "Negritude," but each time it is exploited in critical discourse it acquires a further layer of critical significance which subsequent studies have to take into account.

The seminal study of Negro-African literature in French, Lilyan Kesteloot's *Les Ecrivains noirs de langue française: naissance d'une littérature*, published in 1963 and translated as, significantly, *Black Writers in French: A Literary History of Negritude,* argued that a new literature had come into being:

> With the awakening of the African continent, demanding its freedom, it is time to recognize that black writers of the French language form a comprehensive literary movement. As early as 1948, "Black Orpheus," Jean-Paul Sartre's brilliant preface to L. S. Senghor's *Anthologie de la nouvelle poésie nègre et malgache de langue française* ["Anthology of the New Negro and Malagasy Poetry in French"] saluted the accession of the poets of "Negritude." Today, everything about this poetry, its abundance and quality, its diversity of style and form, its incontestable originality, prompts us to consider these neo-African authors as creators of an authentic literary school. [p. 7]

The particular field of study outlined by Lilyan Kesteloot, "Negro-African literature of French expression," continues to be proposed as a coherent area, made up of a homogeneous corpus of texts. Since Kesteloot's study, however, numerous other secondary discourses have defined or described different "areas," which, they have argued, offer equally coherent fields of study: "neo-African literature," "Negro literature," "African literature," and so on. As in a complex Venn diagram, some texts belong within the area delineated by numerous intersecting circles, while others fall only within one. Léopold Sédar Senghor's poetry, for example, falls within the area of "Senegalese literature," "African literature," "African literature in French," "Neo-African literature," and, more problematically, the "literature of Negritude," itself proposed as a distinct and coherent "literature."[1]

Thus, typological terms of secondary discourses are not simply descriptive terms; they also operate explicitly or implicitly as criteria of evaluation. This is most obviously and explicitly the case where cultural and/or racial criteria are used to define the area, on the one hand, and where what is foregrounded in the secondary discourse is precisely the cultural and/or racial markers, on the other. The way in which Senghor uses the criteria of Negritude (in its Senghorian form) as both typological characteristics of the literature, on the one hand, and criteria of evaluation, on the other, is an important example of this and is considered further in chapter 4.

Senghor's method is relatively explicit. What is more problematical is the way in which Negritude (in numerous guises) surreptitiously conditions critical discourses. Furthermore, Negritude's own instability further complicates any attempt to expose the methods of the secondary discourse. This argument is difficult to summarize in advance of its fuller presentation.[2] The difficulty is partly a matter of historical perspective and the multifarious historical guises in which Negritude exists. While in many of its versions the idea of Negritude is closely associated with a state of being, a specific consciousness, the actual history of the idea itself reveals a quite remarkable instability. Partially reconstructing that history will be implicit in the examination of the secondary discourses associated with the wider literature (marked here as "Negro-African literature in French") within which the literature of Negritude finds its place.

What previous commentators have failed to recognize is that the history of Negritude bears witness to the fact that there is no original base doctrine to be unproblematically uncovered, and in relation to which all other definitions can be seen as simple derivatives or perversions. Commentaries on Negritude are often drawn to investigation of its "origins," that is, to the moments of its first articulation in the texts of Aimé Césaire and Léopold Sédar Senghor, in particular.[3] The quest for synoptic sense, based on their texts, and the abundance of widely differing commentaries subsequently produced on those canonical texts, itself testifies to a history of the continuous adaptation and transformation of those origins. Thus the idea of Negritude cannot be read independently of the numerous commentaries to which it has given rise, and in which it is now diversely embodied. The actual history of Negritude is not the principal concern of the study, but a recognition of its historical character—and the significant effect of this on secondary discourse—is an indispensable feature of the approach adopted here.

A further consequence of the literature's instability as an autonomous subject is that the bibliography of secondary works concerned with it (in all its different formulations) is large. However, because publication has taken place in numerous different countries—in France, Francophone and Anglophone Africa, French Canada, and the United States, in particular—there has been very considerable repetition and overlap between studies.

The history of secondary works here takes account of canonical works (that is, those that have dominated the scholarly debate). Introductions of a seminal kind are treated; later introductory works that offer few original insights and textbooks that, equally, offer little that is new, are the most obvious examples of what has been ignored.

For critical discourse to be valid (and indeed useful in terms of assisting the processes of reading, understanding, interpreting, and judging the literary text) it must make its own operations and assumptions visible. Whether or not Althusser's proclamations concerning the ideological nature of every act of reading (and thereby every act of criticism and indeed writing) are accepted, the context in which "Negro-African literature in French" came into being and now exists is one in which the ideological is often paramount. Riffaterre claims that "the poetic phenomenon, given that it is linguistic, is not simply the message, the poem, but the whole act of communication" (Riffaterre, 1971, pp. 325–326). The literary text issues from a writer (the "place of emission") and is directed to one or more readers (the "place of reception"). The text therefore belongs within a process of communication. This is self-evident. With the risk of oversimplification, it is clear that a literature whose historical conditions of "emission" and "reception" have (at least temporarily) separated the "place of writing" from the "place of reading" poses peculiar problems for literary criticism. Furthermore, in the case of the amorphous literature under scrutiny here, the "place of writing" is a "black place," and the "place of reading," in many cases, a "white place." In 1956, L. S. Senghor wrote in the postface to *Ethiopiques*: "We write primarily, I don't say exclusively, for the French of Africa" (p. 107).[4] Senghor presumably meant those Africans who had French citizenship, but the expression "Français d'Afrique" was ambiguous in 1956; its ambiguity is symptomatic of a wider ambiguity concerning the "place of reception" of the literature considered here.

Alternatively, the aim of the literary-critical activity (according to what the French would term "la lecture universitaire traditionnelle") may be regarded as being to lay bare "the true meaning of the text" or "what the author sought to express." Even if these are the premises of the literary-critical enterprise, the historical, political, social, racial, geographical, and linguistic features of the literature and its own instability as an "autonomous literature" (as evidenced by the instability of its definition and literary history) create numerous and complex problems for literary criticism.

There are further distinctive and unusual features of "Negro-African literature in French" which have a powerful influence on criticism—in particular, the direct political involvement of so many of its writers and their contribution not only to literature but also to the debate surrounding it. Whether what is at issue is "what the author sought to express" or "from where and to whom the discourse speaks" (to take two critical extremes), Senghor's political status is relevant. Whether or not Michel Hausser is correct in his interpretation of how Senghor is read, his point that he is read differently today from the 1950s must be taken into account:

> *Hosties noires* and *Ethiopiques* haven't changed since 1948 and 1956, but these poems were then read as though coming from an artisan of decolonization and of liberation; they are read today as the sign of a politician whose liberal declarations poorly disguise his conservatism. [Hausser, 1979, pp 9–19]

The debate surrounding "Negro-African literature in French," contained within various secondary discourses—literary histories, prefaces to anthologies, articles, essays, theses, introductory manuals, and so on—has always been controversial. This can be explained, in part, politically. However, as with any new literature, secondary discourses have played a crucial "prescriptive" role, either explicitly or implicitly, directing the literature toward particular ends, demanding of its authors particular languages, forms, or attitudes, for example. Just as the precise nature of the relationship between the criteria for the definition of the literary area and the criteria of its evaluation has to be exposed, so the influence of secondary discourse on the constantly evolving literary production itself has to be borne in mind.

Although a number of articles focusing on the criticism and reception of "Negro-African literature in French" have appeared in various periodicals over the years, a colloquium organized by the Université de Paris III in 1978, *Critique et réception des littératures négro-africaines*, was the first important indication that a systematic discipline would develop out of this subject. Three further works should also be mentioned: Bernard Mouralis's *Littérature et développement: essai sur le statut, la fonction et la représentation de la littérature négro-africaine d'expression française* (Paris, 1984), Locha Mateso's *La Littérature africaine et sa critique* (Paris, 1986), and Rand Bishop's *African Literature, African Critics: The Forming of Critical Standards 1947–1966* (Westport, CT, 1988). Although there is an area of overlap between these three works and this book, there are important differences.

Mouralis's publication developed out of his thesis prepared for the Université de Lille III. It retains many of the characteristics of the French doctoral thesis whose principal drawback lies perhaps in its length. In covering a large and complicated area, his work fails to retain an overall coherence of argument. It contains a considerable amount of information, but its multidisciplinary approach means that material is discussed in relatively self-contained sections. It proposes "two interpretations of the African reality: the colonial ideology and the nationalist ideology" and discusses "colonization considered as a sub-culture." The "evolution" and "characteristics of colonial teaching up until independence" are examined in terms of "colonial culture" and "literary creation," and it traces the way in which Negro-African writers were drawn into the metropolitan literary sphere. The second section of the book examines three criteria in the "definition of Negro-African literature": "the criterion of language," "the cultural criterion" (in terms of "the image of Negro-African culture in Senghor and Césaire"), and "the ideological criterion." He provides a brief history of "exotic texts," "colonial literature," "ethnographic literature," and "texts of African origin." Different political contexts relevant to "the elaboration of a discourse on Negro-African literature" are also proposed: "Pan-African," "Afro-Asiatic," and "Tri-continental." The role of *Présence Africaine* and the various Congresses and Debates of the 1950s and 1960s are also examined.

From this relatively brief outline of *Littérature et développement*, it will be clear that there are sections of Mouralis's book which pertain to a study of the "The History and Theory of 'Negro-African' Literature in French." However, the bias of Mouralis's work is toward the broadly "social-scientific," and thus the "literary" is often obscured. As its subtitle indicates, Mouralis's work is a series of detailed essays on what can be broadly described as the sociology of Negro-African literature in French. The questions to which the work addresses itself are:

> To what does one refer when one speaks of "African literature," and what might be the place and function of this phenomenon in the evolution of contemporary black Africa?

Mouralis's work provides another example of a "secondary discourse" operating at a "prescriptive" level. That is, it makes particular demands on literary texts that have not yet, at the time he is writing, come into being. It should, however, be made clear that this study is indebted to Mouralis's pioneering work, which reveals, for the first time, the complex historical, ideological, political, and linguistic framework within which "Negro-African literature in French" operates.

Locha Mateso's intentions in his work *La Littérature africaine et sa critique* are more limited and self-contained. The book is divided into three relatively short sections. The first section, entitled "Problematique de la critique," is in many ways a summary of the major problems of criticism examined by Mouralis. The second section is a short and highly selective "Histoire de la critique littéraire africaine moderne." The final section examines the "Methodes et concepts de la critique littéraire africaine moderne."

Mateso makes clear, in his introduction, that "African modes of reading" are better able to interpret and judge "Negro-African literature in French" than European modes, and this conviction prejudices his account of the history of criticism:

Criticism of African origin is subversive. It proclaims its specificity in terms of its relationship with Western criticism. We will analyze the postulates on which this kind of epistemological severance is based. [p. 15]

It is clearly of paramount importance that there be an "African" criticism of "African literature," and Mateso's desire to discover and analyze "the recurrent models to which Africans refer when interpreting the work of their own people" (p. 217) is of considerable importance. One mark of a significant literature is, however, that it should attract attention outside its national boundaries. To that end, it is important that African literature be "de-colonized," not in the sense of discouraging its study by European critics (though they should not, of course, hold a monopoly) but that their criteria of judgement should no longer be those of the colonist. The cultural and indeed ideological (among many) differences of the European critic must be made visible in the critical discourse.

Similarly, Rand Bishop's excellent study *African Literature, African Critics* is concerned with the "critical standards" proposed by African critics. This leads to a particular analysis of the development of African critical discourse, one that does not, however, take account of what has often been a generative dialectic: debate between African and non-African commentators.

The present study is divided into six chapters, followed by a conclusion. The chapters cover the six major periods in the history of the criticism of "Negro-African literature in French." There is, as always, an element of the arbitrary in the division of a continuum into parts, but it remains a necessary organizational practice. Explanations for the various divisions are given in the body of the text where relevant.

The first chapter, "Discourses Surrounding French Texts 'about' Africa" examines the perspectives of the early critical writings about texts concerned with Africa by both Europeans and Africans, focusing principally on the period from 1870 until the 1930s. Thus it examines the evolution of a literature known successively as "négrophile," "exotique" (defined in a variety of ways), and, finally, simply "coloniale." Literary commentaries written during the colonial period, which corresponds with the period of imperialist expansion during the closing decades of the nineteenth century, stretching into the twentieth century, reveal a growing emphasis on realism, in terms of landscape and customs and, more particularly in terms of "native psychology." This call for psychological realism accounts in part for the very considerable esteem in which the first African writers were held by the first literary commentators. The perspectives of contemporary prefaces are also examined in some detail, as the preface constituted one of the earliest forms of critical response. The third form in which early criticism of African literature was recorded was, of course, in journals and periodicals; these are also characterized.

Chapter 2 describes the beginnings of what can more properly be termed a criticism of Negro-African literature in French, and the chapter focuses on the relationship between the shifting definition of the field and the critical criteria proposed. Concentrating on the years from 1920 until the end of the Second World War, chapter 2 examines the foundations of criticism and isolates the crucial features determining its future development. It is during this period that the close dialectic between literature and criticism establishes itself, a dialectic that becomes increasingly complicated after 1945. The importance of the perspectives adopted by Haitian writers is examined, as is the way in which these ideas were developed by other West Indian writers. The significance of ideas relevant to the Harlem Renaissance is also emphasized. The final section of chapter 2 explores the criteria and objectives proposed by Africans and West Indians living, writing, and publishing in "Negro" periodicals in Paris.

While chapter 4 examines the ways in which changing attitudes to nationalism affected literary criticism during the period 1945–60, chapter 3 focuses on the principally cultural rather than political and examines the concept of Negritude as a criterion for the evaluation of Negro-African literature during the same period. Sartre's seminal essay "Orphée noir," and Senghor's essays on literary criticism collected in *Liberté I: Négritude et humanisme,* are the principal texts around which chapter 3 is organized.

Chapter 4 deals with the period from after the Second World War until 1960, a time in which the question of what constituted a "national literature" was central to most discussions. Before 1945, Negro-African literature was discussed primarily by West Indian and European writers, West Indian critics choosing between a number of different publications as outlets for their work—such as *Les Continents* (Paris, 1924), *La Dépêche Africaine* (Paris, 1928), *La Revue du Monde Noir* (Paris, 1931–32), *Légitime Défense* (Paris, 1932), *L'Etudiant Noir* (Paris, 1935) and *Tropiques* (1941). After the war, African writers and critics began to contribute to the debate; this shift can be largely attributed to the role of *Présence Africaine,* first published simultaneously in Dakar and Paris in 1947. The controversies, debates, and exchanges that appeared during the period to 1960 provide the focus for the fourth chapter. Integrated into this discussion of the evolution of critical debate in *Présence Africaine* is a commentary on the various debates and congresses on Negro-African literature and the ideas and views voiced at these conferences.

Chapter 5 turns to the criticism of Negro-African literature in French during the decade 1960–70. Here, for the first time, it is book-length publications that form the basis of the discussion. Lilyan Kesteloot's sociohistorical work, *Les Ecrivains noirs de langue française* (Brussels, 1963, revised 1965) is discussed at some length due to its seminal nature and the position it continues to maintain as an "origin" of the literary-critical and historical debate. Other significant publications examined in chapter 5 are: Janheinz Jahn's *Muntu: l'homme africain et la culture néo-africaine* (1961),[5] Léonard Sainville's highly polemical *Anthologie de la littérature négro-africaine: Tome I, Romanciers et conteurs négro-africains* (1963), Edouard Eliet's *Panorama de la littérature négro-africaine (1921–1962)* (1965), Robert Pagéard's *Littérature négro-africaine d'expression fran-çaise* (1966), Lilyan Kesteloot's *Négritude et situation coloniale* (1968), and, finally, the British publication *Protest and Conflict in African Litera-ture* (1969), edited by C. Pieterse and D. Munro.

Chapter 6 is entitled simply "The Wider Debate": here, for the first time, a roughly chronological account has been abandoned in favour of discuss-ing more recent works of criticism according to the typology of what they foreground: Negritude as a cultural or ideological phenomenon, the socio-logical, the ideological, and African tradition. Chapter 6 also includes a brief description of the institutional contexts within which secondary dis-courses concerning "Negro-African literature in French" are now pro-duced, in universities in Africa, France, other European countries, North America, and the former Soviet Bloc; a description of a number of major conferences is also given. Although the French have never held an absolute monopoly on research in the field of "Negro-African literature in French," it is only during the past couple of decades that *national* trends in criticism emerge. Thus recent "French" criticism of Negro-African literature is dis-tinct in many ways from recent African works of criticism.

The sophistication of recent studies and the rapid growth in literary-critical activity, particularly in Africa, do not represent the establishment of autonomous literary-critical or historical canons distinct from the canon constituted by those works considered in earlier chapters. Despite the geo-graphical distances between the places of publication of recent studies, and despite the theoretical distance between many of them, the debate remains international and multidenominational. This is in part because the history of the literature and its original constitution was consecrated by earlier works. Kesteloot's history of Negritude has been superseded by (at least) two important French theses, yet Kesteloot's formulation, because it has itself become part and parcel of the "Negritude myth," cannot be ignored. Thus even in a study such as Michel Hausser's long and theoretically complex *Essai sur la poétique de la négritude* (1986), reference is made in the introduction in particular, to the works of Janheinz Jahn, Sartre, Kesteloot, and Senghor. It is the continuing importance of these early studies—whether as touchstones or as the studies that first formed (or de-formed) the area—which warrants the attention they are given in earlier chapters. It is a significant shift in terms of the literary-critical field which suggests the mid-1980s as an appropriate cut-off point. As national appel-lations become more widespread in literary-historical and literary-critical terms, so the notion of a "Negro-African" literature has become less of a concern. It is also the case that "literature" has become the subject of study of other African disciplines, particularly African philosophy (see, for example, the introduction to Tsenay Serequeberhan's recent book, *The Hermeneutics of African Philosophy: Horizon and Discourse*, 1994). The range of publications relevant to literary criticism and theory, belonging to numerous disciplines, becomes ever broader and, arguably, impossible to analyze in any sense globally.

The conclusion, while attempting to avoid the simplistic and reductive, aims to establish a broad overview of the history of the theory and criticism of Negro-African literature in French and draw a number of conclusions from it. The ubiquity of Negritude as an unstable critical trope operative within secondary discourses for approximately half a century is considered. A discussion of the ways in which critical problems have become the generative themes of literary works such as M. a M. Ngal's *Giambatista Viko ou le viol du discours africain* and *L'Errance* is also integrated into the conclusion.

The theoretical, historical, and critical texts to be examined in the study constitute a distinct discipline. They create a particular tradition in the same way as literary texts form a tradition; they can best be elucidated by taking this into account. The theoretical tradition that the book traces demonstrates the reliance on certain textual features: themes, tropes, images, symbols, and so on. These form a textual patina that, if the processes of secondary discourses are to be exposed, has to be peeled away from time to time. This is particularly the case within a discipline as complex and often confused as Negro-African literature in French. One of the hopes of this study is that it will point to the interdependence and self-generative nature of critical discourses.

In the process of engaging with secondary discourses there is a danger that their contradictory and paradoxical features will be denied in an attempt to describe—more succinctly than they themselves do—their approaches and methods. Extended commentary and quotation have often been exploited in place of summary in an effort to avoid a reductive process. This is most obviously the case with the most "difficult" texts: Sartre's "Orphée noir," and recent critical works. To provide a precis of these is often to deny them the very complexity that renders them exciting as texts to be read alongside the "literary" text. It is also to deny them the critically generative features that account for their importance within the critical tradition.

NOTES

1. The area under consideration here will be termed "Negro-African literature in French" (for a basic definition of this term, see note 1 in chapter 1). To some extent, this will automatically condition (in a way that is not always appropriate) what is

foregrounded in the subsequent discussion. Any definition (whether or not it is termed a "working definition") will function in this manner. However, it is hoped that a consciousness of this will, if not minimize its role, at least expose it.

2. This account of Negritude and its operations is in part inspired, perhaps surprisingly, by Christopher Prendergast's account of *mimesis* and its workings, described in *The Order of Mimesis: Balzac, Stendhal, Nerval, Flaubert* (Cambridge, 1986).

3. For a discussion of the "origins" of the word "Negritude" see, among many others, Iyay Kimoni, *Destin de la littérature négro-africaine ou problématique de la culture* (Sherbrooke, 1975), pp. 66–67.

4. All translations are my own, unless otherwise noted.

5. Janheinz Jahn's *Muntu* was first published in 1958, in German. It was not published in French until 1961 and did not enter the French debate until the early 1960s. For this reason it was considered most appropriate to discuss it in chapter 6.

1

Discourses Surrounding French Texts "about" Africa and Africans: The Ubiquity of "Les Sciences Coloniales"

The criticism of the first works of Negro-African literature in French grew out of the discourses that accompanied the appearance of earlier texts written by Europeans about Africa and Africans.[1] Furthermore, the criteria proposed for the evaluation of the first works of literature by Africans were intimately related to the areas within which texts were seen to belong. Where African texts were subsumed under "colonial literature," for example, the criteria used to evaluate the texts were largely those of "colonial literature." Thus an awareness of the different genres made up of texts by Europeans about Africa and Africans explains the contexts within which texts by Africans were first criticized and draws attention to what was recognized as the specificity of writing by Africans. The characteristics by which these texts about Africa were categorized and evaluated by literary criticism are significant in terms of recognizing the ways in which perspectives were to change when criticism focused, for the first time, on works by Africans. It is necessary to observe in what ways *secondary* discourses were aware of a difference, and in what areas this difference was to be found. This should in no way suggest that Negro-African literature in French has its origins solely in European writings about Africa, but rather that the secondary discourses that accompanied the new literature by Africans developed largely out of the perspectives adopted for the exploration and criticism of the earlier works by Europeans.[2]

Among the increasing mass of European writings that appeared from the fifteenth century onward about Africa and her people, there exist a number of relatively distinct genres. These genres did not succeed one another in a

single line of development but existed, in part, in parallel. The two dominant genres are, in fact, in some senses opposed to one another and are thus
best defined in terms of their differences. They are "textes exotiques" and
"textes coloniaux." The body of texts known as "exotic" literature came
into being when contact was first made with foreign places, and it grew
steadily from the sixteenth century onward, reaching periods of particular
productivity during the eighteenth century and at the beginning of the
twentieth.[3] A subsection of exotic writing consisted of a body of works
known as "textes négrophiles."

The most obvious requirement for the definition of the exotic text is that
it display a predominance of particular themes or references concerned
with some "far-away place" which is also largely hitherto unknown. It is
thus expected to describe a landscape, its flora, and its fauna and to provide
details of the ways and customs of a people. Where it diverges from the
"colonial" text, however, is in the tension it reveals—either explicitly or
implicitly—between *two* cultures, one to which the author by implication
belongs and another "foreign" culture. This dualism between the known
and familiar—and the unknown and new—is one of the central characteristics of the exotic text. Introducing a new geographic and human space and
attributing value to aspects of its culture—broadly defined—necessarily
throws into question comparable elements of the culture within which the
author is writing. Solutions to questions of different kinds—principally
philosophical and political—are sought within the context of an alternative
culture.

That the exotic text demonstrates the positive features of the alternative
culture is important as it is through the esteem afforded the other culture—
whether real or largely or wholly imaginary, as in a Utopia—that the culture to which the author belongs is called into question. Thus the exotic
perspective introduces the possibility of a new self-conscious and self-
critical attitude. The extent to which the exotic text tends to value aspects
of the foreign culture is one way in which the exotic text distinguishes
itself from the colonial text. The latter, while also focusing on a far-away
place, tends to denigrate its "indigenous" features in favour of the features
fostered by the colonial culture. (The etymology of the word "denigrate"—
from "niger," black—is fortuitously relevant.) Similarly, adventure stories
that are situated in far-away places can also be distinguished, as the qualities of the place—social, moral, or political, for example—are never a
major concern of the narrative.

Introducing a new geographic space and the people who inhabit it, and
attributing value to both the place and its people's ways—the principal
characteristics of the exotic text—necessarily takes place within a comparative perspective, as the author, and his or her readers, do not belong to
the society at the centre of the discourse. A number of different characteristics arise out of this dualism. In particular, three main tendencies can be

discerned all stemming from this "cultural relativism." The first leads to a general skepticism, stemming from the observation that numerous different approaches to life are all equally acceptable, but none wholly satisfactory. Montaigne's famous essay, "Des cannibales" (*Essai 1*, XXXI) is an obvious example this kind of attitude:

We can thus call them barbaric in relation to the rules of reason, but not in relation to ourselves who surpass them in all manner of barbarisms. [p. 235]

A second response to the cultural relativism introduced by the exotic text leads to a plea for humility and tolerance in attitudes to the "barbarism" of other culture. Jean de Léry, in 1578, writes, concerning his voyage to Brazil:

Nevertheless, having described the anthropology of the Indians, in order that those who read of these quite horrible deeds, performed daily amongst the peoples of the land of Brazil, might also consider carefully what our own great usurers do (sucking the blood and marrow, and consequently eating alive everything, widows, orphans, and other poor persons for whom it would be better swiftly to cut their throats, rather than to leave them to languish) and one would then consider them more cruel than the savages I describe. [chap. 15, p. 56]

In addition to the philosophical response of skepticism, and the plea for tolerance at a moral or political level, the cultural relativism that the exotic text introduced also excited a more radical reaction that compared the so-called civilized man with the so-called savage and concluded that the latter was in fact more "civilized" than the former. The life of the "Bon Sauvage" was regarded as infinitely preferable to the life of the European, and the former's fortune, at having remained outside history and beyond so-called civilization, was observed with envy.

One of the paradoxes of the myth of the Bon Sauvage—common within exotic literature—a myth that aroused so much interest from the sixteenth to the eighteenth centuries (although traces can be observed right up until the middle of this century), is that this same Bon Sauvage was quickly to be forced to submit to the "civilizing" powers of colonialism and was thus also to become not only a "colonisé" but a potential "esclave" and "déporté" also. The dualism "nature" versus "civilization" coincided with the distinction between the colonized and the colonizer, between free man and slave. It was the "texte négrophile" that can be seen as in some sense responding to this paradox.

From the end of the seventeenth century until the abolition of slavery in the middle of the nineteenth, there existed, within exotic literature, a body of work known as "textes négrophiles." These texts—both theoretical and fictional—aimed to draw the attention of the European public to the fate of African slaves deported to America and the West Indies. Generally highly Romantic, novels such as Mrs Behn's *Oronoko* (1688) or Saint Lambert's *Ziméo* (1769) depict the numerous obstacles that stand in the way of the main characters' love, this theme intertwined with overt—and in the case of *Ziméo* fiercely violent—criticism of slavery. The hero almost always conforms to a number of particular characteristics: he is of aristocratic origin, generally preparing for an influential role within his own society at the time of his capture, physically strong and attractive, well educated and consequently of good conscience. Further characteristics of *"le genre négrophile"* include the presentation of detailed descriptions of the violence of slavery. There are frequent and full accounts of the manner in which slaves were captured, of the voyage across the Atlantic, of life in the colonies, including the conditions of work on the plantations, and accounts of slave revolts. The brutality of slavery is thus depicted with grim realism, and a comprehensive view of the life of the slave often given.

Of the various literary genres in which Africa and Africans are at the centre of the discourse, such as "textes exotiques" and "textes négrophiles," it is the "texte colonial" that is the most immediately significant for the development of the criticism of Negro-African literature in French because it was into colonial literature that the first texts by Africans were incorporated, and it was thus within the context of colonial literature that these texts were judged.

Colonial writing first appeared during the period of colonial expansion from the middle of the nineteenth century and continued well into the twentieth century. It was at the end of the nineteenth century that it became an increasingly autonomous genre displaying a strict allegiance to the broader field of the Colonial Sciences; that is, all the various branches of study—political, economic, geographical, sociological, ethnographic, and so on—pertaining to French colonialism. Thus colonial and metropolitan writing remained fundamentally distinct, the former fostered by its own specific journals, published both in France and Africa. The most important are publications such as *L'Afrique française*, first published in 1891, which included brief bibliographical information about colonial writings and, in particular, about letters, and *La Vie*, founded by Marius and Ary Leblond in 1912, which, in a section entitled "La Vie des Colonies," published articles noting and commenting on new publications. The most significant periodical as far as colonial writing is concerned was, however, *Outre-mer,* which appeared between 1929 and 1937. The large amount of space devoted to colonial writing is explained by its broad intentions, overtly stated in the "Avant-propos" and in a short section entitled "Notre programme" which appeared at the front of the first issue. The aims of the journal were made very clear:

The aim which the new Review "OUTRE-MER" sets itself and which its programme defines with clarity and precision, responds, without question, to the needs of the colonial politics of France. We have conquered the land, we have improved it, we have brought about order and peace, we have succeeding in extracting significant profit; it now remains for us to conquer definitively *souls*. . . .

More urgently than ever, the necessity for the representatives of the race that has achieved a superior degree of civilization to commit all their energy to the careful study of the characteristics of the less evolved races, to take note as accurately as possible of the reactions, often so unexpected, produced in response to measures taken on their behalf; to understand, in a word, and in the most general sense of the term, the native mentality.

It is to this indispensable project that the Review "OUTRE-MER" aims to collaborate, an initiative that deserves to be encouraged by all those who hold dear . . . the strengthening of our colonial empire, closely linked to the good reputation of France.

E. Roume,
Gouverneur Général honoraire des colonies,
Président du Conseil d'Administration de l'Ecole Coloniale.

> [*Outre-mer, 1* (1929), pp. 3–5; my italics]

The section entitled "Notre Programme" began: "The study of the principles, general doctrines, methods and current procedures of colonization: such is the object proposed by OUTRE-MER." [p. 7]

In addition to being fostered and encouraged by colonial periodicals, colonial writers looked to their own Association des Ecrivains de la Mer et de l'Outre-mer, founded in 1926 by Louis Bertrand, Marius and Ary Leblond, and Jean d'Esme, and to their own Academy, the Académie des Sciences Coloniales, founded in 1922, whose aim, according to its Statutes, was to:

Excite, encourage, develop, and coordinate study of interest to the colonies and to serve as a centre of work for the intellectual life of the colonies, protectorates, and places of influence. [p. 11]

In addition to their own institutions and periodicals, colonial writers competed for their own prizes: "Le Prix de Littérature coloniale," "Le Prix triennal de Littérature Coloniale," "Les deux Prix du Comité National des Conseillers du Commerce extérieur," and a number of more specific prizes.[4] Colonial writing, as an intrinsic part of the colonial sciences could thus remain self-contained and, in many ways, autonomous.

Colonial writing remained distinct from the metropolitan exotic tradition for a number of reasons. The most obvious factors that lie outside the text are the author's origins and where he or she lived. Colonial writers themselves emphasized this difference for a number of reasons, which will emerge later. This obvious distinction between the exotic and colonial text is nevertheless important as it was familiarity with the "foreign" place that rendered the work of the first African writers eligible for the dubious status of colonial literature, as the following quotation from A. Roland Lebel's *Histoire de la littérature coloniale en France* (Paris, 1931) makes clear:

> Colonial literature: this should be produced either by a Frenchman born in the colonies or one who has spent his childhood there, or by a colonial who has lived there long enough to assimilate the spirit of the place, or, finally, by one of our indigenous subjects writing—it goes without saying—in French. [p. 58]

There are, however, more important differences between the exotic and the colonial genres.[5] Whereas the "texte négrophile" denounced, either implicitly or explicitly, the cruelty perpetrated by so-called civilized societies in their involvement with the slave trade, and defended the rights of the black man, colonial texts tended to present the various myths and stereotypes that served to justify the colonial system.[6] One of the most obvious explanations for the difference in perspective proffered by the colonial as opposed to the "négrophile" writer is that the colonial author was very often an official, working within the colonial system and thus overtly committed to it, as Lebel makes clear in the conclusion of his *Histoire*:

> The colonial vision is an affirmation of moral energy. Colonial literature ... declares itself a reaction against decadentism. ... It [colonial literature] demonstrates the influence of French strength, the powerful beauty of Greater France. Abandoning ... utopias ... it concerns itself instead with ethnic truth and is committed to the study of social and psychological problems on which the conduct of political affairs depend. Not only does it celebrate the glory of the Empire, it also participates in imperial endeavors. [pp. 212–213]

The author of the colonial text was working very much from within—and indeed for—the system and from a position of a certain degree of familiarity with it, whereas the author of the "négrophile" text, on the other hand, like the author of other exotic texts, often had little or no first-hand experience of the place with which his narrative was concerned. This lack of familiarity was one of the features of exotic literature to which the colonial writers objected and, conversely, held their own work to be superior. Thus Lebel writes in his *Etudes de littérature coloniale* (1928):

> Simply because they appear at almost the same time, the tourist and the colonial novelist must not be placed in the same bracket: a distinction has to be recognized. The tourist passes through, a hasty traveller, or even a

French writer seeking to renew a worn-out tradition. If he limits himself to publishing . . . a book of impressions, that is fine. . . . The danger begins when the passer-by, who is often in a great hurry, wants to write a novel in which he claims to give a profound impression of the colony he has visited. There we have, in its entirety, the mistake of the old exoticism, of that superficial impressionism which only takes account of the decor, of clothing, of the exterior features of the ways of the country. [pp. 16–17]

While colonial writers thus emphasized the superiority of their work over texts belonging to "l'ancien exotisme," the colonial texts were always considered within a distinct genre by the metropolitan public and metropolitan critics. This genre was not, in the first place, a truly "literary" genre, but something inferior. Colonial writers were always distinguished from writers of a "purely literary" kind.

That their work failed to have conferred on it the status of "literature," and that colonial writers continued to be regarded as distinct from the mainstream of French writing, might have led to considerable frustration and bitterness. However, colonial writers argued that the criteria that rendered a text "literary" according to metropolitan standards were not criteria to which they wanted their texts to conform. Their writings aimed to fulfil certain very specific and concrete criteria within the context of colonialism:

Alongside politics which, for better or worse, extends across and animates a field that it has not created, alongside commerce which for the time being only timidly draws profit, alongside science which explores with a success that our rivals envy, literature has assumed the task of making this vast domain tangible and concrete by inscribing it, little by little, in ideas familiar to all. . . . It is by means of colonial literature that the French know of the existence of the Empire and understand the relationship between the several colonies scattered around the world. [Lebel, *Histoire*, p. 213]

Furthermore, metropolitan literature was characterized by colonial writers as an unnecessarily complicated and overly sophisticated—and even "old"—literature. Colonial literature would breathe new life and vigour into what was seen as an introspective and narrow literary tradition. Discussing the scope of colonial literature, Lebel thus wrote, in his work *L'Afrique occidentale dans la littérature française depuis 1870* (1925):

From this representation emanates a breath of fresh air that refreshes the all too stuffy air that we breathe. Our literature is very old. The refinements of feeling, the sentimental complications by which attempts are made to re-invigorate old themes, no longer move us. The colonial writer, who seeks out violent and primitive emotions, the battles and fecund victories, strong and generous ideas that the man of action depicts, re-awaken energies in us that are otherwise ignored. In our literature as in our spiritual life, it exercises an invigorating effect. [p. 236]

Thus colonial writers sought to distance themselves from—and deni-grate—exotic literature. There are a number of specific characteristics of the genre which are frequently proposed as its major shortcomings: super-ficiality, subjectivity, and the fragmentary nature of the exotic text.[7] The subjective character of the "exotic" text constituted the first objection. The "exotic" writer, Lebel wrote in L'Afrique occidentale, was:

too subjective, noting only how he is moved before virgin nature, and unknown countries are often no more than a source of new emotion, sometimes no more even than a pretext for description; certainly exotic feelings have sometimes succeeded in exciting some fine works but they have also given birth to mediocre works where "local color" is artificial and the "I" intrudes in a highly vulgar manner. [p. 238]

Implicit in these criticisms of exotic literature are the qualities that they believed their own work offered. Firstly, written by men who had lived in the foreign place for a considerable length of time, almost always working in a professional capacity, their work could offer detailed knowledge of a geographical, sociological, economic, demographic, and ethnographic kind. They therefore drew attention to the "documentary" value of their work, in terms both of providing amateurs with precise information about the region, and, as they themselves pointed out, of fulfilling the important task of providing the necessary knowledge for the continuing colonial domination of the area in question. For example, Lebel writes:

Modern works will assume an ethnographic interest and will translate the psychology of races; in the colonial domain this natural curiosity takes on a more precise significance: it is the expression of the need for intimate knowledge of the country and its people, useful for our domination, to-ward which end our civilizing efforts are directed and, in addition, useful to our educational project. . . . Colonial writers, informed observers . . . will confer on their books a documentary value which, without marring their charm, will increase their interest. Thus particular works will appear that chart the material and social progress of the colony . . . and can go beyond the purely literary domain. [pp. 225–229]

The crux of their argument for the superiority of the colonial text rested, ultimately, on the detailed knowledge of the place which the colonial writer could provide. The first writings by Africans were thus automatically sub-sumed under colonial literature and judged by its standards, and any work that failed to conform to the literature's narrow criteria was judged unsuccessful. René Maran's *Batouala: véritable roman nègre* (1921)—discussed in some detail later on—was considered to have failed because it lacked "objectivity" and failed to meet what Lebel describes as:

the very formula of colonial literature, which attempts to provide, within the form of an objective account, an exact knowledge that furthers the practical knowledge of the black world. [p. 219]

Robert Randau's work *Diato* (1923) is, however, described by Lebel as:

a purely local story, seen from the native perspective, considered with the mentality of a local inhabitant and one that could have been told, if not written, by a native of Casamance. [p. 222]

The apparently important criterion here is that the novel seem *as though* it could have been written (or told) by "*un indigène.*" What really distinguishes the two works is, however, the attitudes to colonialism revealed by the two novels.

One of the more insidious consequences of the annexation of early writings by Africans by colonial literature was that their terminology left little room for a truly "*African* literature." With reference to Randau, for example, Lebel claims, "il compte parmi les plus éminents africains" (p. 213), meaning "Africanists," and refers to the field he is writing about by means of the terms "littérature coloniale," the work of "écrivains coloniaux," "colonialisme en littérature," but also "littérature africaine" (p. 88). There is a sense in which the colonial writers created a monopoly of terms, exploiting a wide variety of descriptions used to designate the area and blurring or obliterating important differences between them. When African writers first began to publish, there was no specific and distinctive term that could be applied to their work; the term "African literature" was ambiguous. This inability to indicate a *difference* by means of nomenclature contributed to the blurring of criteria by which these texts were first judged.

The difference between "la littérature coloniale" and the literature produced by Africans was indicated, not by reference to distinct characteristics of their work but by distinguishing its author from the colonial author. Thus African authors were first known as "écrivains indigènes." Where their texts conformed to the definition of colonial literature, African writers were accepted. In *Histoire de la littérature coloniale en France* (1931), Lebel welcomed the "natives who [are] beginning to write, thus providing their own unmediated witness" (p. 143). The "indigènes" to whom Lebel refers are writers such as Amadou Mapaté Diagne, Bakary Diallo, Félix Couchoro, or Ousmane Socé. Given this new and growing group of writers,

Lebel had to expand one aspect of his definition of "colonial literature" (see above, p. 18).

The extent to which the first texts by Africans were judged essentially by the standards of "colonial literature" can be seen clearly in the first texts to constitute a critical response to African literature: namely, in the prefaces that generally accompanied these first publications by "indigènes." As a genre, the broadly "critical" role, or critical typology, of the preface is characterized by a number of elements. One of its important features is that it constitutes a program for reading: it sets out the perspective that the reader should bring to the text. In certain cases, it also rules out other possible perspectives. It has, therefore, both a programmatic and preemptive function.

In many instances the text—the literary object—was offered as tangible proof of the success of the "mission civilisatrice" of colonialism. Georges Hardy's Preface to Paul Hazoumé's *Doguicimi* (1937), although one of the latest prefaces of its kind, offers an example of almost every feature of such prefaces. The extent to which the novel is proposed as a triumph of French colonialism is made clear by the opening sentences:

> In 1892, French troops commanded by Colonel Dodds occupied Abomey; in 1931, a Dahomean school-teacher, Paul Hazoumé, had accepted for publication a study of the "Blood Pact of Dahomey," by the Institute of Ethnology of the University of Paris, an institution not likely to be indulgent toward poor works. In less than forty years scientific research has become acclimatized to the country of the Amazons. . . . One would need to be blind to fail to see, in the juxtaposition of these two dates, something truly marvellous. . . . For France . . . it is a singular achievement, at such an early point in the colonial venture, to have achieved such intellectual and moral conquests. The case of Paul Hazoumé is not an isolated one. [Preface, p. 9]

The literary work is also offered as an example testifying to the success of the French colonial policy of cultural assimilation; thus the "Frenchness" of the author is emphasized:

> If his coloring did not betray his origin you would take him for a Frenchman of France; everything in his relaxed and lively manner of expression, in his courteous manner, in his easy and careful gestures, in the attractive warmth that emanates from him, is as of one of us. Everything in his bearing, in his conduct, testifies to a scrupulous conscience, well aware of his duties. [Preface, p. 10]

Not only is "Frenchness" in terms of superficial indicators emphasized, a French attitude is also claimed for Hazoumé, an attitude that is manifest in a loyalty to France, "la mère Patrie": "Citoyen français, il ne conçoit . . . au surplus, d'autre patrie possible que la nôtre" (Preface, p. 10). Hardy draws attention to the novel's "objectivity" and the way in which it provides not only accurate documentary evidence about Africa but, more importantly, psychological realism:

> The novel form that he considered appropriate to adopt is deceptive: it is, without question, history . . . exact, perfectly objective, and furthermore psychological history, the only kind that really counts. [Preface, p. 10]

Yet, despite the emphasis on objectivity and historical truth, Hardy comments:

> Rather than dry analyses, which always remain distant from lived experiences, he has preferred to opt for a series of animated and colorful scenes, an animation of facts and actions, a drama that takes us to the very heart of the local society and gradually familiarizes us with mental processes. . . . This method is closer than any other to the truth. . . . It maintains the merits of intelligent "reportage." [Preface, p. 11]

Yet he concludes, "il n'invente rien . . ." (Preface, pp. 10–11). The preemptive dimension of the preface, mentioned earlier, is manifest in the way in which Hardy denies any possible anti-French or anticolonial dimension in the novel (Preface, p. 10). Hardy's Preface ends with an overt statement that it should provide a "program" for how the book should be read, and a plea that Hazoumé be kindly received:

> It is thus in such a spirit that this book should be welcomed and read. . . . I ask, if I may, all the sympathy of the French public for this powerfully original work. [Preface, p. 11]

One of the most marked characteristics of the preface within the context of "indigenous writing" in French is the almost complete absence of literary-critical observations which it displays; also, the preface generally is written not by a specialist in literature but more commonly by specialists in other fields—for example, by ethnographers or linguists. Remarks about the literary language of the text are rare: in almost every case, it is on the presentation of African society and on psychological realism that the preface writer dwells. A condescending, patronizing tone is common, and the emphasis is almost always on an Africa "civilized" by France. There are, however, some remarkable exceptions.

Some preface writers, those with different ideological and political convictions, focus on the meeting of two cultures and openly revile the arrogance, lack of tolerance, and contempt that characterize relationships between Africans and Europeans. Jean-Richard Bloch's "Avertissement," which prefaces Bakary Diallo's *Force-Bonté* (1926), provides a useful example. Bloch opens his "Avertissement" with a description of the author's unusual background:

> Bakary Diallo is no ordinary Black. He is not even an educated negro, a school-teacher, a functionary. Adventure sought him out, like so many others, in his Senegalese grass hut and made him an infantryman. [p. 3]

Bloch then outlines the qualities of the author which he believes the narrative reveals:

> It is in Morocco and in France that he began to babble French. But it is in Africa that his heart opened. And the confidences that he imparts, in a language that is not his own, are dictated to him by means of an admirable simplicity, a spontaneity, a goodness, an openness, a candour, which are the natural perfume of the black soul. [pp. 3–4]

This list of typically African characteristics exists, as the preface writer goes on to say, only "when it [the black soul] is not perverted by oppression of any kind" [p. 4].

Bloch was writing at a time when there was little question as to the superiority of French culture and France's right—even duty—to colonize: his "Avertissement" represents a new departure from the attitudes expressed in prefaces such as Hardy's (later) preface discussed above. Bloch's views were, however, supported by others. G.-D. Périer and G. Dulonge contributed a preface to Badibanga's tales contained in *L'Eléphant qui marche sur des oeufs* (1931), in which they warn against assuming the absolute superiority of the white man over the Black. The first paragraph emphasizes the need for understanding the black man's perception of the White:

> There is no shortage of works on the Congo and its people. But they have all been written by Europeans because the natives, who are in the main illiterate, were not yet writing. It is thus that we never had anything other than Whites' opinion of Blacks. However, we are equally concerned to know what the latter think. [Preface, p. 7]

The Preface's perspective assumes an extraordinary attitude on the part of the reader:

> They are men, women, old people, and children who have ways and customs like other people in the universe. Over the centuries they have themselves made arms, tools, all those objects, in short, necessary for their village life. [Preface, p. 7]

Yet the perspective of the journal *Outre-mer*—proposed in its first issue, quoted above, the supreme need to "conquérir les âmes," and the obvious function of "indigenous writings" in this enterprise—is not wholly absent from the Preface by Perier and Dulonge.

Robert Delavignette, in his Preface to Ousmane Socé's *Karim: Roman Sénégalais* (1948), quotes the great Africanist Théodore Monod: "Le Noir n'est pas un homme sans passé, il n'est pas tombé d'un arbre avant-hier" (Preface, p. 8). Emphasizing the European tendency to overlook the complexity and sophistication of other cultures, Delavignette encourages the reader to embrace the "otherness" of the novel's atmosphere. He introduces the theme of cultural "métissage": the creation of a "civilisation métisse" should be the fundamental aim of the colonial venture.

G.-D. Périer's Preface to Lomami-Tshibamba's tale, *Ngando*, which was published in 1948 and awarded a prize at the Foire Coloniale in Brussels in the same year, reveals a similar perspective. He emphasizes the need for understanding between Black and White. The notion of the "primitive" is rehabilitated, having previously acquired a derogatory meaning, and there is a moving sense of understatement in his words: "We understand, today, that those who were yesterday despised, the Blacks, may also perhaps have something to say, that it is not simply a matter of seeking to instruct them, but also a matter of listening to them" (Preface, p. 11).

More common than the perspective that encourages the reader to see in the work introduced the results of a "métissage culturel," however, is the perspective that presents the African's work as evidence of the rare "accomplishment" of almost complete cultural assimilation. Such is the perspective in the preface to Dim Delobsom's *L'Empire du Mogho-Naba* (1932) by the colonial writer, Robert Randau:

> Consider the efforts necessary . . . to teach French to a Black. His native language is essentially different from ours; he has lived in a narrow social milieu, sectarian, committed to savage and cruel ways. Initially everything is incomprehensible to him, from our way of life to our most simple ideas. So in the presence of his teachers he learns without forgetting anything; his knowledge, acquired and remembered thanks to a prodigious memory, generally remains superficial. More rarely, served by a larger intelligence, he adopts, at least in part, our ways of thinking. This was the case with Dim Delobsom. [Preface, pp. I–II]

A not altogether different discourse was provided by the author of *Le Fils du fétiche* (1971), David Anadou, introducing his own work:

> The Black is neither worse nor better than the other children of Adam. If he is sometimes taken for a "Savage" or a "half-monkey," it is only his lack of appropriate culture and education. The present work is not an apologia on his behalf. . . . It is simply . . . a familiar discussion capable of

showing a glimpse, and from afar, of the very curable ills that hang menacingly over the African continent. [p. 9]

Anadou's introductory note ends with a "homage to the developed countries which continue to effect great works in Africa" (p. 9). Statements of this kind are a recurrent theme within the early prefaces to Francophone African texts.

Where texts by Africans were considered within the context of the colonial sciences, they were expected to conform to the narrow requirements of colonial literature and their principal function was above all to furnish the colonial enterprise with appropriate information. The emphasis was on the factual and the documentary.[8] Beyond the sociological and anthropological detail required of the colonial text was the need for psychological realism: the penetration of "la mentalité primitive." The ultimate achievement open to the colonial text, as Lebel made clear in his assessment in *L'Afrique occidentale* of Randau's work *Diato*, was that it "could have been told, if not written by a native" (1925, p. 222). The disciplines of ethnology and anthropology were precisely concerned with acquiring access to the world of the colonized, and as Périer and Dulonge wrote in their Preface to Badibanga's tales collected in *L'Eléphant qui marche sur des oeufs* (1931), "There is no better way of penetrating the primitive mind than listening to the tales recounted around the camp fire in the evening" (p. 8).

The textual features of these early African writings were worthy of comment only insofar as they testified to the success of linguistic assimilation, as in Randau's assessment of Dim Delobsom, or Jean-Marie Jadot's Preface to Naigiziki's novel, *Escapade ruandaise* (1950), which is presented as an example of the success of Belgian educational provision in Africa. G.-D. Périer goes still further, when he writes in his Preface to Lomami-Tshibamba's *Ngando* (1948):

[if the command of] French reflects on the black disciple, what more obvious evidence of the patient application of his masters of the white race and the value of their literary education? [pp. 13–14]

The fabric of the text is rarely discussed, and any comments tended to be vague and impressionistic.

Received into colonial literature, African writing was thus held in something of a theoretical impasse. While specific features distinguishing it from other literatures failed to be identified, there were no grounds on which to propose the literature as an autonomous field. Yet as long as the literature was seen to belong to another field, these features would not be recognized. The literature can be said to have broken out of this impasse at a precise moment. The initiative came from literature and not from secondary discourse: in 1921, René Maran published *Batouala*, subtitled *véritable roman nègre.* While his famous preface made his views of French colonialism very clear, his subtitle challenged commentators to consider the novel in the light of this appellation. Maran's novel was immediately recognized not by the colonial literary establishment but by the metropolitan literary establishment, winning the Prix Goncourt the year after Proust's *A l'ombre des jeunes filles en fleurs.* For many colonial writers, however, *Batouala* was *de facto* a work of colonial literature, and colonial critics stubbornly embarked on analyzing it according to the principles of colonial literature. According to Lebel, for example, *Batouala* failed to conform to the definition of colonial literature (see above).

Other colonial critics argued that, by awarding the Prix Goncourt to *Batouala*, the metropolitan literary establishment had at last honoured—or at least intended to honour—colonial literature. J. Ladreit de Lacharrière wrote, in a contemporary review in *L'Afrique Française* (1922):

Many of the Academie Goncourt's decisions indicate a conscious or unconscious tendency to elect works that come from French soil. . . . This year our colonial literature, long ignored rather than poor, has had its turn and the Academie Goncourt, not without a battle, has honored Greater France. [p. 36]

The review continues, "But is this truly a 'Negro novel'?" De Lacharrière goes on to argue that Maran's educational background renders him French. The reviewer's more profound objections then appear:

The fact is that, steeped in French civilization, Maran cannot wait to celebrate cruelty; a functionary, he hastens to note how rare, among his colleagues, are "those who cultivate the mind" and how numerous "those who have abandoned all pride" and who sink into "the most abject spinelessness"; a colonial, he delights in emphasizing the "daily baseness" that, according to him, makes up the colonial life; a Frenchman, M. Maran notes how expert France is at sowing desolation because "seven years was enough to ruin from top to bottom, a part of Ouangui-Chari." [pp. 36–37]

The article then focuses on what are considered to be Maran's motives:

Stretched out "on his chaise longue" . . . M. Maran was aiming at exoticism and, an opportunist . . . he wrote a negro novel . . . hoping for a previously unpublished originality. [p. 37]

Reviewers were obliged to consider the implications of describing the novel as a *véritable roman nègre,* and thus Maran forced criticism to discuss new concepts, most obviously the features of the novel that might justify this appellation. De Lacharrière wrote:

M. Maran has taken care to stuff his style with an abundant "little negro" if not simply "negro" terminology. This precaution adds nothing picturesque, as long as it is the case that exoticism does not reside in the vocabulary but in vivid description. . . . The negro vocabulary of M. Maran is dangerous; it underlines the uncertainty and poverty of his French vocabulary. [p. 37]

By 1928 *Batouala* had been banned in the French colonies of Africa. It was Maran's Preface, above all, that had been most overt in its criticisms of French colonialism. Although the novel grew out of the flagrant contradictions that Maran had himself observed between the humanitarian values espoused at home in France, and the atrocities he had observed as a colonial administrator in French Equatorial Africa, it was only the Preface that openly denounced everything to which the administration refers by means of the euphemism "matters that have gone astray" (p. 14). While it was rejected by "colonial" critics, metropolitan critics such as Henri de Régnier and Jacques Boulanger heralded *Batouala* as a major novel. The new element introduced into the critical discourse, more important than the various "literary" criteria that were here for the first time discussed with regard to an African work, was the criterion of "Negro-ness."

A noncommittal anonymous review in the *Nouvelle Revue Française* (January–June 1922, pp. 103–106), for example, uses as its yardstick the extent to which Maran's work can be properly described as a "roman nègre." The review opens with a description of the beginning of the novel, "Batouala, a Congolese negro, wakes. . . ." The review continues in a descriptive vein: "There follows a description of the feast of the ganza or circumcision. An obscene and wilfully bloody celebration. . . ." Having given examples of the basic narrative, the reviewer then sums up his initial reactions:

Such is, in one hundred and fifty little pages, the "true negro novel" promised on the endpaper, the "succession of etchings" that the preface announces and where M. Maran "has pushed objectivity to the point of suppressing all reflexions that might have been attributed to him." [p. 104]

Then follows a paragraph in which the reviewer outlines the "subjects" he considers appropriate to "veritables romans nègres":

the novel about the primitive tribe and its internal fights; the novel about the relations between Blacks and Whites; the novel about the mulatto; the novel about the educated, civilized negro; the novel about the native functionary, etc. . . . [pp. 104–105]

All these "subjects" are, of course, relevant to the novel. The reviewer, however, writes:

> M. Maran chose to write a psychological novel about the negro who is still savage, to note the train of thought, the images, desires, feelings. . . . The success of the first two chapters is remarkable, true interior monologues of his hero. But he has not had the same success in the novel's subsequent chapters. [p. 105]

His later criticisms depend on the extent to which ideas and feelings fail to suggest what is "typiquement nègre" (p. 105).

Maran's *Batouala,* then, provoked a controversial debate and was harshly criticized.[9] Having subtitled his novel *véritable roman nègre*, however, Maran encouraged the development of the concept of an autonomous Negro-African literature governed by its own purposes and displaying particular textual features. *Batouala* having won the Prix Goncourt, the most prestigious prize for the novel within metropolitan literature, it became clear that writing by Africans and those of African descent was not to be the exclusive monopoly of the colonial sciences, and this encouraged a broader criticism to develop. Ten years later, this criticism was to receive the institutional support of the journal *La Revue du monde noir*, published in Paris in 1931, followed by a number of other periodicals crucial to the history of the theory and criticism of Negro-African literature in French. Much of the impetus for the founding of the journal came not from France or Africa, however, but from America and the Caribbean, where new ideas were being formulated about black people, their identity, history, and rights.

NOTES

1. "Negro-African literature in French" is used here to designate a body of texts written in French, which emerged from 1920 onward, produced by Africans or those of African descent, principally West Indians. This basic definition, relying on extra-textual and historical criteria, is a working definition. Various, more specific definitions, dependent on textual characteristics, emerge later. To employ a more textually based definition at this point would be to beg a number of the questions that are explored in the initial chapters of the book.

2. For a thorough study of the "origins," "pre-texts," or "intertextuality" of Negro-African literature in French, see Bernard Mouralis, *Littérature et développement* (1984), in particular Chapter 4, Sections II and III, entitled, "Textes d'origine européenne" and "Textes d'origine africaine." Section III is further divided under the headings, "La littérature orale," "La littérature écrite dans les langues africaines," "La littérature des mouvements messianiques," "Textes produits dans un cadre institutionnel européen," and "Textes heureux."

3. The standard, largely historical work on French exoticism, remains Pierre Jourda's *L'Exotisme dans la littérature française depuis Chateaubriand: Tome II, du Romantisme à 1939* (Paris, 1956). A thorough and interesting examination of the paradoxical features of the exotic text can be found in Régis Antoine, "La Relation Exotique," *Revue des Sciences Humaines, 37* (147) (July–September 1972), 373–385.

4. For a comprehensive listing of the various "Prix Coloniaux" see *Outre-mer, 1* (1929), 240–243.

5. This discussion of the exotic text is partly based on Mouralis's discussion of the differences between "exotic," "colonial," and *"négrophile"* texts; see Mouralis, *Littérature et développement,* Chapter 4, Sections II, 1, 2, and 3. Mouralis's multidisciplinary study, it should be noted, is heavily biased toward the sociological and ideological.

6. Léon Fanoudh-Siefer, *Le Mythe du nègre et de l'Afrique noire dans la littérature française de 1800 à la 2e Guerre Mondiale* (Paris, 1968), is a thorough study, again biased toward the sociological, of the presentation of Africa and the African in French literature (including French colonial literature).

7. The nature of the debate between colonial and metropolitan writers emerges clearly from the huge controversy that surrounded the publication of Pierre Loti's *Roman d'un spahi* in 1881; a similar general debate continued well into the 1930s. For a detailed account of the controversy surrounding Loti's *Roman d'un spahi,* see Lebel's *Histoire de la littérature coloniale* (1931) and *L'Afrique occidentale* (1925). See also for interesting comparison, Fanoudh-Siefer, *La Mythe de négre,* pp. 51–110 and 113–118, and A. Hargreaves, *The Colonial Experience in French Fiction* (London: 1981).

8. "Colonial literature" was confined almost exclusively to prose writings, above all the novel. For an account of the isolated examples of poetry, see A. Roland Lebel, "Poetes de l'Afrique noire," *Outre-mer, 1* (1929), 366–374. The title is ambiguous; as Lebel writes in his introduction:

> Do not misunderstand the title. It in no way refers to storytellers and griots who . . . preserve in black Africa . . . the indigenous oral literature. This little study is concerned only with French authors. [p. 366]

All Lebel can claim for this small body of texts is that "as feeble as it still is, an effort has been made that is not universally without merit" (p. 367). The contradictions of a "colonial" poetry, as a genre belonging to "colonial literature"—with the latter's emphasis on the factual—are made clear in the conclusion of Lebel's own article (pp. 373–374).

9. For a discussion of reactions to *Batouala* in the French press, see R. Fayolle, *"Batouala* et l'accueil de la critique," *Actes du colloque sur la critique et la réception de la littérature africaine d'expression française* (Paris, 1978), pp. 23–29.

2

Critics of the African Diaspora
and Their Contribution to Debates in Paris

The significance of what was later to be known as the American "New Negro" movement or the "Negro Renaissance" (as Alain Locke called it in 1925 in his anthology, *The New Negro*) for thinking in Parisian circles has been described unequivocally by Senghor:

> In the Latin Quarter, in the 1930s, we were influenced, above all, by the ideas and action of the Negro Renaissance, some of whose most dynamic representatives we met in Paris. . . . For my part I regularly read *The Crisis* . . . but also *The Journal of New African History* which devoted numerous articles to material about Africa. But my bedside book was *The New Negro*, "the anthology–manifesto" as Jean Wagner calls it, which Alain Locke had edited. . . . The poets of the Negro Renaissance who influenced us most were Langston Hughes and Claude McKay [*sic*], Jean Toomer and James Weldon Johnson, Stirling Brown and Frank Marshall Davis.[1]

The Crisis was edited by W. E. B. Du Bois, and his work *The Souls of Black Folk* (1903) is often considered one of the earliest expressions of Negritude. In it he denounced the position of Blacks in American society and argued for the need to alter the stereotyped image of the inferiority of the Black—in the minds of both Whites and Blacks. The "New Negro" movement of the 1920s was both literary and social in its concerns.[2] It revealed the awakening of a black identity and advocated the rehabilitation of a dignified past perverted by the ideology of slavery. Thus it promoted a spiritual quest for a cultural wholeness and authenticity, alienated by the dominant American culture. The sense of cultural and spiritual schism, which was to be a crucial motivation for the elaboration of the theories of numerous black writers, Senghor's Negritude, for example, was equally expressed by Du Bois in *The Souls of Black Folk*:

> It is a peculiar sensation, this double consciousness, this sense of always looking at one's self through the eyes of others, of measuring one's soul by the tape of a world that looks on in amused contempt and pity. One ever feels this two-ness—an American, a Negro: two souls, two thoughts, two unreconciled strivings; two warring ideals in one dark body, whose dogged strength alone keeps it from being torn asunder. [p. 3]

It was this experience of confused and contradictory identity which provided an essential catalyst for the Negro Renaissance.

The movement reached a stalemate for a number of reasons. First, it failed to appeal to the black American middle class for whom assimilation into American culture was the obvious means of social advancement. Second, the movement was soon "colonized" by white society and became fashionable among white intellectuals. It was thus reduced to something of an "exotic novelty." The third and perhaps most significant reason for its ultimate demise lay in its failure to develop any socioeconomic ideology, capable of side-stepping white paternalism. On the whole, writers of the Negro Renaissance were published by white publishers. When it became clear that the movement had arrived at an impasse, many black American writers gravitated toward Paris as the centre of their activities, among them Jean Toomer, Countee Cullen, and Claude MacKay whose highly influential novel *Banjo* was published in 1929. In it he made clear that the educated Black was mistaken in thinking that he or she could cross the racial boundary, and MacKay described the destiny of the educated Black as very little different from the destiny of his or her fellow illiterate black brothers. More explicit in its polemic than *Batouala*, *Banjo* replaced the former as the bible of black students in Paris. Senghor sums up his view of the importance of developments in America for developments in Paris when he writes: "It is thus that in terms of the general meaning of the word [Negritude]—the discovery of black values and the recognition for the Negro of his situation—was born in the United States of America."[3] However, the essence and critical typology of "Negro-African literature in French," as advocated and developed by writers in Paris during the 1930s, were in part based on ideas and polemics current in political and cultural debates not only in the United States, but also in Haiti and the French West Indies where, from the end of the nineteenth century onward, political thought was frequently transformed into quasi-literary "programs." It was in cultural and more particularly literary debate, perhaps surprisingly, that ideas developed most fruitfully—and influentially. The first black Republic was in many ways a far greater model in terms of its cultural "program" (although the term is perhaps misleading in suggesting too systematic an approach) than in terms of its unique political history. One of its principal cultural concerns was to define the specificity of Haitian literature, or the literature of the "New Negro."

Oswald Durand is the most important nineteenth-century Haitian writer, and he was recognized by the later "Indigenous" writers as their most significant precursor. Durand praised Haiti's flora and fauna, and his poetry thus represents an overt belief that his native land offered an iconography for poetic celebration. The development of this iconography became a metaphor for faith in his cultural and national identity. He sought artistic inspiration in every aspect of Haitian experience. Later criticism recognized Durand's originality: his emphasis on specifically Haitian experience, peasant culture—and even voodoo rituals. The latter was an unprecedented and striking feature of his verse.

In addition to introducing the flora and fauna of Haiti and celebrating peasant folklore and indigenous practices such as voodoo as subjects worthy of transformation into poetry, Durand also developed themes such as the ambiguity of the mulatto's identity, seen, for example, in "Le fils d'un noir."[4] Durand is also significant for having exploited Haitian Creole: his poem "Choucoune" (1896) is generally recognized as the first successful attempt to write in the island's Creole.

Contemporary Haitian political problems are also an important preoccupation in Durand's work. Patriotism and national consciousness are encouraged in verses reminiscent of the rhetoric of Hugo's political verse. "La Mort de nos cocotiers," for example, draws a parallel between the death of the symbolical indigenous coconut trees and the loss of freedom and idealism in Haiti. It was verse of this kind, which appealed for the defence of the native land and its heroic history, that led to this period being known as the period of l'Ecole Patriotique. No organized poetic movement existed, but many poets were concerned, above all, with extolling a patriotic spirit.

It is against the background of nineteenth-century writers, of whom Durand is the supreme example, that developments in criticism and literary debate in Haiti, at the beginning of the twentieth century, emerge most clearly. Implicit in Durand's verses was a particular view of what Haitian poetry should be. He had introduced specifically Haitian themes and particular national political concerns. These two elements were to become increasingly important in the debate about a national or "indigenous" literature. The Indigenous Movement represented a radically new understanding of what Haitian literature must be. It was preceded, however, by a number of significant literary journals: *La Ronde, La Nouvelle Ronde, La Trouée: Revue d'intérêt général*, followed by *La Revue Indigène: les arts et la vie* and *Les Griots*.

La Ronde has been stereotyped as derivative—much of its work is indebted to French Symbolism—and escapist, in short a typically nineteenth-century manifestation of assimilationist and "alienated" writing. As Michael Dash (1981) rightly argues, however, this is a highly biased view of the journal's contribution to the development of Haitian literature and literary criticism. The poets associated with *La Ronde* were above all preoccupied with the *aesthetic* inadequacies of their precursors. In particular, they identified two problematical areas: the use of "local color," and a utilitarian attitude to literature, two factors that have remained central issues in the criticism of "Negro-African literature in French." While references to local phenomena liberated Haitian writing from the stranglehold of French Classicism, "local color" had—contributors to *La Ronde* argued—been overdone. The authors grouped around the journal believed that a writer who was truly rooted in his native soil did not need to fill his work with local color. It was not that *La Ronde*'s authors despised their local culture, but that they were reacting against a trend that led, in their view, to poetic uniformity and mediocrity. *La Ronde*'s reservations about politically committed poetry were similarly based on the belief that dogmatic commitment debased poetry. *La Ronde* sought to release imaginative creativity and thereby to allow the opening up of what should inevitably be, they argued, a specifically Haitian consciousness.

Although *La Ronde*'s preoccupations were misconstrued by later movements of the 1930s, their credo was not so different, in a number of ways, from that of the Negritude writers, who also sought to break free from any constraints on imaginative creativity; strict allegiance to Realism and materialism, for example, were considered inappropriate by both movements.

La Nouvelle Ronde was founded in 1925 and marked a new departure among Haitian literary periodicals. It criticized the work of the previous generation and sought to renew rather than preserve the Haitian literary tradition. One of the clearest formulations of the journal's position appeared in the July issue in the first year of publication:

> It would have been necessary, for Haitian literature to have existed, for works to have reflected more the aspirations, tendencies, the very spirit of the country. Our elders succeeded in producing works of value. They did not produce works that were truly ours. [Antonio Vieux & Philippe Thoby-Marcelin, *La Nouvelle Ronde*, *1* (July 1925), 30]

La Nouvelle Ronde was published during the period of the American Occupation, when it had become clear that physical resistance was futile. The obvious alternative was to think, to write, and to publish. As one aspect of the American Occupation involved what was seen as an attempt to replace Haitian culture with American culture, it became imperative to define and preserve a properly Haitian literature that could no longer be accused of being an imitation of European models. This was the essence of the thinking behind two other journals: *La Trouée: Revue d'intérêt général* and, more particularly, *La Revue Indigène: les arts et la vie*, both of which first appeared in July 1927.

La Trouée was concerned with literary and more broadly cultural matters, and, as its name suggests, it revealed a more overtly rebellious spirit, as the preface to the first issue, signed "La Direction," stated. The journal's attitude to literature was also made clear in this first issue:

> Literature is not what people think in Haiti. It is not an activity for pedants and for people who have nothing better to do. Both will be banished. Rather it is the cry of a people that wants to say what matters to them. It is not that pastiche agreeably filled with "local color" which some produce, any more than it is that bland delicate writing of some others. It is the expression of Ideas, of our ideas, the ideas of us Haitians. [*La Trouée, 1* (1927), 1]

Although the journal ceased publication before any specific theories of an indigenous literature had been proposed, it made clear, from the first issue, what it believed Haitian literature should not be: namely, imitative or self-consciously bursting with "local color."

The journal published a wide variety of work, ranging from Carl Brouard's prosaic pieces describing Bohemian life, to the more experimental and ambitious works of Jacques Roumain and Daniel Heurtelou. The resources of *vers libre* were also demonstrated in short impressionistic texts, such as Roumain's "Après-midi," which evokes a landscape, etched in rapid, fragmentary images.[5]

Although publication of the *Revue Indigène* lasted only from July 1927 until February 1928, the contribution it made to literary-critical debate was very considerable. The journal publicized ideas current in France and Latin America, while at the same time advocating the need to preserve the cultural integrity of Haiti:

> *We will endeavour to achieve with our review* a faithful and lively picture of the diverse manifestations of contemporary Haitian life and thought. Intellectual and artistic, economic and commercial life. [*Sic*] The Haitian point of view ... and as the word "indigène" ["native"] is made into a term of abuse we reclaim it as a title, the native's point of view. A return to sincerity and the natural, to the living model, to direct description, a perfume more strongly suffused with "haïtienneté" ["Haitianness"], that's what seems to characterize our youthful poetry. [Normil G. Sylvain, "Chronique-Programme," *La Revue Indigène, 1* (1927), 9–10]

In the second issue, Normil Sylvain contributed a more detailed article, entitled "La Jeune littérature haïtienne" (1927), in which he argued against the use of "local color" and suggested a bolder "indigenism":

> True poetry, I find it in the refrains that the black mothers who cradled our childhood sang. . . . Our folklore is rich in such songs. It is the sound of the tam-tam . . . the trembling and sensual rhythm of a lusty meringue . . . which ought to pass into our poetry. [p. 52]

The *Revue* brought together a disparate group of writers, most importantly Emile Roumer, Philippe Thoby-Marcellin, Carl Brouard, Georges Sylvain, and Jacques Roumain. The range of work published is again impressive, finding space for meticulously crafted sonnets, experimental pieces of *vers libre,* and transcriptions of oral poetry. While eclectic in terms of form and anxious to avoid any single orthodoxy, the *Revue* did, of course, reveal particular preoccupations: a strong sense of place dominates numerous poems, and concern for cultural identity and authenticity also stands out. The journal, like the Indigenous Movement associated with it, inaugurated Indigenism, which, like any comparable broadly cultural but also literary and political concept, varies in its definition. Responding to a sense of rootlessness, dislocation, loss of identity, and absence of cultural homogeneity, Indigenism involved a "rooting" of consciousness and an attempt to reinstate the potential of art by reestablishing the artist as the voice of the community. The writers grouped around the Indigenous Movement attempted to rediscover a buried cultural language, still present, but obscured, within the Haitian consciousness. Thus poetry was—as Sylvain, the group's only (and uninspired) theorist, declared—"un instrument de connaissance" that would reconstitute Haitian ethnicity.

A further element in the Indigenist Movement's attempts to redefine and redirect Haitian literature concerns the significance of Africa in Haitian culture. The Indigenists presented Africa as the embodiment of a quintessential cultural wholeness and authenticity. Brouard was one of the first to celebrate his Africanness and to advocate a return to the freedom of African traditions, traces of which remained in Haitian culture. The obvious corollary of this was, of course, opposition to European tradition and the rejection of rationalism, in particular.

The Africa celebrated in Haitian poetry was, of course, largely an abstraction. At a literary-historical level however, it encouraged Haitian literature to be seen within the wider context of a world-wide "black" literature. Thus, by 1928, Paul Morand, in the introduction to his anthology of Haitian writing, *Anthologie de la poésie haïtienne indigène,* encouraged the island's literary aspirations to be compared "aux efforts littéraires de toute votre race, de Chicago à Madagascar" (p. 8).

While the *Revue Indigène* and the Movement married to it avoided any single orthodoxy, inherent in the work of the writers associated with them were specific new ideas about Haitian literature and the range of criteria to which it might conform. Narrow imitations of French models were considered wholly inappropriate and irrelevant, while the "indigenous" reality was to become the focus of attention. In emphasizing parallels with both South American writers and the black writers of the Harlem Renaissance, the *Revue Indigène* also placed Haitian literature within a wider context.[6]

Indigenism was replaced by Africanism as the dominant cultural, literary, and ideological movement in Haiti. The journal associated with it, *Les Griots*, was published from October 1938 to March 1940. Its issues reveal a search for racial specificity, for the authentic biopsychological elements in Haitian culture that were, they argued, fundamentally African. Publications by black writers elsewhere, and in particular the inclusion of four Haitian writers (Léon Laleau, Jacques Roumain, Jean-F. Brière, and René Belance) in Senghor's *Anthologie de la nouvelle poésie nègre et malgache de langue française* (1948), was to give the Griot movement new prestige. Not only did Negritude advocate similar views on race, history, and culture as the Griot movement, but Price-Mars's *Ainsi parla l'oncle* (1928) was being proposed as a crucial and formative "pre-Negritude" text. These concerns belong, however, to a later period.

Haiti's political history, unique in the Caribbean, encouraged a literature in which notions of patriotism, for example, were important even in the nineteenth century, preparing for the concept of a national literature at the beginning of the twentieth century. The patriotic spirit encouraged a reevaluation of the Haitian reality: in terms of landscape, tradition—and history. Independent since 1804, there was real meaning in the notion of a rediscovery of an "arrière-pays culturel," as Edouard Glissant called it. The American imperialist threat to independence encouraged Haitian writers to see the parallels between their literary concerns and those of black Americans, thus allowing for a broader perspective. In the French West Indies, the situation was, of course, very different; here it was within the very specific context of French colonialism that literary developments took place.

Whereas, in Africa, writing by the first Africans was generally prose and was subsumed into colonial literature and judged by the latter's standards, in the West Indies poetry was the dominant genre, initially imitating certain metropolitan French models, those of Romanticism, Symbolism, and Parnassianism, in particular. The poets regarded as worthy of imitation were figures such as Baudelaire, Hugo, Verlaine, Leconte de Lisle, Théodore de Banville, or José-Maria de Heredia. Classical forms, the alexandrine and sonnet, dominated, and the popular themes were conventional—the description of "exotic" landscapes, melancholic meditations in the twilight hours, and so on. Suzanne Césaire, in "Misère d'une poésie: John Antoine-Nau" (1941), an article in the journal *Tropiques* (discussed later), described this imitative and inappropriate literature in the following terms:

> Literature? yes. Hamoc literature. Sugar and vanilla literature. Literary tourism. . . . Come on, real poetry is elsewhere. Far from the rhymes, the laments, the trade winds, the parrots. Bamboos we condemn doudou literature to death. And damn the hibiscus, the frangipane, the bougainvillea. Martinican poetry will be a cannibal poetry or will not be!

In Martinique and Guadeloupe there was little to encourage the idea of a national literature: in both countries the administration and the policy of cultural assimilation were very much against such a development. In *Le Discours antillais* (1981), Edouard Glissant described the atmosphere as one that "triggers non-creativity, reinforced in this case, by the passive consumption of exterior cultural products" (p. 166). No literary journal representing the creativity of colored West Indians was published until 1908, when Oruno Lara organized *La Guadeloupe littéraire*, a branch of a cultural society founded by Lara in Pointe-à-Pitre.[7] His thinking was far from radical, yet, in addition to his tone of gratitude for the "gifts of French culture," he expressed his conviction that his non-French identity could not be wholly contained within the French language and French structures, a contention that was to be reiterated again and again in later theoretical discussions about Francophone Negro-African literature. In the February issue of *La Guadeloupe littéraire* in 1912, Lara wrote:

> How do we impose on ourselves, affirm our personality, when we are obliged to immerse ourselves in a French vision? We live by, we are inspired by, French works; we have a French culture; everything about us, our thoughts, gestures, and hopes are French. How, given the assimilation of our being in French civilization, can we preserve our own character?

This early article posits the central paradox of a Guadeloupan literature in French. Lara implies that assimilation creates a fundamental cultural impasse, preventing the development of an authentic Guadeloupan literature, expressing "our own character." A number of later articles—in particular, Aimé Césaire's "Nègreries: Jeunesse noire et assimilation," published in Paris twenty-three years later and discussed at the end of this chapter—develop the problem of re-discovering an authentic identity beneath or beyond the veneer of assimilation.

Lara advocated a local literature that would be part of a "regional literary movement of the French islands of America," thereby recognizing the importance of situating the (albeit limited) Guadeloupan regionalism he envisaged within the context of other Francophone West Indian literatures. In other ways, however, his thinking remained less forward-looking: he rejected the use of Creole as a literary language and conceived of regionalism as an idealistic, romantic, somewhat lofty patriotism rather than a more fundamental exploration of the Guadeloupan reality rooted in, for example, peasant culture and the oral tradition. Yet, however restricted some aspects of Lara's thinking may now seem, he recognized something that was by no means obvious at the time: that a specifically Guadeloupan identity existed, and that this identity could not be automatically and straightforwardly expressed within the French language and its established literary traditions.

In Martinique, Gilbert Gratiant was aware of an analogous difficulty. He spearheaded the review *Lucioles*, published from 1926 until 1928. The journal brought together colored Martinicans like Gratiant himself, white Martinicans, and metropolitan French intellectuals living on the island. Their primary objective was to make available "original works that take account of our status as Martinicans, either by birth or adoption."[8] *Lucioles* was far from radical in its politics: it benefited from the printing-press of the journal *La Paix*, a dogmatically reactionary publication. *Lucioles*'s literary conservatism disappointed younger Martinicans who had hoped for something less provincial that would draw inspiration from models such as Haiti's cultural example. Concerned neither with indigenous culture nor to reach beyond a small educated minority, *Lucioles*'s limitations were to fuel the conviction of a number of younger writers that a wholly different cultural undertaking was necessary. This was to be nothing less than a "cultural revolution," which was described in *Légitime Défense*, a journal-manifesto published by a group of Martinican students in Paris in 1932. It is against the background of American, Haitian, and French West Indian literary and cultural movements that the three journals crucial to the development of the theory and criticism of Francophone Negro-African literature should be situated. These periodicals—*La Revue du monde noir* (first published in 1931), *Légitime Défense* (which was first published in 1932), *L'Etudiant noir* (the sole number of which appeared in 1935), and *Tropiques* (first published in 1941)—represent the foundation of the theory and criticism of Negro-African literature in French. The editorial boards of these periodicals were dominated not by African intellectuals but by members of the African diaspora, and many of the theories and polemics of the earlier American, Haitian, and West Indian movements found their way directly into the Parisian debate.

La Revue du monde noir was founded by Dr. Sajous, who originally came from Liberia but had spent a great deal of time in Haiti, and Paulette and Andrée Nardal, two Martinican women. The journal's first issue appeared in November 1931, the last in April 1932. The first number opened with a prefatory piece entitled "What We Want to Do":

To give the intellectual elite of the black Race a forum for the publication of their artistic, literary, and scientific works. To study and make known by the voice of the press, books, conferences, and courses, everything that concerns the NEGRO CIVILIZATION and the natural riches of Africa. ... To create for Blacks throughout the world, without regard to nationality, an intellectual and moral link that will allow them to know one another better, to love one another better, to defend better their common interests, and to illustrate their Race, such is the triple aim that "LA REVUE DU MONDE NOIR" will pursue.

By these means, the black Race will contribute with the elite of other races and all those who have been lit up by truth, beauty, and goodness, to the material, intellectual, and moral progress of humanity.

Its motto is and will remain:

> For PEACE, WORK, and JUSTICE.
> By means of LIBERTY, EQUALITY, and FRATERNITY.

And thus, the two hundred million members which make up the black Race, although scattered amongst diverse Nations, will form, on a plane above these, a vast DEMOCRACY, the prelude to universal Democracy. [p. 1]

The above is signed, "LA DIRECTION." The scope of the journal turned out to be more limited than its brief suggests. Published in French and English, its readership was limited to those who knew one of these languages. The areas of the "Black World" paid any significant amount of attention are North America and certain parts of the West Indies. The French colonies of Africa were nowhere discussed, even in 1931, the year of the Exposition Coloniale. A large amount of space was afforded Haiti, partly because of the collaboration of the energetic Sénateur Price-Mars, whose influential book *Ainsi parla l'oncle* was the subject of an article in the third issue.[9] Price-Mars's *Une étape de l'évolution haïtienne* was discussed by Guy Zuccarelli in the journal's fifth issue in 1932 (pp. 28–31). There were also articles on Haitian voodoo: for example, a review-article by René Ménil of W. Seabrook's study *Île magique* (in the third issue in 1932, pp. 26–32). A number of Haitian poems were also published by the *Revue*.

The two dominant preoccupations of the periodical were the French West Indies, on the one hand, and publications about race—about which the Revue developed a strictly defensive attitude—on the other. In literary matters the review reveals a clear bias toward "assimilationist" writing, publishing, for example, a sensitive love story by Etienne Léro ("Evelyn"); the poems by Gratiant, René Maran, and Jules Monnerot offer little to justify their description as "poèmes antillais." Very few articles could be described as literary criticism: titles such as "Point de vue sur le Folklore nègre," by René Ménil, published in the fourth issue, are ambiguous. The "article" is a folktale offered without comment of any kind.

There are, however, one or two exceptions; in particular, Paulette Nardal's "Eveil de la conscience de race," published in the sixth issue of the *Revue* in April 1932 is an important article in terms of the historiography of black Francophone literature. Her article also reveals a particular sociological understanding of how a "new literature" comes about. The article is a comparative study of the awakening of race consciousness among "les Noirs Antillais" and "les Noirs Américains." She begins by pointing to a significant change in attitude:

Scarcely a few years—one could even say months—ago certain subjects were taboo in Martinique. Woe betide those who touched on them: one could not talk of slavery nor proclaim pride in being descended from black Africans without making a fool of oneself or at least being seen as a character. . . . And now this almost contemptuous indifference is changing. [p. 25]

Nardal attributes this shift in opinion to the experience of coming from the West Indies to France:

The sense of rootlessness experienced by Blacks in the metropole where they have not always enjoyed the consideration shown them since the Colonial Exhibition, has given them, despite their French education, a Negro spirit. But this inner state does not have an exterior manifestation. [p. 25]

This tripartite process—alienation from home, followed by discrimination in the metropole on grounds of color, and the resultant acquisition, beneath or beyond their "formation latine," of a distinct "âme nègre"—is quite different, Nardal argues, from the process whereby black Americans develop a race consciousness:

The attitude of West Indians with regard to their own race, so different from that of black Americans, is very obviously explicable in terms of the liberalism that characterizes France's politics in relation to colored people. [pp. 25–26]

Citing the German writer Sieburg's book, *Dieu est-il Francais?*, she continues:

The absence of color prejudice among the French is bound up in their conviction that they will make of the Black, in a relatively short space of time, a true Frenchman. In addition, it was natural that West Indians, coming from a mixture of two races, black and white, imbued with French culture, and ignorant of the history of the black race, would ultimately turn to the element that would offer them the most respect. [p. 26]

Nardal interprets very differently the position in which black Americans found themselves. Although not of pure origin either, "the systematic contempt which white America has always shown them, has pushed them to seek out ... symbols of pride in the history of the black race." Thus, she argues, the race question became their principal preoccupation.

Nardal goes on to explore how these differences in terms of the acquisition of race consciousness between the black Antillan and the black American have affected their respective literatures. In the American case she isolates a number of phases. The first is characterized above all by imitation:

> Blacks can only imitate, in a docile way, their white models. Only certain slaves' stories retain all their freshness and the purity of their original emotion, thanks to the use of an Afro-American dialect. [p. 26]

This is followed by a period in which the anti-slavery struggle generated "a protest literature, one of moral protestation, one where the oratorical genre is well cultivated" (p. 26). In addition, this phase produced a considerable number of documents and memoirs. As for poetry, "Incessant calls for pity characterized poetic production" (p. 27). The year 1880 is signaled as a turning-point, heralding two opposing tendencies:

> On the one hand Dunbar—a poet and novelist, who employs both English and a patois—represents, if one can put it this way, the school of racial realism. On the other Du Bois who continues, in a sense, the literature of social protest claiming for Blacks civic and cultural rights equal to those of Whites. [p. 27]

A final period is represented by those writers whose work reveals a universal purport:

> Modern authors, since 1912, without abandoning Negro themes ... rather make them their inspirational point of departure, universalizing them and, what is still more important, abandoning specifically Negro means of expression, in order to employ the forms and symbols of traditional literature. [p. 27]

Nardal cites MacKay and Langston Hughes as examples with whom readers of the *Revue* will be familiar:

> Our readers ... have been able to see that the Americans, having sidestepped any inferiority complex, calmly express their "individual blackskinned selves, without fear and without shame." [p. 27]

The evolution of Antillan writing, on the other hand, is seen to have taken place within roughly three phases. During the first, "racial preoccupations are not a major concern during the period immediately following the abolition of slavery." The second phase is characterized by imitation of the great French writers, and according to Nardal this period continues until about 1914. Since then "a generation of men can be classed whose racial concerns are primarily channeled into literature, if not their political and humanitarian concerns also" (p. 28). Works belonging to this group include René Maran's *Batouala*; *Les Continents*, described as the "premier journal noir," published in Paris; *La Dépêche Africaine*, described as "le premier journal noir qui ait pu subir l'épreuve du temps" (*Les Continents* lasted only a few months); a history of Guadeloupe, written by Maurice Gatineau, director of *La Dépêche*; Jules Monnerot's *Contributions à l'Histoire de Martinique*; and Césaire Philémon's *Les Galeries Martiniquaises*. Nardal describes these works as concerned with racial questions only at a secondary level:

> None of these works examines the black question itself. They remain tributaries of French/Latin(ate) culture. None of them express their hope in the future of the race, and the necessity of creating a feeling of solidarity between the different black groups scattered across the globe. [p. 29]

Yet more recently, Nardal observes:

> a certain number of our young friends seem to have arrived spontaneously at the last phase that we have noted in the intellectual evolution of black Americans. If they continue to treat purely Western subjects, today it is in an extremely modern form and they try, at the same time, to ennoble characteristic racial themes which our readers will be able to see in a series of very curious poems which we will soon publish. [p. 31]

Nardal's final paragraph is particularly revealing. She begins by asking, "Must we see in the tendencies that we are describing an implicit declaration of war on Latin(ate) culture and the white world in general?" Her reply is unambiguous:

> We are fully conscious of what we owe white culture and we have no intention of abandoning it in favour of who knows what obscurantism. Without it we would not have been able to become conscious of what we are. But we intend to go beyond the context of that culture with the help of learned men of the white race and all our Black friends, to give back to our brothers pride in belonging to a race that is perhaps the oldest in the world. [p. 31]

For Nardal, the *sine qua non* of a "littérature nègre" is "la conscience de race." In America Blacks were forced through circumstance to recognize their racial difference, and this in turn encouraged the early birth of a black literature. For West Indians it was "le sentiment de déracinement" that was to be "le point de départ de leur évolution" (p. 29). Yet the exploration and development of racial consciousness did not, in her view, require a rejection of "la culture latine et le monde blanc en général." It was the journal's belief in a synthesis between Negro-African and European culture which encouraged the appearance of *Légitime Défense*, edited by three former contributors. For them, synthesis represented unacceptable compromise, and the new journal was to promote a very different attitude.

The *Revue* underwrote a new perspective: the concept of "la race nègre," revealing a particular spirit and requiring not only particular social and political changes, but also fundamental changes in consciousness, had been proposed as an alternative to either the narrower regionalisms or nationalisms proposed by journals published in the West Indies and North America, on the one hand, or the French Empire, on the other. Indeed the final sentence of the Preface, "Ce que nous voulons faire," quoted in its entirety above, proposes what is in essence a "Negro nationalism."

The *Revue* probably benefited from a grant from the Ministère des Colonies, and this would be consistent with its relatively conformist spirit and quiet conservatism.[10] From a political perspective, the *Revue*'s attitude to colonialism is particularly revealing: it was entirely reformist in spirit, and fundamental questions about colonialism are nowhere raised. From a cultural perspective, any idea of a complete break with "la culture latine" was ruled out.

In both these important respects *Légitime Défense*, published two months after the *Revue*'s last issue, represented a violent shift in perspective. The frame of reference within which the new journal's contributors were writing was also very different: they were concerned not with a specific "Negro nationalism," but with a small distinct group: that of young, educated, French-speaking West Indians.[11] This group was posited as a representative of the proletariat which should, consequently, fight within existing metropolitan revolutionary organizations, and it was this that led the signatories of the text to commit themselves to the principles of the Communist Party (those of the "IIIe Internationale"). The "avertissement" did, however, recognize a crucial ethnic element in their position:

> if it [the journal-manifesto] is addressed primarily to young Blacks it is because we believe them to have particularly suffered from capitalism . . . and that they seem to offer—*in so far as they have an ethnic personality which is materially determined*—a generally more heightened potential for revolt and for joy. [p. 2; my italics]

Politically, *Légitime Défense* can be seen to follow in the tradition of a number of anti-colonial organizations that existed in Paris from the late 1920s onward: most importantly, the Comité de défense de la race nègre, the Ligue de défense de la race nègre, and the Union des travailleurs nègres. These organizations published, from time to time, various journals or bulletins: *La Voix des nègres, La Race nègre,* and *Le Cri des nègres. La Race nègre,* which appeared irregularly from 1927 to 1986, was produced by Lamine Senghor, Garan T. Kouyaté, and Emile Faure. They advocated the unconditional independence of African colonies, although the means by which this might be achieved caused disagreement: Senghor and Kouyaté believed in solidarity with metropolitan proletariat organizations (in particular the Communist Party) and argued that "the Negro struggle" should be subordinated to the anti-imperialist struggle, while Faure and his colleagues argued for the need to put the anti-colonial struggle first. By 1930, Faure controlled the direction of the journal and based its anti-colonial theories on a rejection of Western political forms (Communism as well as parliamentary liberalism) and advocated the primacy of social forms associated with traditional African societies.

Although *La Voix des nègres, La Race nègre,* and *Le Cri des nègres* advised their readers about important literary publications and *La Race nègre* printed extracts from, for example, Lucie Cousturier's *Des inconnus chez moi* and André Gide's *Voyage au Congo,* the Parisian anti-colonial associations of the late 1920s and 1930s were little concerned with literary matters: the development of a black literature was not seen as a crucial element in the anti-colonialist struggle. While almost politically orthodox by the standards of the more specifically political "negro" journals of the day, *Légitime Défense* introduced important new literary perspectives. In the historiography of the criticism of Francophone "Negro-African literature," *Légitime Défense* is thus of crucial significance.

The journal-manifesto consisted of twenty-two pages: the first fifteen were made up of a preface, followed by articles of a general nature, but including a number of articles of literary criticism. The remaining pages contained poems by Etienne Léro, René Ménil, J. M. Monnerot, and Simone Yoyotte. The literary-critical articles defined and proposed a model for a new "littérature antillaise." They were concerned with both form and content. Broadly speaking, they advocated Surrealism in place of Symbolism or Parnassianism, in terms of the former, and a new authenticity, in terms of the latter. Two articles in particular serve to demonstrate the new perspectives introduced: Ménil's "Généralités sur l'écrivain de couleur antillais" (pp. 7–9) and Léro's "Misère d'une poésie" (pp. 10–12). Ménil observes that:

If, by accident, the colored West Indian exploited for economic gain, turns his activity toward literature, his works manifest a dreary tendency to be the same as those of the white colonizer. [p. 7]

Nor does the West Indian writer attempt to imitate contemporary metropolitan writers; on the contrary, "they generally express feelings that the best authors ceased to express long ago" (p. 7). This state of affairs, Ménil goes on to write, is generally seen as a consequence of the French policy of assimilation:

> The French West Indies have, over the centuries, assimilated the lessons of French civilization to such a degree that at the present moment black West Indians can now only think like white Europeans. [p. 7]

Yet complete "assimilation" is, Ménil argues, an impossibility. Therefore, the West Indian loses his original identity but will always fall short of the identity projected by his French education as desirable. The literature that emanates from this experience of simultaneous "cultural abnegation" and "assimilation" is *objectivement hypocrite* (p. 8). Consequently, "this abstract literature interests nobody, neither the White because it is nothing more than a feeble imitation of slightly out-dated French literature, nor the Black for the same reason" (p. 8). Ménil's article is, thus far, reminiscent of Oruno Lara's 1912 article quoted earlier. However, Ménil's recommendations are rather different from Lara's. The former suggests the themes and emotions that he believes to be appropriate to West Indian literature:

> The feelings of the cane cutter in front of the implacable factory, the feelings of loneliness of the Black worldwide, revolt against the injustices which he often suffers above all in his own country, love of love, love of alcohol-induced dreams, love of inspired dances, love of life and joy, the refusal of power and the acceptance of life, etc., etc. [p. 8]

In his concluding paragraphs Ménil describes the two distinct lines along which literature develops:

> One of these directions goes toward the world and the bounty of the world, expresses fundamental needs, seeks to change existence, is addressed to those who suffer from the same passionate feelings (of hunger, of love, of servitude, etc.). A utilitarian literature. [p. 8]

This sentence has a footnote that indicates what is meant by the term "utilitarian literature": "The proletarian writers of the U.S.S.R.; in France the Surrealists and some others." The other possible line of development is described somewhat ambiguously: "the other direction abandons the world to move toward the purest part of each being. The attitude of the sleeper who does not care about the perils of the world" (p. 9). In weighing up the two options he concludes:

> An imbalance occurs in favour of the abstract because the colored West Indian expresses the feelings of another, because the power of passion and

imagination are unknown to him. It is thus appropriate for the black West Indian to recognize firstly his own passions and only to express himself, to opt for the opposite of the utilitarian, for dreams and for poetry. While pursuing his aim he will come across fantastic images . . . poems, stories, the jazz of black Americans and works of the French which, through effort and by means of the power of passion and dream, have captured the freshness of Africa. [p. 9]

A further footnote refers the reader to the French authors Ménil has in mind: "Lautréamont, Rimbaud, Apollinaire, Jarry, Reverdy, les dadas, les surréalistes."

Ménil's argument remains largely implicit: he suggests that the act of writing a "littérature utile" will fail to liberate the colored West Indian: he will simply be expressing "les sentiments d'un autre." What is required is the freeing of "les puissances de passion et d'imagination." Here Ménil implies that these "forces" emanate from an authentic self. The liberation of "ses passions propres" will come about by means of dreaming and poetry: these activities will allow the West Indian writer to recognize aspects of himself with which, due to French assimilation, he has lost touch.

In examining the position of the West Indian writer and the possibilities for an authentic West Indian literature, Ménil's article serves to focus the abstract and polemical statements made in the initial "avertissement." In particular, his text reveals the extent to which Surrealism is advocated not as an orthodoxy, but as one technique—among a number—likely to allow for appropriate West Indian themes and to liberate a specifically West Indian consciousness.

Commentators have tended to base their statements about *Légitime Défense* and its contribution to the literary and critical debate on the journal's preface which, composed in the manner of a manifesto, makes polemical statements—in the abstract. Ménil's article, while applying some similar elements, reveals a fundamentally broader and more flexible interpretation of them. Even when critics have discussed the individual articles of *Légitime Défense*, there is often a tendency to discuss only those features of the article in every way consistent with the prefatory remarks. For example, in *Littérature et developpement* (1984), Mouralis writes:

Two articles more specifically concerned with literature, those of René Ménil . . . and Etienne Léro . . . illustrate this perspective in a particularly clear way. [p. 237]

The perspective that Mouralis has outlined, based on quotations from the preface, is described in the following terms:

On the cultural level Blacks must become aware of the alienation and training of which the proletariat is everywhere a victim. Within this context the adherence, again "without reserve," to Surrealism appears, to the *Légitime Défense* group, to be the most effective means of bringing about the concrete acquisition of his rights to "human expression." In these conditions it is not thus on the basis of race awareness, but on the basis of class awareness, that an original literature produced by Blacks could be born and develop. It will no doubt draw inspiration from a lucid examination of the lot of the black man but it will not be, in principle, specifically Negro-African because the black writer is invited, from now on, to situate his work within the double problematic of Surrealism and the revolutionary activity of the Third International, that is to say within a context that goes beyond the strictly Negro-African field. [pp. 236–237]

This is to exaggerate the extent to which *Légitime Défense* advocated the sublimation of racial concerns in favour of the concerns of class, capitalism, and International Communism. In summing up his discussion of the journal, Mouralis concludes:

Such is the manner in which the writers who participated in the production of *Légitime Défense* posed the problem of the origin of a literature produced by Blacks. It is why it seems to us pointless, definitively, to ask, following L. Kesteloot or Ngal, whether *Légitime Défense* constitutes a withdrawal—because of its adherence to Communism and Surrealism—in comparison with the positions of *La Revue du Monde Noir* and in comparison with those that the Negritude movement would later take. What matters to us is to note that *Légitime Défense* defined, in a particularly clear way, the necessary relationship between literature and politics and that this allowed it to clarify cogently the conditions that may give rise to a new literature. The development of the Negritude current has been seen by some critics as a reaction against, and denial of, the theses of *Légitime Défense*. It would be true to say that *Légitime Défense* was from the beginning one of the forms that Negro-African literature was going to take, one which, precisely, refusing a narrowly cultural "rooting," present for example in Senghor, Birago, Diop, B. Dadié, placed at the forefront criticism and the spirit of revolt, and to which should be attached notably Césaire, Fanon, Marcien Towa, Mongo Beti. [pp. 238–239]

While Mouralis's account is not wholly inaccurate as far as the preface and Léro's article are concerned, Ménil's article is quite different in its emphasis. It is precisely concerned with a specific "enracinement": that of the West Indian writer. The means by which this might be achieved include the resources of Surrealism. In advocating certain specific models, Ménil does not list writers concerned with the problems of the proletariat, as would be consistent with Mouralis's argument, but rather writers "who have conquered the freshness of Africa" (p. 9). It is sufficient to point out that Césaire's journal *Tropiques*, published from 1941 until 1945 in

Martinique, is testimony to Césaire's own belief in the crucial need for cultural "enracinement," devoting as it did, considerable space to articles on, for example, the flora and fauna of the island: a very literal "enracinement."[12]

Etienne Léro's article "Misère d'une poésie" opens with the following statement: "It is profoundly inaccurate to speak of a West Indian poetry." For Léro, the *sine qua non* of a "poésie antillaise" is that it should in some sense be a national poetry, expressing national concerns, and that it should not be the preserve of a small minority:

> The bulk of the population does not read, write, or speak French. Some members of a mulatto society that is intellectually and physically bastard-ized, literally nourished on white decadence, have made themselves, for a French Bourgeoisie which uses them, the ambassadors of a mass which they stifle and, what is more, one that they disown because it is too dark-skinned. [p. 10]

The extreme mediocrity of West Indian poetry is thus, Léro argues, "closely bound up with the existing social order" (p. 10). The assimilated West Indian, he goes on to write:

> stuffed to bursting point with white morality, with white education, with white prejudices, exhibits in his slim volumes the image of his own in-flated self. [p. 10]

Above all the West Indian poet strives, in his verse, as in his behavior, not to "faire comme un nègre." "He makes it a point of honor that a White can read his book without guessing his skin color" (p. 10). As a consequence: "the foreigner will search in vain for an original or profound accent, the sensual and colorful imagination of the Black, the echo of the hates and hopes of an oppressed people" (p. 10). For Léro, it is the black American poets above all—Langston Hughes and Claude MacKay in particular—who offer a useful example, "les deux poètes noirs révolutionnaires." They have introduced into their poetry "the African love of life, the African joy of love, the African dream of death. And already young Haitian poets are producing verses swollen with a future dynamism" (p. 12).

In her article in the *Revue du monde noir*, Paulette Nardal expressed her belief that the basic condition for a "littérature nègre" was the acquisition of a "conscience de race." Ménil, in his article "Généralités sur 'l'écrivain' de couleur antillais," reveals a not dissimilar conviction that a worthwhile West Indian literature will be the product of writers who recognize their own passions, who learn "de n'exprimer que [eux-mêmes]." Léro, on the other hand, sees literary renewal only as the consequence of political and intellectual liberation:

> From the day when the black proletariat achieves its right to eat and to an intellectual life, only from that day on will a West Indian poetry exist. [p. 12]

All three articles, Nardal's, Ménil's, and Léro's, reveal a concern for the "origins" of Negro-African literature and all three point to the texts of the Negro Renaissance in the United States as influential models. A proud consciousness of race, based partly on the antiquity of African civilization, is also stressed as crucial to the development of an authentic and worthwhile literature. Outmoded French forms are seen as fundamental hindrances to a new literature, and, in the case of the two articles in *Légitime Défense*, a Surrealist poetics is proposed as appropriate—no doubt partly because such a poetics was avant-garde and revolutionary, but also because there appeared to be a consonance in both the political and what might be termed the temperamental. The Surrealist rejection of rationalism, materialism, and Christianity coupled with Surrealism's revolutionary aims were peculiarly germane to black writers' preoccupations. The revolutionary aspects of Surrealism were also particularly relevant to their concerns. Interest in the exploration of the unconscious also chimed in with black writers' concern to discover, beneath their assimilated exteriors, their authentic selves. It was in advocating a revolutionary Surrealist poetics that *Légitime Défense* moved beyond the *Revue du monde noir* in literary terms, and this is, of course, consistent with the later journal's more radical politics.

L'Etudiant Noir, which appeared three years after *Légitime Défense*, in March 1935, introduced further new theoretical ideas about the essence and function of Negro-African literature. The journal, for a long time supposedly *introuvable*, has given rise to extraordinary speculation on the part of a number of critics: the record has now been set straight in the theses by M. Steins and J. Costissela.[13] The journal was a corporate publication produced by the Association des Etudiants Martiniquais en France and was the successor to the Association's *Bulletin*. It contains three particularly important articles, including Léopold Senghor's text, "L'Humanisme et nous: René Maran." In it, Senghor proposed some of the ideas that he was later to develop as the fundamental principles of his conception of a "Negro Humanism." In particular, in the opening paragraph, he wrote:

> Humanism should lead to the discovery and knowledge of self, to a "black humanism" in our case, which I willingly define: a cultural movement that has the black man as its objective, Western reason and the Negro spirit as instruments of research; because both reason and intuition are necessary. [p. 3]

Aimé Césaire's article "Nègreries: jeunesse Noire et assimilation" (p. 2) argues for the need for authenticity: "La jeunesse Noire ne veut jouer aucun rôle; elle veut être soi" (p. 2). He goes on to describe three stages in the Negro's history:

> Negros were first enslaved: "idiots and brutes" it was said. Then a more indulgent gaze fell on them; people said to themselves "they're worth more than reputation suggests" and attempts were made to educate them; they were "assimilated." . . . Young negros today want neither enslavement nor assimilation, they want emancipation. . . . During these two periods the Negro was equally sterile. Emancipation is, on the contrary, action and creation. Black youth wants to act and to create. [p. 2]

This leads Césaire to a similar conclusion to Senghor's:

> They [black youth], want to have their poets, their novelists who will tell them about their unhappiness, their greatness; they want to contribute to universal life, to the humanizing of humanity; and for that, once again, you have either to preserve yourself or find yourself. [p. 2]

Etienne Léro, in his article in *Légitime Défense* discussed above, suggested that some form of political liberation would have to precede the birth of an authentic literature. For Césaire, writing is itself an act of liberation and self-determination; it is an act of "self-authentication":

> But to be yourself you have to fight; firstly against your wayward brothers who are afraid of being themselves. . . . Then against those who have just silenced them. . . . Finally to be yourself you have to fight yourself. [p. 2]

For Césaire, the *sine qua non* of an authentic black literature is the refusal of assimilation: the act of writing can, itself, constitute that refusal.

There is one further article in *L'Etudiant Noir* of importance to the development of the criticism of Negro-African literature, L. Sainville's "Un livre sur la Martinique." He begins by stressing the extent to which literature can pose important social questions. Having stated that "in the West Indies we must find a formula for a good black literature," he then proceeds to discuss the example of Lafcadio Hearn's work, *Esquisse martiniquaises,* which he describes as "an account (or memories) of a traveller, and an account which is above all 'folkloric' describing our customs and strange superstitions" (p. 4.) Sainville also expresses his admiration for Hearn's accounts of Martinicans at work, in particular the descriptions of women at work:

> He does not fail to emphasize the admirable courage of the robust "tray" carriers of vegetables, meat, or bread which, from Monday to Sunday inclusive, guarantee the island's grocery-provision; nor does he neglect to

speak of the jolly washer-women of Roxelane who practice their trade, sometimes risking their lives. [p. 4]

Sainville explains that:

> The author is not a proletarian guided by the doctrine and a technique of a proletarian author. However this traveler is animated by such a strong sympathy for Martinique—its landscapes, its people—that he ends up giving a lesson to all those . . . who have wanted . . . to make Martinique known. [p. 4]

Despite references to "a proletarian author," "social questions," and other similar subjects, Sainville nowhere describes Hearn's work, or what he is advocating as a model for Martinican literature, as "Socialist Realism." Nor had Ménil in his article in *Légitime Défense* used this term, referring instead to a "littérature utile." The critical vocabulary, at this stage, would appear to be lagging behind critical awareness.

Between them, Senghor, Césaire, and Sainville had suggested the broad outlines of a Negro-African literature. For Senghor what was required was "a cultural movement which has the black man as its objective, Western reason and the Negro spirit as its instruments of research": literature would find its place within such a movement. In suggesting a synthesis of "Western reason" and "the Negro spirit," Senghor was reiterating Paulette Nardal's conviction, expressed in her 1932 article "Eveil de la conscience de race," published in *La Revue du Monde Noir*. She warned against the rejection of "la culture latine": this would, she argued, bring "un retour à l'obscurantisme." However, there was a need to "dépasser le cadre de cette culture." Césaire stressed the need to overcome assimilation in order to "vivre, . . . agir et créer." Writing was proposed as an act of liberation in itself and as an act of self-determination. Sainville is most specific in his recommendations, suggesting that detailed description of daily life, of work, festivals, and traditions guarantees the authenticity of "une bonne littérature nègre." Although not mutually exclusive, the fundamental aspects of these three articles were to develop as distinct positions within Negro-African literature: Senghor and Césaire's into the poetic theories associated in particular with Negritude, and Sainville's into a predominantly political theory of Negro-African writing more relevant to the novel.

La Revue du Monde Noir, *Légitime Défense*, and *L'Etudiant noir* are crucial texts in the history of the critical and theoretical discourse concerning Negro-African literature in French. The ideas expressed within them were, clearly, influenced by the Negro Renaissance and its emphasis on the need to rehabilitate black culture and the black identity. Equally, the ideas of Haitian intellectuals, shaped by a unique political history and explored in a number of notable periodicals examined earlier, fed later debate in Paris. Haitian poetry and poetic commentary sanctioned the exploitation of new poetic themes associated with cultural contexts not previously celebrated in French verse. The importance of Africa within the Haitian literary consciousness further emphasized the extent to which Africa would be at the centre of Negro-African literature in general, as will become apparent in subsequent chapters. Although very different, literary developments in the French West Indies also made their contribution to debates in Paris, in particular in their discussions surrounding questions of cultural identity and the role of French in the quest for such an identity. Directly or indirectly, ideas and the movements associated with them were to shape in significant ways the discourses of the Parisian periodicals that established the theoretical basis for a Negro-African literature in French. That basis was to be rapidly built on and developed after the Second World War.

During the war, however, one major journal was inaugurated: *Tropiques*, organized by Aimé and Suzanne Césaire, René Ménil, and Aristide Maugée, and published between April 1941 and September 1945.[14] The importance of the magazine for the cultural and political awakening of Martinique has been amply described by a number of critics.[15] Debate has tended to focus, however, on the extent to which the journal should be regarded as a vehicle for Negritude, on the one hand, or orthodox surrealism, on the other. A. James Arnold has argued convincingly in *Modernism and Negritude* (1981) for a view of *Tropiques* as a point of synthesis of both (pp. 73ff.). One of the advantages of regarding the journal in this light is that it allows for the diversity of concerns displayed by articles. The journal was concerned both with a relatively narrow regionalism and with a very much more outward-looking perspective. In the "Présentation" of the first issue, Césaire wrote:

> Silent sterile land [Terre muette et stérile]. It is ours of which I speak. And my hearing registers the frightening silence of Man in the Caribbean. Europe. Africa. Asia.

This dualism corresponds to the journal's desire, on the one hand for a thorough *enracinement*, and on the other to incorporate philosophical and literary ideas associated with European modernism. (As the title suggest, this is a question investigated in Arnold's study.) The former is represented, for example, by E. Nona's "La Faune précolombienne des Antilles françaises" (1944) or H. Sthele's "Les Dénominations génériques des végétaux aux Antilles françaises: histoire et légendes qui s'y attachent" (1944).

In an article in the first issue, Ménil (1941) explained the paradoxes of a simultaneously introspective and universal poetry:

> The tree has access to the world not from the outside, but from its innermost being, through its roots. . . .
>
> And one penetrates the reality of men and things as one penetrates inside oneself. . . .

Here Ménil argued for a wholly new poetics, a poetics that by exposing the individual self would open the way to "l'accès au monde." Furthermore, he described the poet's commitment in terms that would later be posited as fundamental to the ontology of Negro-African literature: "To create, it is necessary to engage not with the clouds of our conceptual lives, but with the course of our own individual and collective daily lives." This "engagement" necessitated a new authentic art, fundamentally different from the modes and forms of earlier Martinican literature: "It is only by means of a total conversion of our esthetic attitudes that we will be able to pass from a formal conception of our art to our actual art."

Thus despite the war, and more particularly living under representatives of the Vichy regime on Martinique (1941–43), *Tropiques* stimulated important discussion and published a number of significant literary texts, Césaire's "Les pur-sang," for example. The journal was not, however, known to a public outside the island although one or two accounts of it appeared in *L'Arche* (Etiemble, 1944, pp. 137–142). It was the journals discussed earlier, *La Revue du Monde Noir, Légitime Défense,* and *L'Etudiant noir,* that established the theoretical basis of Negro-African literature in French, and it was this foundation that was built on after the war.

NOTES

1. L. S. Senghor, "Problématique de la négritude," Colloque sur la négritude, held in Dakar, Senegal from April 12 to 18, 1971, under the auspices of the Union Progressiste Sénégalaise, *Présence Africaine* (1972) (hereafter *P.A.*); also printed in *P.A.* 78 (1971), 3–26, and in *Liberté III: Négritude et civilisation de l'universel* (Paris, 1977). References are to *P.A.,* 78 (1971), 12–14.

2. For an account of black American writing of the 1920s see, for example, Samuel W. Allen, *The American Negro Writer and His Roots* (New York, 1960).

3. Senghor, "Problématique de la négritude," *P.A.,* 78 (1971), 10.

4. Oswald Durand, *Rires et Pleurs I*, extracts reprinted in Louis Morpeau, *Anthologie d'un siècle de poésie haïtienne 1817–1925* (Paris, 1925); Kraus reprint (Nendeln, 1970), pp. 105–107.

5. J. Roumain, "Après-midi," *La Trouée, 3* (1927), 1; reprinted in C. St-Louis and M. A. Lubin, *Panorama de la poésie haïtenne* (Port-au-Prince, 1950); Kraus reprint (Nendeln, 1970), pp. 393–394.

6. For a detailed account of the relationship between the *Revue Indigène* and the Harlem Renaissance, see M. J. Fabre, "*La Revue Indigène* et le Mouvement Nouveau Noir," *Revue de Littérature Comparée, 1* (1977), 30–39.

7. *La Revue des colonies* (1834–1842), partly written by colored West Indians, was principally concerned with the abolition or reform of slavery, rather than literary matters. For a description of the journal, see Régis Antoine, *Les Ecrivains français et les Antilles: des premiers pères blancs aux surréalistes noirs* (Paris, 1978), pp. 214–216.

8. G. Gratiant, quoted by Antoine, *Les Ecrivains*, p. 356.

9. Guy Zuccarelli, "Un Portrait du Docteur Price-Mars," *La Revue du Monde Noir, 3* (1932); Kraus reprint (Nendeln, 1971), pp. 22–25.

10. It is Régis Antoine who mentions this (*Les Ecrivains*, p. 361). It is unclear whether it was in conversation with Paulette Nardal that this emerged or whether his statement is based on some other authority.

11. A number of other journals paid some attention to literary and more broadly cultural matters: *Le Paria: organe de l'Union intercontinentale* (1922–1926), *Le Libéré* (1923–1924), and *Les Continents*, founded in 1924 by René Maran and Kojo Tovalou Houénou. The last was significant in reproducing work by Langston Hughes and Countee Cullen. The Association des Etudiants Ouest-Africains organized *causeries* modeled on those of the Etudiants Annamités; Ousmane Socé Diop advocated the need for an authentic West African literature, but his ideas never took detailed shape.

12. For example, E. Nona's article, "La Faune précolombienne des Antilles françaises," *Tropiques, 10* (1944), 42–52, and H. Sthele's long article, "Les Dénominations génériques des végétaux aux Antilles françaises: histoire et légendes qui s'y attachent," *Tropiques, 10* (1944), 53–87; *Tropiques* is discussed in some detail at the end of this chapter.

13. Martin Steins, "Les Antécédents et la genèse de la négritude senghorienne," unpublished Thèse d'Etat, Université de Paris III, 1981; Joseph Costissela, "Genèse et évolution de la négritude: des mouvements nègres à Paris (1919–1939) à Léopold Sédar Senghor (1928–1971)," unpublished Thèse d'Etat, Université de Paris IV, 1982.

14. References are to the reprint of the original edition of *Tropiques* in two volumes (Paris, 1978).

15. A. J. Arnold devotes a chapter to *Tropiques* (Chapter 3, "Poetry and Cultural Renewal: *Tropiques*") in his study *Modernism and Negritude: The Poetry and Poetics of Aimé Césaire* (Harvard, 1981).

3

Negritude and Literary Criticism

The period between the end of the Second World War and 1950 is charac-terized by a number of specific events relevant to the continuing develop-ment of a Negro-African literature and, more particularly, to its theory and criticism. Firstly, the simultaneous appearance in Paris and Dakar, in November 1947, of the review *Présence Africaine*. It was also in 1947 that Césaire's *Cahier d'un retour au pays natal* was first published in book form, prefaced by André Breton. In the same year, Léon Gontran Damas published the first anthology of poetry from the French Empire, *Poètes d'expression française 1900–1945*. The framework within which the col-lection's thirty-five poets were presented differs significantly from that of Léopold Sédar Senghor's *Anthologie de la nouvelle poésie nègre et mal-gache de langue française* (published a year later), as their respective titles indicate. Both anthologies suggested particular and relatively homogene-ous "fields"—the field of poetry from the French Empire (also referred to by Damas as "poésie coloniale d'expression française"), and the field of Negro and Malagasy poetry.

It was the later collection, however, that was to be of greater literary and literary-critical significance, particularly as Senghor's anthology was pref-aced by Sartre's penetrating and theoretically rich text, "Orphée noir." Rapidly superseding Breton's preface to Césaire's *Cahier*, Sartre's essay raised questions about the nature and scope of Negro-African literature which have shaped the criticism's development and which remain impor-tant touchstones in literary-critical discussion. Most significantly, these questions were associated with the concept of Negritude, exploited by

Sartre as a highly ambiguous term. It was this very ambiguity that guaranteed Negritude a place as a major critical trope within subsequent secondary discourses. Obscuring and expanding its relevance and significance for Negro-African literature in French, Sartre's essay encouraged a diversification of argument, a widening of the debate.

Unlike the ephemeral periodicals that appeared in Paris between the First and Second World Wars, *Présence Africaine* has been published without major interruptions since 1947 and remains a highly influential journal in the field of Negro-African studies. The journal can be best considered in three phases: from its foundation to 1950, from 1950 to 1955, and from 1955 onward. In 1950, difficulties with the regularity of the journal's appearance, and a sense that major issues had been broached in too rapid succession for thorough discussion, led the journal to abandon regular publication in favour of "special numbers." In 1955 the journal sought to alter its position in a more fundamental way, as the "Liminaire" published in the April–July issue makes clear (pp. 5–7). Here the editors expressed their concern to promote issues of *nationalism*, above all: "It takes very little imagination to understand that our common national aspirations are the very foundation of our unison in the face of a formidable colonialist." From 1955 onward, nationalism was to provide the focus for much that was discussed in *Présence Africaine*. This shift in emphasis was also visible at the various Congresses and Debates of the 1950s, discussed in the following chapter.

Returning to the journal's inauguration, however, the list of members of the "comité de patronage" indicated the intellectual orientation of the new publication: André Gide, Paul Rivet, Th. Monod, P. Maydieu (director of *La Vie intellectuelle*), E. Mounier, L. S. Senghor, P. Hazoumé, Richard Wright, J.-P. Sartre, A. Camus, Michel Leiris, and Aimé Césaire. The editorial board was made up of B. Dadié, Cissé Dia, Ayouné, G. Balandier, F. D. Sissoko, Mamadou Dia, Paul Mercier, Meye, H. Panassié, A. Sadji, T. Serpos, and M. Sillaret.

The first issue, an impressive 196-page volume, opened with an article by the journal's director, Alioune Diop, entitled "Niam n'goura ou les raisons d'être de *Présence Africaine*" (1947):

> This review does not align itself with any single philosophical or political ideology. It intends to be open to collaboration from all well-meaning men (white, yellow, or black), who are concerned to help us to define African originality and to hasten her acceptance into the modern world.

These two objectives—the definition of African originality or specificity, and the promotion of Africa's entry into the modern world—were to be achieved through the publication of three types of texts:

"Presence Africaine" is made up of three essential parts. The second, to our minds the most important, will be made up of African texts (novels, short stories, poems, plays, etc.). The first will publish works by Africanists on African culture and civilization. ... The last part, finally, will review works of art or essays concerning the black world. [p. 7]

The bias of the review was thus heavily cultural, and literary texts were clearly seen as the major means by which "l'originalité africaine" could be defined and Africa promoted in "le monde moderne."

The review recognized the need to reach an African audience:

In founding this organ we have had in mind, principally, African youths. They lack intellectual nourishment. Few echoes of the European life of the mind reach them.

This, however, was not the journal's principal preoccupation:

But, let it be understood, this is not the true point of departure of our enterprise. The idea goes back to 1942–43. A certain number of students from overseas were in Paris—at the heart of the suffering of a Europe questioning itself on its essence and the authenticity of its values—we formed a group to study the situation and the characteristics that defined us.

Neither white, nor yellow, nor black, incapable of returning wholly to our original traditions or of assimilating ourselves into Europe, we felt we were constituting a new race, mentally half-caste, but one which had not become familiar with its own originality and had scarcely taken this into account.

Uprooted? We were in so far as we had not yet thought out our position in the world and were abandoned between two societies, unrecognized in both, strangers to both. [p. 8]

It was his conviction that both African and European culture could be enriched by a more profound understanding of the respective riches of the two civilizations:

We need to know what an ideal is, to choose one and to believe in it freely, necessarily, and in terms of the life of the world. We need to grasp the questions that are asked at a global level and think about them with everyone, so as to find ourselves one day among the creators of a new order.

It was thus that the "racist period" could be brought to an end. In terms of audience he declared:

It is first and foremost in the French people that we have confidence: I mean to say in all those well-meaning men who are faithful to the most

heroic French traditions and who have committed their lives exclusively
to man and his greatness. [p. 14]

The broad humanism and relatively conciliatory tone of Diop's article
should not suggest an unwillingness on the part of the journal to confront
controversial issues. While the first number contained E. Mounier's curiously naive article "Lettre à un ami africain," it also included inflammatory
pieces by Sartre ("Présence noire," discussed below) and by Georges
Balandier ("Le Noir est un homme", pp. 31–43). Similarly, while Diop
wrote, in "Niam n'goura," "Our review is also proud to be French, to exist
within a French context" (p. 12), P. Naville, in his article "Présence
Africaine" made clear the limits of such an intention:

> In France a specialist press exists which talks a good deal about Africa; it
> is what is known as the "colonial" press. But we do not want to know
> Africa through them. We only have confidence in those newspapers or
> reviews that transmit directly the hot and vibrant voice . . . which is yours.
> [p. 45]

Criticism of France's racial attitudes were most overtly discussed in
Sartre's article "Présence noire" (pp. 28–29). He began by referring to
France's complacency and willingness to criticize the positions of other
Western powers. The Martinicans or Sengalese who came to France might
be treated as equals, Sartre argued, but "how numerous were they?" (p. 29).
Sartre went on to oppose the difference between the way in which
Blacks are treated in France as opposed to in Africa or the West Indies. A
double standard operated, Sartre argued, whereby in France Blacks were
regarded as exotic curiosities enlivening the atmosphere at a party, whereas
in Africa there was no contact between Africans and French families. Similarly, whereas in France Africans appeared to be reasonably well-heeled
students, in Africa a labourer would be lucky to earn in a month enough to
buy two kilos of meat. Most French people, he argued, had no experience
of Africa and thus lived in a happy state of ignorance:

> Out there; but we don't go and see; we are like the puritan who wants to
> eat meat as long as he can believe it grows on trees and will always refuse
> to go to the abattoirs, the real origin of the steaks he is served. [pp. 28–29]

Thus Sartre proposed that *Présence Africaine*'s greatest service would be
simply to paint an impartial picture of Blacks in French Africa. There was
no need for anger, polemic, or revolt, he maintained, the truth was all that
mattered: "That will be enough for us to feel on our faces the torrid breath
of Africa, the bitter smell of oppression and misery" (p. 29). Sartre's brief
text turned finally to the crucial question of the role of French culture and

the French language in the Francophone African undertaking, drawing attention to a fundamental paradox within Negro-African writing in French, one that he further exploited in his essay "Orphée noir" and was to become a major focus of one branch of later literary criticism associated with Negritude. Sartre wrote:

> Let us avoid seeing in these creations of the spirit a homage to French culture. . . . The truth is that blacks are trying to get in touch with each other by means of a cultural world that has been imposed on them and one which is strange to them; they must re-tailor the garment completely. Everything about it is uncomfortable and constraining, right down to the syntax, and yet they have learnt to use it and even to know the tool's inadequacies. A foreign language inhabits them and steals their thoughts; but they turn around, within themselves, and face the theft; they master within themselves this European chatter and, finally, in accepting the degree to which they are betrayed by language, they mark it with their imprint. [p. 29]

Above all he admired the fundamental aim of their project: to conquer in and by the language of the colonizer. Later, in "Orphée noir," published in the following year, he developed further the point that, in using French, African writers were opening up new semantic seams and enriching the tools used by the French writer also. In "Présence noire," he wrote simply: "Every Black who seeks to paint himself using our words and our myths, that's a bit of fresh blood circulating in this old body" (p. 29).

Between November 1947 and December 1949, seven issues of *Présence Africaine* were published. Their contents were very much as Diop had suggested they would be, and the journal introduced otherwise little-known or unknown poets, dramatists, novelists, storytellers, and essayists. Certain debates also took place within the earlier issues: for example, the "Mythe du nègre" was explored in the second and fifth issues. Articles of literary criticism were, however, rare in the journal's first phase. The emphasis was on introducing writers, on demonstrating what existed by way of Francophone African writing. From 1950 onward, as mentioned earlier, regular issues gave way to the publication of special numbers devoted to particular themes. The first, *Le Monde noir* (nos. 8/9), was a catalogue of African cultural phenomena presented from a variety of different points of view: anthropological, sociological, artistic, economic. The next two volumes were concerned with *L'Art nègre* (nos. 10/11), and *Haïti, poètes noirs* (in which both the African elements in Haitian culture and new Negro-African poetry were examined). These were followed by volumes subtitled *Le Travail en Afrique noire* (no. 13), *Les Etudiants noirs parlent* (no. 14), *Hommage à Jaques-Ricard-Mollard* (no. 15), and *Trois écrivains noirs* (no. 16). The last brought together Mongo Beti's *Ville cruelle*, Sadji's

Nini, and Jean Malonga's *Coeur d'Aryenne.* Although most of the articles contained in these special issues were to affect the context within which Negro-African literature was seen to belong, in turn affecting literary-critical practices, their influence was not great. There is, however, one exception: Albert Franklin's "La Négritude: réalité ou mystification?" (1953). Subtitled "Réflexions sur 'Orphée noir'," Franklin's article is considered later, after discussion of Sartre's important text. Not only do Franklin's "Réflexions" demonstrate the controversy aroused by Sartre's article, they also serve broadly as an example of *Présence Africaine*'s perspective at that time.

In the same year as the foundation of *Présence Africaine,* Léon Gontran Damas published his anthology, *Poètes d'expression française 1900–1945.* His introduction offered important critical insights into the new "area" that was taking shape and was itself shaped by Damas' selection. The primary objective of the work was straightforward: "In publishing the present collection, we have tried to give an overview of the movement of overseas poetry in French" (p. 7). The area proposed is thus overseas poetry in French and includes text from Africa, Madagascar, Réunion, Guadeloupe, Martinique, Indochina, and French Guyana. The introduction made clear that presenting a representative sample had been a major preoccupation:

> We have contented ourselves ... with including poets who are either classical or modern in inspiration, irrespective of poetic doctrine, obeying only our intention to publicize a hitherto unknown literature. [p. 7]

What emerges, however, is that the texts reproduced in the anthology were to be presented, not only because they employed a shared language, but, more importantly, because they all emanated from a particular sociopolitical context: that of French colonialism. This also explained, Damas argued, the poetry's own obscurity: "The colonial system has not so far allowed normal contact, not only between the Metropole and the colonies, but also amongst the colonies" (p. 7). The primary intention of the anthology was to make the poetry of these ignored "cultures franco-indigènes" (p. 8) available for the first time.

Damas made various observations about the range of poetry included. He pointed out that while apparently very different, the texts bore witness to a very considerable common desire for individualism. This he recognized particularly among the younger generation, for whom he had greatest sympathy. Their search, he argued, was not simply for novelty, but for a new form of art: "For these last, art is no longer a representation but a creation" (p. 9). The work of younger poets represented an end to a "reign of imitation" (p. 9). Their work was a reaction against "the excesses of colorful romanticism, and of symbolism," and Damas continued, "what follows the artificial formula is one that is automatic, original, and human" (p. 9). Central to this new enterprise was a different conception of the role of the artist and his responsibilities. This difference was associated with a new need for a functional art:

> Poetry has a task to fulfil, it must be more and more of its time, it must be concerned with the passionate examination of the problems of modern life and must not be afraid of risking being ahead of, and deeper into, the expression of ideas, passions, and suffering that afflicts society in general and colonial societies in particular. [pp. 9–10]

Damas declared that a new period had begun, one in which submission and inhibition no longer had a place, one in which the oppressed had a responsibility to become self-conscious, to become aware of his or her rights and duties as a writer, novelist, storyteller, essayist, or poet. The resultant poetry would be suffused with certain themes, which Damas cataloged:

> Poverty, illiteracy, the exploitation of man by man, the social and political racism that the black or yellow man suffers, forced labour, inequalities, lies, resignation, swindling, prejudice, smugness, complacency, coward- ice, resignation, crimes committed in the names of liberty, equality, frater- nity, there's the theme of this indigenous poetry of French expression. [p. 10]

The designation "poésie indigène d'expression française," unlike earlier designations, drew attention to the *solidarity* of those peoples colonized by the French, a solidarity based on common suffering. Although not associ- ated with race (in Damas' argument), it was this notion of a common suffering which Sartre was to point to as a key feature of Negritude.

While Damas presented an impressively comprehensive list of the con- cerns of "la poésie indigène d'expression française," his literary-critical observations remained thematic rather than stylistic, except in his discus- sion of Etienne Léro's work. A significant section of Damas' introduction was devoted to what were described as the innovative efforts of Léro and his review *Légitime Défense*; large extracts from the journal were repro- duced. Damas pointed out that for Léro "the extraordinarily mediocre char- acter of West Indian poetry was intimately bound up with the existent social order" (p. 12), and then went on to demonstrate how Léro had broken out of the assimilated order and had shown a new way forward:

> Etienne Léro innovates in this period when his essentially poetic spirit knew how to triumph over a culture that might have tripped him up as it had more than one of his elders—who had furthermore been gifted. . . . Thus with him, poetry in the West Indies ceases to be romantic or sym- bolist. It is no longer expansive but becomes analytical. The poet leans

on himself, looks again by means of psychoanalysis within himself. [p. 14]

Léro's achievement was not, however, the result of a complete break with French literary practices, as the analysis of *Légitime Défense* in the previous chapter made clear. Damas wrote:

> With him, and it is he who properly opens up the way, surrealism encourages the expression of the first frolics of thinking. A value system is established between poetry of the unconscious and the evolution of human utterings. [p. 14]

Yet, Damas argued, Léro's adoption of Surrealist techniques did not imply a betrayal of his origins. While he borrowed, among other features of Surrealist practice, the technique of automatic writing, a predilection for the fantastic, the description of dreams, and so on, Léro did not lose sight of his origins: "He represents, above all, an instinctive reaction against western civilization and a class lyricism which he condemns above all." While acknowledging Léro's debt to the precursors and advocates of French Surrealism, Damas also stressed the influence of Afro-American writers—for example, Langston Hughes and Claude MacKay.

Damas's introduction ended with a summing up of Léro's achievement:

> It is to him alone that Colonial Poetry of French expression owes its new blood. . . . Now it testifies to a desire to be nearer life, to deepen . . . the sense of the evolution of the country and its oppressed people, to scrutinize with a more open and fraternal gaze the face of humanity. [pp. 15–16]

It was only in the penultimate sentence of the introduction that Damas made overt the thrust of his argument, which had thus far remained implicit: "More and more Politics and Literature interpenetrate and their synchronism is made more and more apparent in the works of the representatives of the new school" [p. 16].

One of the most surprising features of Damas' 1947 anthology is the difference between the excited polemic of the introduction and the considerably less revolutionary tone of almost all the poems included. Damas' text, like Léro's in *Légitime Défense*, must be seen, above all, as a *call* for a particular kind of poetry, situated in a particular relationship with social and political concerns. His emphasis was less on what the anthology actually included, than on what it should include: its tone was prescriptive rather than descriptive.

By definition, an anthology must offer a certain coherence. Texts or authors or both must share similarities at some level. The coherence of Damas' anthology was based on the common cultural context from which the texts emanated. This he described as a "culture franco-indigène." In addition the area was described as "poésie coloniale d'expression française," "poésie indigène d'expression française," and as constituting a "mouvement poétique de langue française d'outre-mer." It is thus above all the context of French colonialism which provided the focus for the anthology, and race or color are not factors that Damas referred to in his introduction; indeed the anthology included poems by poets of various colors, including white.

The rationale for Senghor's *Anthologie de la nouvelle poésie nègre et malgache de langue française*, published the year after Damas' anthology, was very different. As its title suggested, the race of the authors whose work was included was to provide the coherence for the collection. This emphasis on the racial suggested a pan-Negrist perspective, in turn making appropriate the exploitation of Negritude as a focus for the anthology.

Sartre's introductory essay "Orphée noir," although very different from Damas' introduction, also sought to establish the relationship between the political and the poetical and in particular the nature of poetic "engagement." The most fundamental difference between the two texts stems from the different "areas" that the two anthologies cover, one described as "la poésie coloniale d'expression française" and the other as "la poésie nègre et malgache." Unlike Damas' text, Sartre's is deeply rooted, therefore, in the opposition between Black and White.

Sartre began by describing the humbling experience of being a "poetic subject": "for the white man has enjoyed for three thousand years the privilege of seeing without being seen" (p. 7; page numbers refer to S. W. Allen's translation). But this is not the poets' first concern: "It is to black men that these black poets address themselves" (p. 11). He described the poetry of the anthology as "neither satirical nor imprecatory. It is a taking conscience [taking stock of self]" (p. 11) and this observation prepared the way for the overall thrust of his argument; the first section ended with the following statement:

> It is necessarily through a poetic experience that the black man in his present situation must first take conscience [become aware] of himself and, inversely, why Negro poetry in the French language is, in our times, the sole great revolutionary poetry. [p. 11]

Etienne Léro and Damas had essentially advocated a revolutionary Negro-African poetry, one that was in line, above all, with contemporary Surrealist practice. Sartre was arguing not that Negro-African poetry should be revolutionary, but that it *necessarily* is so. This he explained in the second section of his text.

Analyzing the significance, or lack of significance, of poetry for the white proletariat, he concluded:

> Without doubt, the oppressed class must first become conscious of itself. But this taking conscience is exactly the opposite of a re-descent into one's self; it has to do here with a recognition in and by action of the objective situation of the proletariat, a situation determined by the varying circumstances of production and distribution. United by an oppression which weighs upon all, by a common struggle, the worker scarcely knows the interior contradictions which fertilize a work of art but which, on the other hand, tend to vitiate action. [p. 13]

The position of the Negro, Sartre argued, was of course in many ways similar: both the Negro and the white worker are victims of the capitalist system. The decisive shift in Sartre's argument, which separated his position from that of Léro and Damas, among others, concerned the extent to which *race* distinguishes the Negro's predicament from that of the white proletariat:

> The black man is a victim of it [oppression], inasmuch as he is black, in his role as colonized native or as a deported African. And since he is oppressed in his race and because of it, it is first of his race that it is necessary for him to take conscience [stock]. [pp. 14–15]

Sartre then pointed to the fundamental difference between the "prise de conscience" necessary for the liberation of the white worker and the black worker. The nature of the awareness that Marxism attempted to instil in the white worker was based on the nature of profit, on the objective characteristics of the proletarian's situation. Whereas,

> the "interested" contempt which the white worker displays for the Negro ... pierces him to the depth of his heart, it is necessary that the Negro oppose to it a more just view of black *subjectivity*. Thus the consciousness of race is primarily based upon the black soul, or rather, since the term recurs often in this anthology, on a certain quality common to the thoughts and to the behaviour of Negroes and which is called *Negritude*. [pp. 16–17]

Exploiting a key Sartrean term, he went on to argue:

> The Negro who vindicates his Negritude in a revolutionary movement places himself, then and there, upon the terrain of Reflection, whether he wishes to rediscover in himself certain objective traits growing out of African civilizations, or hopes to find the black Essence in the wells of his soul. [p. 17]

The term "Reflection" is not used here to mean "conceptualized thought" but, rather, a "mirror-image":

The black who calls his brothers of color to take conscience [stock] of themselves seeks to present to them a model image of his Negritude and will plunge into his soul to extricate this image which he is seeking. He wishes to be at the same time a beacon and a mirror. [p. 17]

Negritude will be felt rather than known. Distorted by the medium of white culture, both immediate apprehension and total coincidence are impossible. The resultant poetry "has nothing in common with the effusions of the heart; it is functional" (pp. 17–18). Furthermore, the poems of Senghor's anthology, unlike an anthology of "white poetry" which might contain "one hundred different subjects according to the mood and the concern of the poet, according to his condition and his country," had one underlying purpose: "from Haiti to Cayenne, a sole idea—to make manifest the black soul. Negro poetry is evangelic, it comes bearing glad tidings—Negritude is found again" (p. 18). Returning to the concept of Reflection, and introducing the paradox of assimilation, he wrote:

However, this Negritude which they seek in the abysmal depths does not fall of itself under the regard of the soul. In the soul nothing is given. The herald of the black soul has passed through the white schools. ... It is from the shock of the white culture that his Negritude has passed from immediate existence to the state of reflection. [p. 18]

A further complication was then introduced: "But by the same token he has more or less ceased to live it. In choosing to see that which he is, he has split himself in two, he no longer coincides with himself" (p. 18). The idea of the "exilé" assumed the status of a topos, for it is the black man's sense of exile from himself that prompted him to action. Equally he is in exile in Europe and, in the case of the Black in Port-au-Prince, already exiled from Africa. Earlier, Sartre had pointed out that linguistically, by using the French language, the black poet was also in exile. This theme, together with that of slavery, the opposition between Africa and Europe, and what he described as the "division manichéiste du monde noir et blanc," offered great potential as poetic themes.

Sartre's discussion of the paradox of a Francophone Negro poetry re-emerged in a section that began with an account of the relationship between the fight for political independence and the promotion of national languages. Most ethnic minorities in the nineteenth century, he pointed out, at the same time as fighting for their independence were passionately committed to the resuscitation of their national languages. The relationship between national identity and national language was then proposed; Ireland was the example: "But to be Irish, it is also necessary to think Irish, which means above all, to think in Irish" (p. 22). Moving from the particular to the general, and then to the case of the black author, Sartre argued:

> The specific traits of a Society correspond exactly to the untranslatable locutions of its language. Now that which dangerously threatens to curb the effort of the Negro to reject our tutelage is that the apostles of the new Negritude are constrained to edit [write] their gospel *in French*. [p. 22]

The resultant paradoxical position in which the Francophone black poet found himself was succinctly described: "And since words derive from ideas, when the Negro declares in French that he rejects French culture, he takes in one hand what he has pushed aside with the other" (p. 23). Sartre then suggested that this borrowed language conformed to a number of broad characteristics and that these characteristics were likely to be fundamentally at odds with the characteristics of black consciousness. French syntax and the vocabulary of the language had been forged in a far-removed place and time in response to quite different needs and to describe quite different objects. These were inappropriate to the black man's anxieties and fears. The French language and French thought were, Sartre argued, analytical. What if, he asked, "What would happen if the black genius should be [turned out to be] preeminently synthetic?" (p. 23). The solution to this apparently inescapable paradox lay not in language, in the French sense of *langue*, but in language, in the French sense of *langage*. Firstly, Sartre pointed out that:

> It is not true, however, that the Negro expresses himself in a "foreign" tongue . . . since he is perfectly at ease in it when he thinks as technician, as a scholar or as a politician. [p. 24]

The "strangeness" of the language was manifest rather in the "slight but constant unhedging [gap] which separates that which he says, when he speaks of himself, from that which he wishes to say. . . . The white words drink up his thought as the sand drinks blood" (p. 24). This sense of the inadequacy of prose, of the distance between what the writer wants language to articulate and what it does actually articulate, was not, Sartre argued, unique to the experience of the black poet but, on the contrary, constituted a fundamental aspect of every poetic project:

> He can scarcely express his Negritude *in prose*. Yet it is common knowledge that this feeling of failure before the language when considered as a means of direct expression is at the source of all poetic experience. [p. 24]

It is at this point in the argument that Sartre was able to introduce the inherently and, he argued, inescapably "revolutionary" characteristic of the modern French poetic idiom and black Francophone poetry in particular: "from Mallarmé to the Surrealists, the profound aim of French poetry appears to me to have been the auto-destruction of the language" (p. 25). This was a reaction to the realization that "language is, in essence, prose; and prose, in essence, failure" (p. 25). Returning to the case of the black poet, he wrote: "To the ruse of the colonist, they answer by an inverse and similar ruse; since the oppressor is present even in the language they speak, they will speak this language to destroy it" (p. 26). Whereas the contemporary European poet attempted to purify language, to "return it to nature," the black poet's objective was to "de-Frenchify" the language: "he smashes them [words] together, he breaks their customary associations, he couples them by force" (p. 26). Not only would the black poet strip words of their Frenchness, he would also strip them of their *whiteness*: "It is only when they have disgorged their whiteness that he adopts them, making of this language in ruins a superlanguage solemn and sacred, in brief, Poetry" (p. 26). Thus there was something peculiarly and fundamentally poetic both about "the aim of the Negro to camouflage [to depict] himself" and the manner in which he uses "the means of expression at his disposal" (p. 27). This, Sartre argued, was through force of circumstance:

> His situation incites it; even before he dreams of singing, the light of white words reflects upon him, polarises itself and alters. No aspect of this is more apparent than in the use he makes of the two coupled terms "black-white" which simultaneously cloak the great cosmic division "day and night" and the human conflict of colonist and colonial. [p. 27]

Thus:

> The Negro will to learn to say "white as the snow" to express innocence, to speak of the blackness of a look, of a soul, of a crime. Let him open his mouth and he condemns himself, except insomuch as he sets himself to destroy the hierarchy. And if he destroys it in French, he poetizes already. [p. 27]

Where modern French poetry was characterized by its *destruction* of language, black Francophone poetry was characterized by its *negation* of language. Sartre summed this up in a characteristically dense passage:

> Destruction auto-da-fe of the language, magical symbolism, ambivalence of concepts, all of modern poetry is there under its negative aspect. But it is not a gratuitous game. The situation of the black, his original "laceration," the alienation which a foreign intellect imposes upon him under the name of assimilation, place him under the obligation to regain his existentialist integrity as a Negro or, if one prefers, the original purity of his existence, by a progressive ascent, beyond the world of discourse. Negritude, as liberty, is the basic concept and the point of departure; the task is to cause it to pass from the immediate to the mediate, to develop its theme. It is thus for the black to die, of the white world to be reborn of the

black soul, as the platonic philosopher dies of the body to be reborn of the truth. This dialectic and mystic return to origins necessarily implies a method. But this method does not present itself as a neat packet of rules for the direction of the spirit. It becomes one with him who applies it. It is the dialectic law of successive transformations which will lead the Negro to coincidence with himself in Negritude. It is not something for him to *know*, nor to tear from himself in ecstasy but to discover and at the same time to become that which it is. [p. 31]

Access to what Sartre called "this original simplicity of being" is afforded by two distinct methods, one objective, the other subjective. These in turn are represented by two distinct types of poetry. The first is described as "une négritude objective" expressed in customs, the arts, song and dance: "The poet as a spiritual exercise submits himself to the fascination of primitive rhythms, and allows his thought to run in the traditional forms of black poetry" (p. 32). In a lyrical passage, Sartre evoked "tam-tams" and "nocturnal drums," "tribal story-tellers," and the "oral tradition." Poets of "objective Negritude," he concluded, like "the blacks of Africa," still existed within a rich mythical context. Francophone black poets do not exploit these myths for entertainment as the white poet might exploit popular songs. On the contrary, "the black poets of the French language are not amusing themselves with these myths as we are doing with our songs. They yield to their hypnotic spell in order that, upon the words of incantation, Negritude, magnificently evoked, should surge forth" (p. 33). Sartre contrasted this "objective poetry" with the poetry of Aimé Césaire:

Césaire has chosen to the contrary, to re-enter into himself backward [to turn in on himself]. . . . He will descend beneath words and meanings—"to think of you I have placed all words at the mount of piety"—beneath daily activities and the plan of the "restitution" beneath even the first reefs of revolt, the back turned, the eyes closed, to touch his feet finally in the black water of dreams and of desire, and to let himself drown in it. [p. 33]

Referring to Surrealist method, Sartre introduced Etienne Léro, whom he described as the first black poet to have experimented in this way. Comparing the two poets, however, served only to throw light on what Sartre saw as the profound originality of Césaire's poetry, as opposed to Léro's which he described as "exercises of a student, they remain rigid imitations, they fail 'to surpass themselves,' indeed to the contrary they close in upon themselves" (p. 35). In describing the inadequacy and inefficacy of Léro's Surrealist method, Sartre revealed the purpose or function to which this method should, by implication, be dedicated. In Léro's poetry there was something gratuitous about the Surrealist image. Two distant terms were brought into relationship in the hope that this random process would reveal a hidden aspect of Being. But, Sartre argued, Africa was nowhere evoked in

Léro's poetry and this was its great failing. "The liberation of the black man" and/or the evocation of Africa were thus specific characteristics that Sartre expected of black poetry. The first was the primary characteristic of a "subjective poetry," such as Césaire's; the second, the defining principle of "objective poetry." Sartre then revealed a further preoccupation as a reader of Francophone Negro-African poetry: if Léro's poems were removed from the context of the anthology and the author's name was hidden, a reader, whether black or white, would be unable, Sartre argued, to distinguish Léro's poetry from that of a European contributor to *La Révolution surréaliste* or the *Minotaure*. Sartre implied that the fact that Léro's racial characteristics were not visible in the fabric of his poetry rendered it inferior to Césaire's. Sartre was thus, by implication, demanding a specific and distinct black poetic project. Césaire, he argued, did not destroy all culture, but white culture. What his poetry brought to light was not the aspirations of all, but the revolutionary aspirations of the oppressed Black. Furthermore, rather than focusing on the cerebral, his poetry touched a particular form of "concrete" humanity. Sartre went on to describe his technique as that of an "automatic committed writing." This was further qualified by an apparent contradiction in terms: Césaire's writing was described as a "committed automatic and *directed* writing." By this he meant not that Césaire's writing was mediated through the intervention of reflection, but rather that there was a relentless consistency and obsessiveness conveyed by Césaire's words and images. Contrasting the white Surrealist and Césaire once more, he wrote: "At the bottom of his soul, the white surrealist finds release; at the bottom of his soul, Césaire finds the fixed inflexibility of vindication and of resentment" (p. 37). Césaire's undertaking could thus be distinguished from that of the white Surrealist, and this rendered his work superior to that of Léro. Indeed, Sartre implied that Césaire's work was more perfectly Surrealist than European Surrealism:

> In Césaire the great surrealist tradition is achieved, takes its definite sense, and destroys itself. Surrealism, European poetic movement, is stolen from the Europeans by a black who turns it against them and assigns it a rigorously prescribed function. [pp. 38–39]

Returning to the concepts of objective and subjective poetry, Sartre summed up his assessment of Césaire's poetry in terms of its Negritude. His words did not describe Negritude, did not point to Negritude, did not copy it from the real as an artist copies a model. Césaire's words created Negritude, composed it beneath the eyes of the reader. Thus Negritude became a thing, a tangible object taking shape before the reader. Here the "subjective" and "objective" methods that Sartre had earlier proposed came into relationship with each other:

The subjective method which he has chosen joins the objective method of which we have spoken above; he thrusts the black soul outside of him at the moment when others try to interiorize it. The final result is the same in the two cases. Negritude, it is this distant tom-tom in the nocturnal streets of Dakar, it is the voodoo cries of a Haitian worshipper which slide to the edge of the precipice, it is the Congo mask. But it is also this poem of Césaire, slavering sobbing glazed, writhing in the dust like a severed worm. This double spasm of absorption and excretion beats the rhythm of the black heart in all the pages of this collection. [p. 40]

Defining Negritude further, Sartre remarked that "this complex notion is, at its core, Poetry pure" (p. 40). A little later it is described as "a certain affective attitude in regard to the world" (p. 41). Finally, Sartre characterized his description of Negritude: "to employ the language of Heidegger, is being-in-the-world of the Negro" (p. 41). The following section of Sartre's complex and wide-ranging essay contrasted the ontology or consciousness of the black as opposed to the white workman, focusing initially on the difference between the white and black tradesman's relationship with the tools and skills of his trade. While the white workman may not own his tools, he owned his techniques. The black workman, on the other hand, owned neither. It is in this context that Sartre quoted the following famous section of Césaire's *Cahier d'un retour au pays natal* where he described his black brothers as:

Those who have invented neither powder [gunpowder] nor the compass
Those who have tamed neither gas nor electricity
Those who have explored neither the seas nor the skies

[pp. 42–43]

What might be seen as an absence, a failure, became according to Sartre, "a positive source of riches" (p. 43), because:

A technical rapport with Nature reveals it as a quality pure, inert, foreign; it dies. By his proud refusal to be become "homo faber," the Negro restores life to it. [p. 43]

A little later, Sartre referred to Bergson's distinction between intelligence and intuition and quoted Césaire again: "Conquerors omniscient and naive" (p. 44). The final paragraph of the section made explicit what had earlier been suggested:

Of technique [the tool], the white knows all. But this merely scratches the surface of things, it is unaware of the substance, of the life within. Negritude, to the contrary, is a comprehension through sympathy. The secret of the black is that the sources of his existence and the roots of Being are identical. [p. 44]

In the subsequent section, Sartre expanded on these various relationships with nature:

Techniques have contaminated the white worker, but the black remains the great male of the earth, the sperm of the world. . . . To labor, to plant, to eat, is to make love with nature. [p. 45]

Sartre then offered a quotation from Léon Laleau:

Under the sky the conical drum laments
It is the soul of the black
Heavy spasms of man in passion, viscous sobs of love
Violating the calm of night.

[p. 46]

This quotation was then used to re-situate his earlier remarks about the relevance of Bergson's philosophy. This is a common stylistic practice of Sartre's, making isolated quotation from his texts a problematical practice. Having earlier implied the relevance of Bergson, holding that "upon reading this poem, one cannot help but think of the famous distinction which Bergson established between intelligence and intuition" (p. 44), and having provided a quotation from Césaire that largely confirmed Bergson's distinction, Sartre wrote:

We are here, far from the chaste and asexual intuition of Bergson. It no more concerns being in sympathy with life, but being in love with all its forms. [p. 46]

Further distinctions between white and black metaphysics followed. Statements such as "For the white technician, God is primarily engineer. . . . The rapport of the creature with the creator is never carnal" (p. 46) contrasted with notions such as that "For our black poets, to the contrary, being comes from non-being as a rising phallus. Creation is an enormous and perpetual coition" (pp. 46–47). Quotations from Jean-Joseph Rabéarivelo, the Malagasy poet, and from Césaire were presented as evidence for Sartre's descriptions of black metaphysics. Furthermore, the symbolism that encapsulated this metaphysics accounted, according to Sartre, for the greatest originality of black poetry. This was based on the profound unity of vegetal and sexual symbolism which contrasted with the "mineralization of the human," visible in contemporary European poetry.

There were, however, further important motifs; one of these was the theme of suffering: "To the absurd utilitarian agitation of the white the black opposes the long authenticity of his suffering" (p. 49). It is through suffering that the black race was "a race elected [a chosen race]" (p. 49). And Sartre continued, "one could . . ., name Negritude a Passion" (p. 49). Combining this with Nietzsche's "dionysianism," he wrote:

> As the dionysian poet, the Negro seeks to penetrate beneath the brilliant phantasies of the day and encounters, a thousand feet under the apollonian surface, the inexpiable suffering which is the universal essence of man. If one wished to systematize, one would say that the black merges into all of Nature insomuch as he is sexual sympathy with Life, and that he vindicates himself as Man insomuch as he is the Passion of suffering in revolt. [pp. 49–50]

Systematizing further, and revealing his conception of the basis of the black ontology and its manifestation in black poetry, Sartre wrote:

> Perhaps it is necessary in order to understand this indissoluble unity of suffering, of eros, and of joy, to have seen the Negroes of Harlem dance frenetically to the rhythm of the blues, which are the most desolate songs of the human race. It is the rhythm, in effect, which cements these multiple aspects of the black soul; it is that which communicates its nietzschean lightness to these heavy dionysian intuitions; it is the rhythm in the tomtom, in jazz, in the throbbing of these poems, which expresses the temporal aspects of the Negro *existence*. [pp. 50–51]

Sartre then returned once more to the theme of suffering, and in particular to slavery. This experience was also to be found at the heart of the black ontology:

> From one end of the earth to the other, the blacks, separated by the language, the politics and the history of their colonizers, have in common a collective memory. [p. 53]

This memory of slavery suggested Christian parallels:

> And in a certain sense I see well enough the rapprochement one can make of a black conscience with a Christian conscience; the iron law of slavery evokes that of the Old Testament, which relates the consequences of the original sin [of original sin]. The abolition of slavery recalls that other historic fact: the Redemption. [pp. 53–54]

The parallels were, however, misleading, as "the first fact of the history of the Negro is indeed a sin, but the black is an innocent victim" (p. 54).

Having explored the apparent similarities between the experience of slavery and Christianity, Sartre turned to colonialism and Christianity; they, he argued, were no more reconcilable, because the Black's experience of slavery made it clear to him that "suffering is the common lot of men and that it is no less unmerited by them (p. 55). Through the suffering of slavery, the Black man discovered a truth unknown to or disguised by Christianity:

> suffering carries within itself its own refusal; it is in essence refusal to suffer; it is the face of the shadow of negativity, it opens itself toward revolt and toward liberty. [p. 55]

This process also introduced a historical perspective because:

> At a blow, the Negro historicizes himself to the measure by which the intuition of suffering confers upon him a collective part and assigns to him an objective in the future. [p. 55]

This historical dimension of Negritude was of extreme significance:

> Strange and decisive divergence: the *race* has transmuted itself into historicity: the Present black explodes and temporalizes himself; Negritude inserts itself with its Past and its Future in the universal History; it is no more a *state*, neither even an existential attitude; it is a Becoming. The black contribution in the evolution of humanity is no more a flavor, a taste, a rhythm, an authenticity, a cluster of primitive instincts; it is a dated enterprise, a patient construction, a future. It was in the name of ethnic qualities that the Black was recently claiming his place in the sun; at present it is upon his mission that he bases his right to life, and this mission, exactly as that of the proletariat, comes to him from his historic situation. Because he has, more than all others the sense of revolt and the love of liberty. And because he is the most oppressed, it is the liberation of all that he necessarily pursues when he labors for his own deliverance. [p. 57]

The difficulty, as Sartre saw it, was that this threatened the very homogeneity of Negritude that he had thus far proposed. On the one hand Negritude was "a lost innocence which had existence only in a distant past," and on the other "a hope which will realize itself only in the bosom of the City of the Future" (pp. 57–58). Sartre dwelt on the concept of Negritude, posing questions rather than offering answers. In one revealing passage, for example, he referred to Negritude as similar to all anthropological notions.

His next point concerned his well-known statement that "the Negro . . . creates an anti-racist racism" (p. 59). This was then framed by a crucial section:

Negritude appears as the weak stage of a dialectical progression: the theoretical and practical affirmation of white supremacy is the thesis; the position of Negritude as antithetical value is the moment of the negativity. But this negative moment is not sufficient in itself and the blacks who employ it well know it; they know that it serves to prepare the way for the synthesis or the realization of the human society without racism [races]. Thus Negritude is dedicated to its own destruction, it is passage and not objective, means and not the ultimate goal. [pp. 59–60]

Having quoted an extract from a poem by Jacques Roumain in which a loyalty to Africa is balanced against a loyalty to the "fellow workers of every land" (p. 60), Sartre argued that the next step in the argument resulted in the disappearance of Negritude: "that which was the the ancestral and mysterious boiling of black blood, the Negro himself in fact, would be recognized as a geographical accident, the inconsistent product of a universal determinism" (p. 61). A little later, a further paradoxical, contradictory, typically Sartrean definition of Negritude was proposed:

Negritude is not a state, it is pure surpassing of itself; it is love. It is at the moment that it renounces itself that it finds itself. [p. 62]

Sartre's pronouncements on the parallels between race and class were summed up at the very end of the essay:

The definition of class is objective. . . . Whereas for the Negro, it is at the bottom of his heart that he finds race and it [is] his heart which he must tear. Thus Negritude is dialectic; it is not only nor primarily the unfolding of atavistic instincts; it represents the surpassing of a fixed situation by a free conscience. [pp. 62–63]

Finally, Sartre's essay returned to poetry, and the relationship between all that has been said about Negritude, and the poetic text itself:

Negritude fashions itself in a tragic beauty which finds expression only in Poetry. Because it is a living unity, dialectic of so many opposites, because it is a Complex, rebel to analysis, it is only the multiple unity of a song and the flashing beauty of the Poem, which Breton names a "fixed exploding," which can manifest it. [p. 63]

Negritude was further defined as "the content of the poem" and "the poem as thing of the world, mysterious and open, indecipherable and suggestive." Sartre went further: "it is the poet himself," and still further:

Negritude, triumph of Narcissism and suicide of Narcissus, tension of the soul outside of its culture, words and every psychic fact, luminous night of non-knowledge, deliberate choice of the *impossible* and of that which Bataille names the "torture" [agony], intuitive acceptance of the world and rejection of the world in the name of the "law of the heart." . . . Upon this one occasion at least, the most authentic revolutionary program and the purest poetry derive from the same source. [p. 64]

Sartre's final paragraph offered various ideas on the future of Negritude and its allegiances. If for the sake of the Revolution the black poet decided to define himself first and foremost as a proletarian rather than as a Black, then would the source of this great poetry dry up, he asked, and he ended by declaring:

Let us salute today the historic chance which will permit the blacks to "raise relentlessly the great Negro cry until the foundations of the world shall tremble." [p. 65]

Sartre's typically complex and often elliptically argued essay offered a wide range of sometimes complementary, sometimes contradictory descriptions and definitions of Negritude. The relationship between Negritude and Negro-African literature was also proposed in a number of at times mutually exclusive configurations. Rather than clarifying Negritude, these paradoxes in Sartre's polemic stimulated the secondary discourses surrounding Negro-African literature. The sophistication of "Orphée noir" and its paradoxical features encouraged the incorporation of quotations from the essay into a wide range of different arguments, and many of Sartre's observations became the touchstones for relatively distinct critical approaches, as will emerge in later chapters. For example, the paradoxes of a non-French literature written in French have been seen by some critics of Negro-African literature as paramount. A further instance of his important critical legacy is his discussion of the relative significance of race and class in considering the African or West Indian writer's allegiances. This question was greatly to influence later discussion of the context in which Francophone Negro-African literature should be considered. Two schools emerge in this regard, one favouring the cultural (and racial), the other emphasizing class and situating Negro-African literature within the context of the literature of the proletariat. Negritude's historicism, expounded in "Orphée noir," was also seen by later critics as a crucial point of departure for any discussion of the concept. While few critics would deny the extent to which Negritude belongs to a particular historical moment, works that discuss Negritude have guaranteed its survival not as a contemporary literary doxy but as a highly versatile literary-critical trope. This versatility was guaranteed, to a large extent, by the multiplicity of meanings with which Sartre endowed Negritude in his seminal essay. In addition, in emphasizing

Negritude (in one instance) as a sociopolitical force or ideology, Sartre assured its place within political (as well as cultural and literary) debate.

One example of how Sartre's essay was to fuel that debate is provided by an article published in *Présence Africaine* in 1953. This text also serves as an illustration of the journal's contribution to literary-critical debate at that time. Appearing in the special number, *Les Etudiants noirs parlent*, Albert Franklin's article "La Négritude: réalité ou mystification?" is subtitled "Réflexions sur 'Orphée noir'." Franklin's concern with Negritude stemmed from his contention that:

> Negritude has surpassed the stage of a simple speculative mental attitude, because today there are Africans who exploit it, either openly or insidiously, to justify their political acts. [p. 287]

He began by referring to Negritude's origins in the work of "a young generation of black poets writing in French of whom the best-known representatives are Léopold Sédar Senghor and Aimé Césaire" (p. 287). But, he continued, "Negritude seems to us only really to become a substantial theory with a study by Jean-Paul Sartre" (p. 287). Locating Negritude's origins as a crucial theoretical term in Sartre's "Orphée noir," Franklin outlined six elements of Negritude identified by Sartre:

—anti-racist racism
—sense of collectivism
—rhythm
—sexual conception
—ancestor-worship

[p. 288]

Franklin considered each of these in turn, denying their absolute and inherent association with black consciousness and accounting for them either in terms of the material conditions of the black man's circumstances or in terms of white misconception, myth, and prejudice.

Franklin was above all concerned with the political corollaries of Negritude as his conclusion made clear:

> For the liberation of Black Africa, any study of weapons which does not itself stipulate as a condition to remain as far as possible within the limits of reality by drawing on the methods of historical materialism, will end up a mystification, as is the case with Negritude.

Secondly, Franklin argued that improving the material conditions of black people was one of the most effective means of combating racism. Finally, he declared that:

the oppressed of every nation ought to create and reinforce, across the entire world, an effective solidarity. It is a crime when, to favour a legitimate nationalism . . . some wish to encourage Negroes to brush aside the hand offered by the white proletariat, the theory of Negritude leads precisely to that. [p. 303]

Finally, Franklin denied categorically Negritude's political contribution to the fight against oppression:

> In this struggle, the theory of Negritude is not designed to help us because it is "rest, a magical holding to ransom of the world," that is to say abandon, anguish, despair. [p. 303]

Franklin's article is symptomatic of a new pragmatism with regard to cultural matters characteristic of many of the articles published in *Présence Africaine* from the early 1950s onward. This pragmatism was not, however, totally unchallenged as the Debates and Congresses of the 1950s, examined in the next chapter, reveal. Literary criticism was not tailored exclusively to the requirements of the Black Revolution, and although many literary critics and writers were preoccupied by the need for "engagement," the nature of that "engagement" was to become a controversial subject of debate, focusing the literary-critical issues of the 1950s.

4

Nationalisms and Literary Criticism: The Nature of Literary "Engagement"

The major contributions of the 1940s to the theory and criticism of Negro-African literature in French had been the publication of anthologies by Damas in 1947 and by Senghor in 1948 (prefaced by Sartre's important text), and the inauguration, again in 1947, of the journal *Présence Africaine*. The function of all three publications was, most obviously, to introduce (and thereby to promote) a new cultural phenomenon. Furthermore, the two anthologies (in line with anthologies as a genre) implied a certain homogeneity among the texts presented, and both works were accompanied by critical introductions that argued for and explained (in ways that were not necessarily the same as those of the anthology itself) this homogeneity. In a not dissimilar way, *Présence Africaine* proposed to cover a specific literary area, and again, like the anthologies, implied that this area constituted a unified field. During the 1950s, the criteria used to define the coherence of the literary area proposed by both Damas's and Senghor's anthologies, and the wider context within which *Présence Africaine*'s literary discussion had taken place, were all to be explored in greater depth.

By the 1950s, *Présence Africaine* had become the major forum for the discussion of Francophone Negro-African literature, and the emphasis was no longer simply on drawing attention to a new literary event. A number of concerns focused the debate on Negro-African literature and encouraged a more profound exploration of the literature's specificity and ontology, on the one hand, and its many anomalies, on the other. Much of the discussion concerned the nature of artistic "engagement."

Three events of the 1950s concentrated the major areas of literary-critical and theoretical discussion of the 1950s: a "Débat autour des conditions d'une poésie nationale chez les peuples noirs," which took place in 1955/56, and the two *Congrès internationaux des écrivains et artistes noirs*, which took place in 1956 and 1959.[1] The subjects that dominated these debates and the polemics to which they gave rise need careful investigation, for it is often the case that the tenacity that holds a subject at the centre of the debate points to a hidden and more controversial area, related to the apparent subject of discussion, but distinct from it. For example, embedded within literary-critical discussions of the 1950s is the question of the primacy of race or class in terms of the black writer's allegiances.

Thus in the "Débat," the fundamental question was not so much which poetic *forms* Negro-African poetry should assume in order to be consistent with its nationalistic concerns, but within which *ideological context* it should situate itself: within an international proletarian literature or alternatively within the literature of Negritude. Similarly, the layering of debate at the first *Congrès* obscures crucial controversial areas, giving rise to major points of disagreement. For example, the relative weight attributed to African as opposed to colonial culture, in considering the African writer's heritage, is fundamental to an understanding of the contributions of Senghor and Césaire. Neither writer is explicit in this regard, but the difference in their emphases points to a fundamental issue in the theory of Negro-African literature. In order to constitute an autonomous and distinct literature, Senghor advocates the writer's immersion in his or her Negro-African heritage. By conveying a sense of cultural richness and historical perspective, the African writer will, simultaneously, undermine the colonizer's derogatory discourse. Césaire, on the other hand, advocates a direct confrontation with colonial culture. Only by engaging with it will the Negro-African writer be free to assume his or her own authentic cultural identity. At the second *Congrès* there were also important areas of disagreement, again disguised beneath more obvious (and less insidious) points of contention. There, it was the political corollary of the genres which was the fundamental (but once again not explicit) literary-critical contention.

Louis Aragon's article, "D'une poésie nationale et de quelques exemples," published in *Les Lettres Françaises* in December 1953 (followed by further articles on the same subject, published in one volume, *Journal d'une poésie nationale* and accompanied by an anthology of texts serving as examples), was the catalyst for *Présence Africaine*'s "Débat autour des conditions d'une poésie nationale chez les peuples noirs." Aragon's text, which advocates the use of traditional French verse-forms in order to convey a sense of French nationalism within French poetry, reveals an awareness of the ramifications of his argument for Francophone poets of non-French nationality ("Cela s'étend à tout le domaine français qui passe les frontières"). A few lines are devoted to the cases of Tristan Tzara, Charles Dobzynski, and Belgian writers, but he does not refer to the complex position of the Francophone Negro-African writer. It was René Depestre, the Haitian, who took up a position in the debate as a black Francophone writer. His "Lettre à Ch. Dobzynski," published in *Les Lettres Françaises* in June 1955, in turn prompted Aimé Césaire to write a "Réponse à Depestre, poète haïtien: éléments d'un art poétique," which introduced the debate into the columns of that journal.

Integrated into Aragon's original article, "D'Une poésie nationale," were three poems, including one by Guillevic, all of which conform to the traditional rules of versification. Chosen by Aragon, they served as illustrations for his article which attempted to explain and justify his own practice as a poet, which, since 1940 and more particularly since the Occupation and Resistance, had been characterized by an increasing commitment to the traditional forms of French poetry. Aragon's article takes a critical look at the development of French poetry since 1850 and seeks, in particular, to implicate "l'individualisme formel en poésie" in his criticisms of contemporary French poetry. For Aragon, "traditional French verse" is "an essential *donnée* of the heritage of our people, where the national character of our poetry is expressed in its fullness" (p. 32). However, at a certain historical moment, an increasingly fragmented poetry (that of the Moderns), a poetry that for Rimbaud, Apollinaire, Spire, or Eluard had been difficult to achieve, authorized the following generations of poets, who had no experience of traditional forms, to write "directly." Elsa Triolet, Aragon continued, had drawn attention (in an article in *Les Lettres Françaises*) to the impression given by contemporary poetry of being translation. This, Aragon argued, testified to its "denationalized" quality. If great care was not taken, contemporary poets would lose:

> the carnal, living link with the nation, which is the very genius even of the language of prose, that which is by definition *untranslatable* . . . and which thereby creates the *national* greatness of a poetry. [pp. 32–33]

Vers libre is itself a "forme dénationalisée," whereas the work of Eluard, Guillevic, Pichette, Dobzynski, and Gaston Baisette, written in traditional forms, represents a new development which Aragon describes as "a kind of galvanizing of the national mentality" that gives the French consciousness "its song, its voice, its demanding strength" (p. 33).

Had it not been for René Depestre, Aragon's pronouncements on national poetry would very probably have remained a source of controversy within the French metropolitan poetic debate alone. Depestre's "Lettre à Ch. Dobzynski" was written in response to his reading of Aragon's collection of essays. In the main, Depestre found himself in sympathy with Aragon's reasoning, but his position as a black Francophone poet involved additional complications—in particular, the role of Negro-African culture in a West Indian or African poetry written in French:

> It would be an error on our part, a lie to our *nationality*, to ignore the *African* shutter which features at the window of our national traditions. This presence of Africa, of African rhythm, in all the manifestations of our artistic sensibility, should determine in large measure the forms to which we have recourse to exalt the life of our people, its struggles and hopes. [p. 5]

Depestre's first step toward resolving this difficult problem (the complexity of which Depestre fully acknowledges) involves seeing the "engagement" of Negro-Africans with the French language as an irreversible historical, political, and sociological event. The Negro-African poet must then, on the one hand, distance himself from both "l'individualisme formel" and "le cosmopolitisme" and, on the other, examine in detail the constituent elements of his culture in order to isolate those most useful to him in his elaboration of a poetry at once "réaliste et révolutionnaire." For Depestre, Aragon had shown the way that Haitian poets should follow, allowing for the incorporation of "*données* foreign to the French context." Their obligation was, according to Depestre, "to penetrate the essence . . . in order to discern in the cultural patrimony which comes to us from Africa, that which can be harmoniously integrated into the French prose tradition." The position outlined in Depestre's article is, in itself, of no great significance in terms of the history of Negro-African literary criticism and theory. Advocating that racial and cultural elements be to some degree subordinated to a French linguistic framework, Depestre's ideas for Haitian poetry scarcely represent a development from the principles outlined by the Indigenous Movement some forty years earlier. However, his article did serve to launch what was to become a major exchange of views, voiced in a series of texts published in *Présence Africaine*. The polemical crossfire initiated by Depestre threw up a number of crucial questions significant to Negro-African literary history.

Aimé Césaire had written a preface for Depestre's collection of poems *Végétations de clarté* (1951). When Depestre published his "Lettre à Ch. Dobzynski," Césaire took the opportunity to announce officially (if obliquely) his reservations about Aragon's (and Depestre's) ideologically motivated regimentation of poetry, by publishing "Réponse à Depestre, poète haïtien: éléments d'un art poétique" in *Présence Africaine* (nos. 1–2, 1955). In the poem, Césaire alludes to his fear that Depestre's adaptation of Aragon's poetic norms will lead to the abandoning of the values of Negritude which he believed to be so central to Haitian culture; he therefore appeals to Depestre:

might it be
that the rains of exile
have slackened the skin of the drum of your voice

[p. 113]

Césaire does not disguise his belief that Depestre would do better not to align himself with the dogmatic Marxist critical-realist line of the Communist Party advocated by Aragon. The poem also makes clear that the ever-present danger of exoticism militates against traditional forms (p. 114). Césaire goes on to explore the question of "l'individualisme formel" and demonstrates, throughout the text, the ambiguity of the poetic "je"—that it is the expression of West Indian culture and history rather than an indicator of any "individualisme."

In "Réponse à Depestre, poète haïtien," Césaire brought into focus a number of fundamentally important questions, not just for Negro-African poetry, but for any poetry that is in some degree "committed." While he had always held that poetics and politics cannot be wholly separated, he drew attention to two perennial problems: firstly, can ethnic and cultural differences exist within the unifying forces of the Marxist polemic; secondly, can innovative forms be used to express socialist attitudes? These two questions, which Sartre had, of course, addressed earlier in "Orphée noir," were to remain central to the critical debate surrounding Negro-African literature, and poetry in particular, and they remain important critical issues today.

Aware of the importance of the questions raised by Césaire's poem, *Présence Africaine* organized a "Débat" to which Césaire, along with many other writers, contributed. His paper, "Sur la poésie nationale" (no. 4, 1955), reveals his principal concern: to define not the "national" in poetry in general, but the significance of the debate on "la poésie nationale" for Francophone West Indian and African writing. Thus he begins by identifying what he considers to be a fundamental paradox in Depestre's position as a Haitian writer. The question is, once again, as in his "Réponse à Depestre," the place of Negritude (in this case understood simply as "African culture," broadly defined), within Haitian culture, and consequently poetry. Having confirmed that the African contribution should play a significant role in the elaboration of a West Indian poetry, Depestre's argument, Césaire explained, led him to write:

"Aragon illuminates by his genius, by his example, the direction which should be ours, Haitian poets, by leaving us the responsibility . . . to use *données* foreign to the French context." And he adds: "We must penetrate the meaning of his direction in order to discern, in the cultural domain, which comes to us from Africa, what can be harmoniously integrated into the French context." [p. 39]

For Césaire, this implied that the French contribution takes precedence: "If this sentence has a meaning it is that henceforth, for Depestre, what is essential is the French heritage, the French base" (p. 39). Only those elements of African culture which can be readily absorbed into the French tradition would be retained. Certain parts are rejected, others are retained, those precisely which could be harmoniously integrated into the French poetic tradition. Anything that cannot be readily incorporated is left aside, Césaire argued, and thus regarded as being of little value. For him, this was an inexcusable reversal of priorities: "it seems to me that Depestre, under the pretext of aligning himself with Aragon's positions, falls into a detestable assimilationism" (p. 39). The debate is supposed to concern the "national" in poetry, but, Césaire reasoned, Depestre's position was paradoxical because while attempting to commit himself to a "national poetry," he allowed his thoughts to be imprisoned within ready-made forms that exude "du *cosmopolitisme de la rhétorique internationale*" (p. 40). Where specific poetic forms were concerned, Césaire went on to ask: "Because, in the end, what have the sonnet, the epistle and other fixed forms to do with a national African or West Indian poetry?" (p. 40). Within a broader context, he maintained that defining the "national" in poetry was an extremely precarious task:

> National? Why should the alexandrine be more national than the verses of the Chanson de Roland? Why should Boileau be more national than Rimbaud? Why Déroulède more national than Apollinaire? Why rhyme more national than free verse? [p. 40]

Césaire then considered what he described as Depestre's "formalisme" (his imagery referred back to the "Réponse à Depestre"):

> Because in the end it is formalism to think that there is a pre-established form, a finished mould into which the poet only has to introduce his experience. [p. 40]

Césaire was equally suspicious of those who believed that Africa could proffer a specific form into which experience could be neatly poured. In considering the idea of formal prerequisites for Negro poetry, Césaire pointed to two extremes, both of which would fail the Negro poet: assimilationism and exoticism.

> To think that there is an African form into which the poem must, whatever the cost, be made to go, to think that it is a matter of forcing our experience as modern Negro poets into this mould fabricated in advance, seems to me to be the best way of landing up, not this time in assimilationism, but in something which is no less serious: in exoticism. I repeat, it seems to me that the problem is badly put and that here the defect is inherent. [p. 40]

For Césaire any "prescription" for poetry was counterproductive and the question of a "national poetry" wrongly formulated: "Let poetry be—that's all" (p. 40). Finally, by referring to his understanding of the poet's position in society, Césaire revealed his conviction that a genuine poet's work would, necessarily, communicate a form of nationalism:

> I'm told: "but we need a national poetry and, in particular, an African or West Indian poetry." I reply that it's a tautology. I believe that if the poet commits himself wholeheartedly to the poem, I think that his poetry, if he is African, cannot be other than an African poetry; that if the poem is good ... the poem cannot but carry the mark of the poet, his essential mark, that's to say a national mark. Who, more than the poet, is of his time, his milieu, his people? [p. 41]

Césaire concluded by arguing that black writers, like all writers, had a responsibility to innovate and to follow their own poetic intuitions:

> We are big enough to run the risks and perils of the great adventure of freedom; let our poetry exist at that price: *our right to take initiatives* including our right to make mistakes. I speak of poetry. And of the Revolution too. [p. 41; Césaire's emphasis]

Depestre replied to Césaire in a further article published in *Présence Africaine*, "Réponse à Aimé Césaire: introduction à un art poétique haïtien" (no. 4, 1955). In this long piece he developed a number of the ideas first expressed in his "Lettre à Ch. Dobzynski." Here it becomes clear that what is at issue is not so much the *form* within which the literature should be written, but the cultural or ideological context within which it should situate itself: the context of Negritude or, alternatively, that of international communism. Associated with this is the question of whether race or class should dominate the definition of the literature. If the former, then Negritude is the appropriate ideology; if the latter, an international political program. Depestre's first important point concerns the concept of "black poetry," which itself must be based on some notion of the homogeneity of black culture. The national character of a culture, Depestre argued, is not based on linguistic homogeneity, nor on racial homogeneity, but, in the final analysis, on the historical conditions of development peculiar to each country. If that source of nationalism is ignored, the danger will be, Depestre contended, that "we will risk falling under the sign of 'Negritude'" which, on the one hand, ignores the diversity of the material conditions of evolution and, on the other, considers the creative sensibility of Blacks within a homogeneous cultural bloc.

For Depestre, the notion of a "poésie noire" is a myth as confused as "la notion métaphysique de négritude" (p. 45). So as not to proceed in a contradictory manner, Depestre limits himself to discussing the case of the nationalism of Haitian culture and poetry. His first point is that Haitian culture cannot be satisfactorily regarded as an amalgam of European and African culture. Rather, Haiti is made up of two distinct, coexistent cultures. Any unity that might have been encouraged by the liberation of the slaves, Depestre argued, had been rapidly destroyed by the class struggle. The dominant group was committed to the imitation of French and North American culture. Thus two cultures confront one another in Haiti. Not, as one might expect, African culture and French culture, but rather a Haitian culture with nationalist aspirations, on the one hand, and, on the other, a poached cosmopolitanism to which the ruling classes shamelessly aspire. Thus it is not, Depestre argued, French culture per se that needed to be questioned, but the way in which it is used within Haitian society. Similarly, certain practices associated with "la culture nationale en formation," in particular certain escapist religious traditions, needed to be viewed with considerable caution. Given the complex dualism of Haitian culture, relying on a return to Haiti's African roots (associated with the literary practices of Negritude) would not guarantee an authentically Haitian poetry. The Haitian case should, rather, be viewed within a global framework. As such, French could be an important vehicle. Thus Depestre argued for the elaboration of a poetry that would be qualitatively distinct from the double heritage of France and Africa.

If Depestre's position, in considering the context within which black literature should be written and received, can best be described as privileging class rather than race, and the political rather than the cultural, Senghor's polemic, in his article solicited by *Présence Africaine*, "Suite du débat autour des conditions sur la poésie nationale chez les peuples noirs: Réponse" (no. 5, 1955–1956), advocates reliance on the potential of Negritude, as the literary (and consequently literary-critical) mainstay of black literature.

Depestre had advocated formalism in poetry and realism in prose writings, and Senghor's most serious reservations concern the former's plea for realism: "Depestre's weakness, to speak frankly, is to have chosen as his point of departure a realism invented by, and made for, the West." Senghor insists on the available resources of "le réalisme négro-africain":

> Does he have to be told that there is a Negro-African realism? . . . Does he have to be told that there is a Negro-African imagery, that is to say a style, and that the tradition to assimilate—I use an active verb—is not French? [p. 80]

He then turns to the question of formal prerequisites. Aragon's original article had advocated a return to the traditional forms of French poetry.

Senghor, like Césaire, emphasizes the indivisible nature of form and content. Where the cultural nature of the "essence" is concerned, Senghor declares: "But the essence of a Negro, even though influenced by history and by much else besides, remains incontestably Negro" (p. 80). It is here that the greatest difference between Depestre's position and Senghor's lies. The former denied the homogeneity of the black creative sensibility; Senghor, on the other hand, proceeds from the Negro's common Negritude. This in turn suggests (to Senghor) that the black poet should draw on his or her Negro-African heritage as the authentic source of cultural riches.

It is in connection with the Negro-African heritage available to the black writer that Senghor introduces a work he has recently prefaced, published by Présence Africaine, R. Colin's *Contes noirs de l'Ouest Africain* (1957), from which he quotes at length. Relevant to the debate about "la poésie nationale" are his ideas about Realism and its capacity to express "reality." Senghor is categorical in his denial of Realism's monopoly on truth. Historically, he continues, Realism, which turned into Naturalism with Zola, was the method of novelists of the second half of the nineteenth century. "It is true," Senghor argued,

> that it [the novel] claims itself to be objective because it is scientific. The novel "creates itself, emerges alone from materials." But, we know that materials are not presented, at first sight, like a photograph: they are chosen, reinvented. The writer has his subjectivity intervene. . . . In truth realism is only a subjectivity which, falsely, likes to think of itself as objective. . . . Realism becomes pure negativity. "The determinism of the naturalist novel," wrote Sartre, "crushes life, replaces human action by one-way mechanisms." [pp. 80–81]

Senghor then comments on the methods of the African folktale, explaining that the African storyteller interprets neither things nor people: they remain "things." Nor does he relate his experiences or comment on "the facts"; he presents them but does not dominate them. "Using a language where the roots of the words are concrete," he explained, "it is enough to *name*" (p. 82). Thus the Negro-African tale may or may not be "Realist":

> Realism if you like, but spiritualized and incarnated; spiritualized because incarnated, in a word *social*. It is still the best definition of a true socialist realism.

Why then, Senghor asked, do contemporary writers and storytellers look elsewhere when all they need can be found within the popular literature of Africa? The positions outlined by Senghor and Depestre represent the two extremes in the "Débat autour des conditions d'une poésie nationale chez les peuples noirs."

Gilbert Gratiant's article, "D'une poésie martiniquaise dite nationale" (no. 5, 1955–1956), which like Senghor's article, was solicited by *Présence Africaine*, is a carefully considered piece that advocates compromise—and indeed patience. Echoing Césaire, his main point, with reference to poetry in general, is that "toute bonne poésie est ensemble nationale et universelle." Turning to the specific case of Martinique, he states plainly: "I don't believe that there is a Martinican nation, but there is a Martinican country whose reality is a syncretism" (p. 86). Unlike Depestre, Gratiant maintains that this syncretism combines both French and African elements:

> In concrete terms that means that the poetry of Martinican poets should be, taken as a whole, a poetry which is faithful to Africa in terms of what Africa has experienced by way of pain and retains by way of inspiration, in terms of what she commands by way of sensibility and rhythm—faithful to France in terms of what she has had, still possesses and will develop tomorrow, in terms of generosity—in terms of what she has by way of . . . a sense of the universal;—faithful to Africa in terms of what she has by way of spirit and fantasy. [p. 87]

Gratiant also considers the question of the poetic forms appropriate to a national poetry, and here he disagrees with Depestre's position, "when he says that he wants to 'meditate' on the traditional forms of French poetry" (p. 87). This is not to say that Gratiant underestimates the French heritage available to Francophone Martinican poets. On the contrary, according to Gratiant, Martinique is also a province of French culture, and the Martinican poet may, simultaneously, and providing he is in no way compromised by the consideration, participate in the enriching of French literature in the same way as a Parisian or provincial writer.

While arguing for a position of compromise, it was Gratiant who introduced into the debate the question of the role of Creole in a national Martinican poetry, a question relevant to Durand much earlier (see chapter 2). Historically, Martinicans are bound to Creole, the only popular language, the only mother-tongue. Thus by using Creole the Martinican writer can plumb the depths of the Martinican consciousness. Thus, Gratiant argued, his poetry will be truly nationalistic, more nationalistic than any other Martinican poetry. The relationship between language and nationalism was clear. He concluded:

> Martinique is an authentically bilingual country and what she can propose that is more fundamentally "national" in terms of expression, will be Creole poetry. Better still, Creole can serve as a cultural link between the various islands of the West Indies, whether French or English. [p. 89]

Seen in this way, Creole offers the potential not only for a strengthened

Martinican nationalism, but for a West Indian nationalism. Clearly Gratiant sees the political corollaries of literary and linguistic choices within a West Indian context, whereas Senghor's emphasis is within an international Negro-African context and Depestre's within the context of an international proletariat.

David Diop also contributed a brief article, "Contribution au débat sur la poésie nationale" (no. 6, 1956), to the "Débat autour des conditions d'une poésie nationale chez les peuples noirs," which served equally as a preface to his collection *Coups de pilon*. The piece has, therefore, received a wide readership. He begins by giving a working definition of poetry:

> It [poetry] is the harmonious fusion of the tangible and the intelligible, the means of realizing by sound and sense, by the image and rhythm, the intimate union of the poet and the world which surrounds him. Poetry, the natural language of life, bursts forth and renews itself only through its contact with the real. It dies beneath corsets and imperatives. [p. 113]

Nor does Diop have faith in Depestre's (and Aragon's) strictures concerning form. No particular form can be relied on to convey a sense of nationalism, nor will a traditional form necessarily render a poetry "popular" (p. 113). Diop provides a succinct description of his understanding of what constitutes the "national" in general, before considering its implications for poetry:

> The "national" in this context is not defined by exterior markings but by psychological particularities, by habits of thought born of given conditions of life and which, filtered through the personal genius of the author, reveal a culture common to men living in a same nation. [p. 113]

Diop discusses the relationship between national character and various poetic forms, and while he believes it to be undoubtedly true that "at a certain period in France the alexandrine had been the poetic form most commonly employed" (pp. 113–114) and that "numerous chefs-d'oeuvre are witness to it" (p. 114), he believes that as the nature of the national character changes, so the forms within which it will be best expressed will also need to change; neither can remain static. What the poet must consider, therefore, is not an exterior reality and the form in which it can be best expressed, but rather: "if the poet draws from the best of himself that which reflects the essential values of his country, then his poetry will be national" (p. 114). Furthermore, his poetry will thereby have meaning, Diop argues, beyond the poet's own country. It will be a message accessible to all, transcending national boundaries. The starting-point must be what Césaire describes as "'the right to take initiatives,' that is to say freedom of choice and action" (p. 114).

In the second section of Diop's brief article, he considers the genesis of Negro-African poetry in French, and its likely future. In his final sentence he writes: "It is only thus that we can fully exercise our responsibilities and prepare the renewal of our civilizations" (p. 115). These are, by implication, the primary concerns of the poet. Historically, during the colonial period, the African artist has been deprived of access to the history of his own civilization and its languages. He is, therefore, in a dangerous position:

> The African artist, deprived of the use of his language and cut off from his people, risks being no more than the representative of a literary current . . . that of the conquering nation. His works will be, as a result of inspiration and style, the perfect illustration of the politics of assimilation, which will no doubt provoke the warm applause of a particular criticism. In point of fact, these praises will go above all to colonization which, when it can no longer hold its subjects in slavery, makes docile intellectuals exploiting Western literary modes. Which is, besides, another subtler form of bastardization. [p. 114]

The usual response to such a presentation of the apparently inescapable position in which the Francophone African writer finds himself would be to advocate the rediscovery and integration of the African cultural heritage. This Diop recognizes as the "Negritude" solution. Again, however, Diop sees serious contradictions. By attempting to remain faithful to Negritude, the African artist may fill his work with words borrowed from his native language and be too concerned with revealing a "typical" consciousness. Hoping to regenerate the great African myths, complete with the beating of tam-tams and filled with tropical mystery, the writer will simply be creating a reassuring image designed to please the colonial bourgeoisie. "That's the best way," he argued, "to fabricate a 'folkloric' poetry, which only in salons where 'Negro art' is discussed will people declare themselves enraptured" (p. 115). According to Diop, the African writer must avoid both assimilation and "a facile Africanism" (p. 115). Thus, the Francophone African writer is in an invidious position and one that will be rectified only by social and political change. His role must, therefore, be to promote that change:

> He knows that by writing in a language which is not that of his brothers, he cannot truly translate the "deep song" of his country. But by affirming the presence of Africa with all his contradictions and faith in the future, by fighting through his works for the end of the colonial regime, the black artist writing in French is contributing to the renaissance of our black cultures. [p. 115]

For Diop the existence of a Francophone poetry is tangible evidence of the African writer's subjugation. In an Africa free from constraints, he maintained, it would not occur to a writer to express his feelings and those of his people in any language other than his own. African poetry of French expression, Diop ventured, "cut off from its popular roots is, historically, condemned" (p. 115). His responsibility is, therefore, an interim one: "to paint the man whom he lives alongside, and whom he sees suffering and fighting" (p. 115).

The debate was moved on by the West Indian, Georges Desportes, in a later issue of *Présence Africaine* (no. 11, 1956–1957). Instead of repeating much of what had already been said, Desportes chose rather to consider what he describes as a "the judicious formula given . . . by Césaire: *The experience of the modern Negro poet*" (p. 88). As far as the question of language is concerned, Desportes considers that "for the time being we can only express ourselves in French" (p. 88). One of the many consequences of this, he believes, is that "we must take into account the views of French critics" (p. 88). Yet, according to Desportes, to gain the approval of French criticism "you have . . . to leave your skin at the door" (p. 88) because "only that which is in the French character and illustrates the genius of the 'race': that's to say national and classical" (p. 88) is acceptable. But it is not the West Indian writer's concern to "nourish, deliberately, French literature" (p. 88). The cultural affiliations that, as a West Indian, Desportes believes he has, are in part French but, more importantly, Creole and African. As a Creole, he considers himself somewhere between French and African, but participating in both. In addition to these racial complications, Desportes writes, should be added "antagonisms of class" (p. 89). Thus Desportes seeks not to deny the importance of either race or class but rather to balance their sometimes opposing, sometimes complementary forces. He concludes the section on the nature of the West Indian identity by writing that he has "a Creole heart, African feet and a French head" (p. 89). What is the relevance, therefore, of "French classicism" (p. 89)? What is required is, rather, "Both a new content and a new style" (p. 89):

> Inherently revolutionary, of anticolonial thinking, anti-exotic, antiformalist. To conclude, we need a role for ourselves in this world and a life for ourselves; a poetry made for us and dealt with according to our own sensibility; because, truly, *we have to choose* completely independently and with initiative, we have to celebrate our freedom. [p. 89; his emphasis]

Quoting Césaire's article "Jeunesse noire et assimilation," published in the first issue of *L'Etudiant noir*, Desportes declared: "We want to live, to create and to act" and, he adds, "[we want] to impose our influence on the world" (p. 89). He concludes the first section of his article with a reference to the important question of audience:

> But a poem will be all the more powerful, richer, if it can hold the maximum attention—on all fronts—whether of the most cultivated man, answering all the questions of his critical perspective, while at the same time systematically satisfying the demands of a popular sensibility. [p. 90]

In the second section of his article, entitled "Positions et Propositions," Desportes embarks on a brief examination of the forms in which the spirit of modern man has manifested itself since 1900: the cinema, radio, posters, advertisements, notices, painting, architecture, music, jazz, etc. His most significant conclusion is that truly modern forms of expression are particularly stimulating creatively. West Indian poets should, therefore, abandon traditional poetic forms and concentrate instead on modern forms of expression. By exploring these forms, the West Indian poet would create what Desportes describes as "a material lyricism" rooted in an understanding of the real world, that is to say, drawing on the images, symbolism, and signs—the semiotics—appropriate and familiar to modern man.

In January 1957, *Présence Africaine* considered that with Mustapha Wade's article, "Débat autour des conditions d'une poésie nationale chez les peuples noirs: autour d'une poésie nationale" (no. 11, 1956–1957), the debate could be brought to a close. His article began, "I have never liked false problems." Wade's straightforward text argued for the need to study African languages in depth, to explore their potentialities and standardize their morphologies. In the meantime, using French as a "go-between," what must be spoken must be the language of the people which Wade characterized as "vibrant, colored, clear, direct and simple, hard, explosive, frothing, and muscular." The people must be listened to, he counselled, in order that the language of poetry might in turn speak to them.

A brief "Conclusion" to the debate was published in the same January issue of *Présence Africaine* (pp. 100–101). It was both a résumé of the debate and an attempt to synthesize the various positions taken. The "Conclusion" claims that the *Premier Congrès international des écrivains et artistes noirs*, which had taken place during the course of the debate in *Présence Africaine*, had allowed certain disagreements to be resolved. Depestre, for example, no longer felt any fundamental disagreement with Césaire:

> in the field of lyricism, and its Negro possibilities, nothing, absolutely nothing, when it comes to the fundaments, will separate me from the aesthetic position defined, last year, by Aimé Césaire. [p. 101]

He believed, like Césaire, that the poet's "right to take initiatives" should be preserved in all domains. The way forward was, Depestre explained, by means of "the fuller understanding of the past." This was the only way to produce authentic work.

By the end of the debate, all those writers asked were prepared to confirm that they, and they alone, were in a position to define Negro-African poetry. Yet, at various levels there were, nevertheless, areas of disagreement that *Présence Africaine* disguised. The notion of what constituted "engagement" was one notable area in which definitions varied considerably. David Diop used the term in a strictly militant sense, whereas for Césaire, for example, "engagement" described the poet's full communion with his poetry. Most importantly perhaps, the debate on "la poésie nationale" testified to the optimism shared by participants, in the future of African poetry.

During the course of the debate, a number of questions that had been raised at the first Congress were explored at greater length (see note 1). The importance of political affiliation as opposed to racial or cultural affiliation was again a major area of dispute. Organized by *Présence Africaine*, the Congress took place in Paris, in the Amphithéâtre Descartes at the Sorbonne, from 19 to 22 September 1956, and was attended by sixty-two delegates, from the United States, the Caribbean, Francophone, Anglophone, and Lusophone Africa, and India. Most of the conference was taken up by papers, followed by debate. Contributions addressed three main themes, each one discussed on a separate day of the Congress. The first day was devoted to drawing up an "inventory of the riches of Negro-African culture'; the second to the "present crisis of this culture"; and the third to "perspectives for the future." Proceedings of the conference were published in the journal (no. 8–9–10, 1956). Price-Mars, Rector of the University of Haiti and author of *Ainsi parla l'oncle*, occupied the chair and was introduced by Alioune Diop. In his brief speech of thanks for the privilege of presiding over the conference, Price-Mars summed up the intentions of the Congress: "to affirm, exalt, to glorify the culture of black peoples" (pp. 7–8). This was to be done through recourse to a number of disciplines, namely, history, sociology, literature, poetry, and human geography (p. 8).

The first substantial contribution was Alioune Diop's "Séances d'ouverture" (pp. 9–18), in which he considered the black man's shared history, dominated by slavery, racism, and colonialism. In spite of the oppression of the past and the injustices that continue, Diop emphasized that, in the words of Lévi-Strauss, "there is no people without a culture" (p. 12). The way forward is thus to explore the black cultural heritage. He also pointed to the need for a forward-looking cultural initiative in addition to retrospective historical investigation: "We have . . . to arouse . . . new values, to explore together the new worlds born of the meeting of peoples" (p. 15). One of the most fundamental experiences shared by the delegates of the conference, Diop went on to say, was their ambiguous relationship with European culture, the culture of the colonizer. Whether believers or atheists, Christians or Muslims or Communists, they all had the common sense of being frustrated by Western culture, Diop declared. "Jean-Paul Sartre," he said, "many years ago, already noted that the French language stole the thoughts of the Negro poet" (p. 15).

Diop also touched on the multifaceted question of the intellectual's relationship with his traditional culture and emphasized the extent to which traditions must not only be rediscovered but, more importantly, constantly reinvented: "The classics of a people have to be recreated and therefore re-thought, re-interpreted by each generation" (p. 16). In concluding, he pointed to the three major concerns of the Congress: "essentially we are going to voice together and to assess, the riches, the crisis, and the promise of our culture" (p. 17). Diop made clear that this was not a matter of the scholarly research of folklore. The politically explosive element of the undertaking was clearly spelled out:

> How can the black world and its writers be given a voice when it is clear that the least song, regardless of how deeply felt by the author, contains an explosive power sufficient to call into question the colonial order, even the structures of the Western world and of the wider world? Let's not fool ourselves. We live in a period in which artists bear witness and where they are all more or less committed. [p. 17]

He then stated unequivocally a fundamental criterion for the evaluation of African art, one that was to become highly controversial: "Every great work by an African writer or artist will bear witness against racism and the imperialism of the West" (p. 17).

The antithesis of Diop's approach to African art, is represented by Senghor's paper, "L'Esprit de la civilisation ou les lois de la culture négro-africaine" ["The spirit of the civilization, or laws, of Negro-African culture"] (pp. 51–65). Where for Diop political change will allow for a cultural renaissance, for Senghor the cultural has the force to bring political change. The "African renaissance," Senghor argued, would be less the work of politicians than of Negro writers and artists. Experience had shown, he argued, that cultural revolution was the *sine qua non* of political liberation. If white America had made concessions to Negroes, it was because writers and artists had rehabilitated Negro dignity. Similarly, Senghor argued that if Europe was beginning to pay attention to Africa, it was because, from now on, her sculpture, music, dance, literature, and traditional philosophy were making their impression on an astonished world.

Thus where Diop concluded that the African work of art was great insofar as it bore witness to the West's racism and imperialism, thus laying the emphasis on a negative dialectic with Western culture, Senghor's emphasis was on the need to assert the cultural integrity of the African artefact, in other words advocating a positive dialectic with African culture. For Senghor the spirit of Africa animated the best artists and writers from both Africa and America. Where they were conscious of Negro-African culture and were inspired by it, they raised themselves to an international level. Where they turned their backs on "Mother-Africa," Senghor claimed, they lowered themselves. What constitutes "l'esprit de la civilisation négro-africaine" is thus what guarantees the authenticity—and quality and success—of the African work of art. The major part of Senghor's article explores African cultural specificity, the Negro ontology.

Senghor's well-known criteria of Negritude are far-ranging. He begins with the sensual nature of the African. He is a man of nature, a sensual, a man with his senses open. He senses rather than sees, "he senses himself" (p. 52), Senghor explained. This does not, however, deny him the power of reason: "The Negro . . . is not stripped of *reason* . . . but his reason is not discursive; it is synthetic. It is not antagonistic; it is sympathetic" (p. 52). Thus "white reason" is characterized as "analytical through use," whereas "Negro reason" is "intuitive through participation" (p. 52). "It is this physiopsychology of the Negro," Senghor goes on to argue, that explains his metaphysics and thus his social life to which both literature and art belong. And citing Father Placide Tempels as his authority (*La Philosophie Bantoue*, 1948), Senghor explains that in black Africa social life is based on a group of logically coordinated concepts. He then introduces the quintessentially Senghorian concept of "la force vitale." At the centre of the system, "il y a *l'existence*," that is, life. And he continues, "It is the ultimate gift, . . . the expression of the vital power. The Negro identifies being with life; more precisely with the vital force. His metaphysics are an existentialist ontology" (p. 53). It is within the context of other social activities—religion, sacrifice, the family, and clan—that Senghor introduces literature and art: "It is within social activity, underpinned by a religious sensibility, that literature and art become very naturally integrated" (p. 55). Literature and art are "the most useful expression . . . of the techniques of craft" (p. 56). To support this conviction, Senghor refers to Camara Laye's famous novel of 1953:

Remember, in *L'Enfant noir*, Laye's father forging gold jewelry. The prayer, or rather the poem which he recites, the eulogy sung by the griot while he works the gold, the blacksmith's dance at the end of the process, it's all these—poem, song, dance—which *brings to fruition* the work and which makes it a *chef d'oeuvre*. [p. 56; Senghor's emphasis]

Senghor also mentions the question of "engagement," but uses the term idiosyncratically:

Because they are functional and collective, Negro-African literature and art are committed. . . .

They commit the *person*—and not simply the individual—by and in a collectivity, in the sense that they are techniques of *essentialization*. They engage him in a future which will from then on be present, an integral part of self. . . . Once again, the artisan–poet is situated and he commits, with himself, *his* ethnicity, *his* history, *his* geography. [p. 56]

The aesthetic is not, however, wholly overshadowed by the functional. African art is not purely utilitarian, and the word beauty, contrary to what some ethnologists have argued, does exist in African languages. The truth is, he argues, that "the Negro-African assimilates beauty into goodness, or above all into usefulness" (p. 57). There are, however, differences between the European and African artistic intention. If, for both the Negro-African and the European, "the great rule is to please," "the one and the other do not find pleasure in the same things." Within the Graeco-Roman esthetic, which survives in the Western European esthetic until the end of the nine-teenth century, art is "imitation of nature," "corrected imitation." In black Africa, on the other hand, art is explanation and knowledge of the world. This Senghor describes as "explanation and knowledge of the world, that's to say *sensory participation in reality*." Where the European takes pleasure in *recognizing* the world by means of a reproduction of the object, desig-nated as "subject," the Negro-African takes pleasure in *knowing* it "by the image and rhythm." Senghor returns to these last two—"l'image" and "le rythme"—again and again in his writings as the two essentials of Negro-African aesthetics: "they are the two fundamental traits of Negro-African style." Here, as elsewhere, he stresses the distinctive nature of the African image which is not "image-equation" but "image-analogy," a "surrealist image." The Negro-African is horrified by straight lines, by the supposed "right word." As Aimé Césaire rightly points out, "two and two make five." Senghor then explains that "the object does not signify what it represents, but what it suggests, what it creates" (p. 59). If the mention of Surrealism in turn suggests further parallels with European literary modes, this is mis-leading, because the "Surréalism" of the image is not the same as the European Surrealist image. The latter is empirical, the former mystical, metaphysical. Senghor then quotes from Breton's *Signe ascendant*: "'The poetic analogy'—understand the European Surrealist analogy—differs fundamentally from the mystical analogy in that it in no way presupposes, through the fabric of the visible world, an invisible universe set to make itself manifest. It is wholly empirical in its approach." The Negro surrealist analogy, on the other hand, "presupposes and manifests a universe made hierarchical in terms of the vital forces" (p. 59). Rhythm is of equal impor-tance, and so too is the relationship between rhythm and image. The latter depends on the former for its effect, "here, rhythm is consubstantial with the image; it is it which completes it, in unifying, in a whole, sign and sense, the flesh and the spirit" (p. 60). Rhythm is described in the following terms: "It is the architecture of the self, the internal dynamism which gives form, the system of waves which the self emits to address Others, the pure expression of vital force" (p. 60). It is not until the concluding paragraph of Senghor's address that it becomes clear that Senghor is not only proposing these features as characteristic of Negro-African literature and art, but suggesting that these are necessary features of all significant Negro-African artistic production:

> The spirit of Negro-African civilization animates, consciously or not, the best Negro artists and writers today, whether from Africa or America. Where they are aware of, and inspired by, Negro-African culture, they raise themselves to international standing; where they turn their backs on Mother Africa, they degenerate and become weak. [p. 65]

The essential element of Senghor's critical system is thus the extent to which a work reveals its Negritude. As he writes elsewhere, "the artistic or literary work is admirable and beautiful only in so far as it conforms to the genius of the race."

Senghor's paper stands out from the bulk of the papers given at the Congress because of its breadth. His efforts to characterize "la culture négro-africaine" can be contrasted with Amadou Hampate Bâ's attempts to explore and characterize no more than the "Culture Peuhle" (pp. 85–97).

Of the twenty-seven papers given at the Congress, only seven concern literature specifically, although many have a bearing on literary matters. Of the seven devoted specifically to literature, only two deal with Francophone contexts: L. T. Achille's "Les 'Négro-Spirituals' et l'expansion de la culture noire" (pp. 227–237), and J. S. Alexis's "Du réalisme merveilleux des Haïtiens" (pp. 245–271). However, Césaire's paper, "Culture et colonisation" (pp. 190–205), while more political than literary in its focus, nevertheless discusses problems of greater significance to the Negro-African writer than the more obviously "literary" contributions. His text has exerted considerable influence over Negro-African authors.

Césaire's paper sought to reconcile apparently conflicting views. The principal point of disagreement among participants of the Debates and Congresses of the 1950s concerned the concept of Negro-African culture and the role of politics within it. His text "Culture et colonisation" explored these two phenomena and sought to define the relationship between them. His contribution was prefaced by a short section in which he defended the legitimacy of the conference in bringing together diverse members of the "Negro-African" world. In reply to those who asked: "what is the common denominator of an assembly that unites men as diverse as Africans from black Africa and North America, West Indians, and Madagascans?"

[p. 190], Césaire replied, "la situation coloniale." For him the problem of black culture is linked inseparably to the problem of colonialism: "Because all the black cultures are presently developing in the particular conditions which are a function of the colonial, or semi-colonial, or para-colonial, situation" (p. 190). Unlike Senghor, Césaire emphasizes the relationship between nationalism and culture, rather than race and culture. For Césaire "there is no culture other than the national" (p. 191). However, this does not rule out the concept of a "Negro-African" culture, because "one can talk of a large family of African cultures which merits the name of a Negro-African civilization" (p. 191). Césaire then considered "the concrete conditions in which, today, the problem of black cultures is posed" (p. 191). For him these were constituted by the colonial situation. The question therefore became the extent to which the colonial context influences the development of those cultures with which it came into contact. Césaire's answer to this question was unequivocal:

> a political and social regime which suppresses the auto-determination of a people kills, simultaneously, the creative power of that people. [p. 194]

The Bandoeng conference was, in these terms, of political but also extreme cultural significance. "It has been," Césaire argued:

> a peaceful uprising by peoples who have been starved not only of justice and dignity but also of that which first and foremost colonization took from them: culture.

He went on to outline the process by which colonialism destroys the culture of the colonized, emphasizing in particular the fate of indigenous languages:

> The "psycho-logy-petrified" language, it's been said. No longer the official language, the administrative language, the language of schools, the language of ideas, the indigenous language undergoes a demotion which thwarts it in its development and sometimes even menaces its existence. [p. 194]

Césaire rounded off this part of his paper by concluding that "all colonization translates into, with more or less delay, the death of the colonized society's civilization" (p. 196). His next concern was to refute the idea that the colonizer simply replaces the indigenous culture with his own, and from here he went on to consider a further possibility, "that of the elaboration of a new civilization, a civilization that owes something to Europe as well as to the indigenous civilization" (p. 200). Césaire holds that this theory is erroneous because "it depends on the illusion that colonization is a contract between civilizations like any other and that all borrowings are the same" (p. 200). Referring to Nietzsche's ideas on cultural homogeneity, Césaire argues that the fragmentary nature of a colonized society leads to cultural sterility. Césaire quoted the following passage from Nietzsche:

> Culture is above all the unity of artistic style in all a people's manifestations. To know a good deal and to have learnt much, is neither a necessary means of culture nor a mark of that culture and, if need be, this is closer to being a feature of the opposite of culture, barbarism, which means the absence of style or the chaotic jumble of all the styles. [p. 201]

This indictment of colonial culture is not, Césaire argued, an exaggeration. In his own words, he described the state of colonized cultures in bleak terms:

> Thus the cultural situation in the colonized countries is a tragic one. Everywhere where colonization interrupts, the indigenous culture gradually becomes sickly. And, amid the ruins, what is born is not a culture, but a kind of subculture, a subculture that, because condemned to remain marginal in relation to European culture, and to be the lot of a small number of people, with an "elite" placed in artificial conditions and deprived of the revitalizing contact with the popular culture, has no chance of blossoming into a real culture. The result is the creation of vast territories of empty cultural wilderness. [p. 203]

A formidable challenge therefore lies before all "men of black culture." But for Césaire, it is not a question of choosing between "autochthonous tradition and European civilization," between "fidelity and backwardness or progress and rupture" (p. 203). His paper ended without a straightforward prescription for the future, but his tone was, nevertheless, hopeful. Despite describing the contemporary "cultural chaos":

> Our role is to say: liberate the creator who alone will organize this chaos into a new synthesis, a synthesis that will merit, this time, the name of culture, a synthesis that will be a reconciliation with, and a surpassing of, the old and the new. But we are here to speak and to claim: give the peoples a voice. Let the black peoples take the great stage of history. [p. 205]

Césaire's paper, like most of the papers delivered at the first Congress, identified more problems than it proposed to solve.

The second Congress, on the other hand, was more purposeful. Organized by the Société Africaine de Culture, it took place in Rome from 26 March to 1 April 1959. Its objectives were publicized in an "Appel: Unité et responsabilités de la culture négro-africaine" ["Call: Unity and responsibilities of Negro-African culture"], published the year before (no. 24–25, 1959, pp. 9–17):

> Our first Congress of 1956 took as its central theme: the crisis of culture. Our principal concern then was to situate responsibilities and to dissipate ambiguities. It is mistakenly, in fact, and under the influence of colonialist interests that the peoples of the West accepted the notion of peoples without culture. . . . This year, our concern has a less critical and more constructive character. In 1956 we diagnosed what was wrong. In 1959 we are proposing a solution: the solidarity of our peoples. [p. 9]

This solidarity was to be defined and promoted in a number of ways. First, the negative discourse of Western culture had to be recognized. The authority of Western culture betrayed the personality, interests, and aspirations of black people, the notice declared. Second, a canon of texts was to be drawn up, to serve as a stock of relevant cultural references or "totems." The significance of Descartes, Shakespeare, Dante, and Goethe, for Western people, lay as much in their status as familiar "totems," the totems of a "large family." Regardless of their absolute worth (or indeed complete insignificance), these works constitute the foundations of a culture. The Pantheon of African totems had still to be drawn up, a Pantheon made up of both Ancients and Moderns. A "community of evidence," a subtler mainstay of stable cultures, was also to be established:

> A society always fosters ideas, beliefs, and judgements that are accepted and have no need of justification or apologetics. These judgements and beliefs create the atmosphere and lines of force that inspire all creation. . . . Every writer is a prisoner (even if he denies this) of the ideology and the *Weltanschauung* of his society. With our peoples we must then rethink our communal "evidence." [p. 9]

Finally, the Congress would encourage the development of a "communauté de style et d'expression," one that would naturally be wholly consonant with Negro-African consciousness. The genuine style of a society was, the text continued, a faithful reflection of its spirit at a particular moment of history. Emanating from the depths of its being, the totality of expressive forms represented by the genuine style of a people in turn had its effect on the spirit of that people, as it came to grips with new experiences. Thus the vocabulary, the genres, and the themes of the people translated and satisfied the people's developing aspirations. It was thus from among the people that writers should look for their inspiration, for their resources of expression (p. 11).

The emphasis of the Congress was very much on cultural *difference*. The role of artists and writers in defining and promoting that difference was made very clear. With reference to the four objectives outlined, the "Appel" stated:

All these original contributions: authority and responsibilities, great men and totems, evidence and value judgements, vocabularies and styles, must simultaneously *distinguish* us from others, explain us to others, and join us, and allow us to articulate ourselves, to the human family. Hence the interest in constituting a real population of writers and artists, subject to its own laws, having its own specific tasks and conscious of the historical importance of its role in the world which will (as a function of the irruption of peoples of color onto the scene of global responsibilities) redefine the laws and structures at once of culture, economics, and world politics. [p. 11; my italics]

The prescriptive tone of this section of the "Appel" draws attention to the way in which Negro-African writing has, since early in its development, evolved alongside a forceful secondary discourse, attempting to shape it according to its own ideas. This in turn encouraged a particular self-consciousness among writers and an awareness both of the literary-critical criteria that would be brought to bear on their writing and an awareness of the context within which their work would be seen to belong.

In the "Discours d'ouverture," the organizers of the Congress asked participants to address two principal areas. First, they asked: "What alterations or falsifications has the power of colonialism or racism inflicted on your discipline?" and, second, "What inspiration can your art or your discipline legitimately expect of the present aspirations of black peoples?" (p. 13). Similarly, in the opening address, Alioune Diop stressed the importance of African sources of influence for African writers. Although African artists' admiration for Western artists might be entirely legitimate, they risked losing touch with their people if they failed to find their source of inspiration among the latter.

Aimé Césaire's paper, "L'Homme de culture et ses responsabilités" (pp. 116–122), developed various ideas that he had first presented during the debate on "la poésie nationale" with René Depestre. Adamant that writing should not be directed toward specific predefined political goals, Césaire emphasized the paramount importance of creativity. Césaire suggested that what was required was not a messianic conception of the artist or writer. Nor did he believe that the artist or writer was a nation-builder or even a creator of nationalistic values. The issue was very much simpler:

The man of culture is he who by *creation* expresses himself and creates form. And this *expression* itself, by the very fact that it is *expression*, hence brought to light, creates or recreates—dialectically—in its own image the feeling of which it is, all in all, no more than the emanation. [p. 117]

Where other contributors encouraged writers to *incorporate* particular
political perspectives into their work, Césaire argued that the act of writing
was, for the African, a political act per se. Any cultural creation, because of
its very *creativity* was, by definition, a destabilizing force, a disturbing
force. First and foremost it shook the colonial hierarchy, because it transformed the "colonized," the "consumer," into a "producer." Colonialism
had sought to remove the initiative from the colonized people: to create
was to assume the power of initiative, once again. This was why, Césaire
argued:

> the colonizer can only regard all true indigenous artistic creation with
> suspicion. He can try to adjust to it. He can even try to use it. But, deep
> down, every indigenous creation is, for the colonizer, strange, therefore
> dangerous. If one wants one proof among many it is sufficient to remem-
> ber the beginnings of Negro literature in France thirty years ago and the
> scandalously hostile reaction provoked by a René Maran or a Rabearivelo.
> . . . Their mere existence constituted a scandal. [p. 118]

The act of writing also had profound psychological ramifications for
both the colonizer and the colonized. In the same way as it was dangerous
for the colonizer, it restored confidence in the colonized, thus making up
for the loss of confidence and the sense of inferiority that the experience of
colonialism instils in its subjects. Thus, Césaire declared, "We must create"
(p. 118). He was also clear that writers and artists should be concerned not
only with the colonialism of the present, but also with future political
independence and its attendant challenges.

Césaire had avoided being drawn into a debate on form, as he had been in
the "Débat autour des conditions d'une poésie nationale." A number of
other papers, on the other hand, concentrated on one form in particular, that
of the novel: for example, U. Pierre-Louis, "Le Roman française contemporain dans une impasse: perspectives comparées du roman d'Haïti, des
peuples noirs et de l'Amerigne latine" ["The Contemporary French Novel
in an Impasse: Perspectives Common to the Haitian Novel, and Black and
Latin American Peoples"] (no. 27–28, pp. 57–68) and Léonard Sainville's
"Le Roman et ses responsabilités" ["The Novel and Its Responsibilities"]
(no. 27–28, pp. 31–48). Pierre-Louis's paper considered the formal requirements of the Negro-African novel and drew parallels with the choices open
to Negro-African poetry. Referring back to the "Débat autour des conditions d'une poésie nationale," he argued that the practical recommendations
made during that debate were relevant to the novel also:

> No enrichment is possible, no recognition of self can be envisaged, no
> seizing of daily life can be practiced, if the novelists do fully recognize,

from the start, this undeniable fact, . . . that is that content engenders form. [p. 61]

The form chosen for the Negro-African novel, Pierre-Louis argued, should be appropriate to the Negro-African spirit: "Is it not the case that sobriety, the desire for coherence and control, express an idea of man and life which sterilizes creative Negro potentialities?" And he concluded that the experience of black novelists, in particular Ibero-Americans and West Indians, exposes the poverty of traditional novel forms, based on Cartesian reason and its attendant features: balance, sobriety, and proportion. He continued:

At this stage of our critical approach, under the tree of popular African, Ibero-American, and Haitian culture which is in full flower, which is triumphing in painting, popular tales, folkloric songs, and in the nuggets of wisdom of proverbs, what matters is to regraft artistic forms, a pictorial, poetic and novelistic aesthetic that will be better and better in tune with the diverse and contradictory character of the personality, intelligence, and sensibility of the black and West Indian peoples. [p. 67]

Rather as Senghor's contribution to the "Débat autour des conditions d'une poésie nationale" emphasized the need for Negro-Africanness in Negro-African poetry, so Pierre-Louis emphasized the need to find a novel-form appropriate to the Negro-African spirit. Within the debate, Senghor's paper had contrasted with Depestre's contribution which emphasized class rather than race. Similarly, Sainville's contribution to the second Congress, "Le roman et ses responsabilités," emphasized the ideological requirements of the African novel. The novel genre, he argued, had particular political concerns:

We have to study the responsibilities of the novel. By that I think we have to understand the function which it [the novel] ought to fulfil in the formation and development of the nations that are now taking off or, being born to liberty and material progress, are freeing themselves from the intolerable yoke of colonial or semi-colonial servitude. [p. 37]

He made clear what he considered the duty of the novelist to be:

Our originality is our desire to work for . . . the construction of a cultural world, the translated expression of the thought and sensibility of peoples who were yesterday still alienated, or whom the forces of oppression continue to divert from their genius. [p. 38]

Sainville ended his paper by emphasizing the need for novelists to explore and extol black cultural values and the black heritage, in addition to stressing the need for the novel of protest: "The Negro-African novel is above all a protest, the protest being more or less precisely formulated" (p. 43).

At the end of the Congress, the various specialized commissions who had been asked to explore various issues, gave their summaries. The literary body had prepared a dense text, "Résolution concernant la littérature" (no. 24–25, pp. 387–392), in which they described the seven areas that they had briefly examined. First, they had considered "the state of the vernacular literatures of black Africa and countries peopled by Africans." Second, they had considered the confrontation of "traditional cultures with the forms of Western culture, within the unhealthy and more often barbaric context of colonization." Their third consideration had been the "situation of the black writer in the modern world." Here they cited the problems of language, of audience, and of publishing. Considering "the general literary context in which the black writer signs himself up" (their fourth area of discussion), they recognized the importance of "the conscious or unconsciously felt influence of the traditional cultures of black Africa." Local and national frames of reference were, the commission argued, of importance also. In terms of literary forms, writers were encouraged to "surpass the fixed literary structures such as they emerge from the literary history of the West." The commission went into greater detail in discussing what it considered to be the "collective" concerns of African literature in contrast to Western literature:

> The affirmation of the individual, that is to say the demands of an inner freedom, is today linked to the affirmation of peoples in the form of a quest for national sovereignty, and common ambition, for the future. Negro-African literatures are thus capable of promoting new literary forms, at odds with the dominant character of Western literatures where, too often, the individual is considered to be the absolute, necessary, and sufficient end. [p. 389]

In discussing a fifth consideration, "the responsibilities of the black writer toward his people," the commission outlined the need for the development of indigenous languages. In addition, their report stressed the writer's obligation to "the true expression of the reality of his people, for a long time obscured, deformed, or denied in the course of the period of colonization." Furthermore:

> This expression is so necessary in the present circumstances that it demands of the black writer or artist a particular definition of the notion of commitment. The black writer can only participate in a spontaneous and total way in the general movement outlined earlier. [p. 389]

The commission's final point concerned the fostering of African theatre, and the "Résolution" ended with more practical recommendations, further emphasizing the prescriptive tone of the Congress.

More so than the debate of the mid-1950s and the 1956 Congress, the 1959 Congress made certain demands on the Negro-African literature of the future. The context within which Negro-African literature was discussed at this later Congress, and the characteristics recommended for it, were, naturally, to be a major influence on the literary criticism of the 1960s. The vocabulary developed to steer and monitor the nascent literature in turn shaped the criticism that met that literature as it emerged as a major body of texts.

Thus the contributions of the debate of 1955/56 and the two Congresses of 1956 and 1959 to literary criticism were highly significant, if somewhat oblique. Literary criticism is generally a retrospective process, involving the analysis or judgement of existing texts, but the emphasis of the three events considered here was very much more prescriptive and concerned with hypotheses. Underlying the discussions were questions about the shape the literature *should* take and, implicit in this, the criteria that would be brought to bear on the literature as it developed.

For some writers (and the fact that so many of the participants were primarily writers rather than critics is significant), the evaluative criteria that would be brought to bear were very much associated with political concerns: Depestre's argument, for example, was essentially that of the Marxist critical-realist and was based on his rejection of the concept of a coherent "poésie noire." Césaire's position was more complex and is consequently more difficult to summarize briefly. His texts develop around abstract concepts, and he does not conceal his unwillingness to solve the mysteries of creativity. Similarly, Gratiant argued that "all good poetry is both national and universal." For Senghor, the criteria of Negritude were proposed as evaluative literary-critical criteria.

The opinions expressed at the first Congress were no less diverse. Diop, for example, in his opening address, emphasized the need for the African work of art to testify to the West's racism and imperialism. Senghor's paper, on the contrary, stressed the need to explore and convey a sense of the richness of "la civilisation negro-africaine." Césaire's paper was particularly important in attempting to grasp the central point of contention among contributors. For Césaire, writers should not choose between autochtonous tradition and European civilization, between loyalty and backwardness or progress and alienation, but rather should aim toward "a new synthesis, a synthesis that will be reconciliation with, and a surpassing of, the old and the new."

By the end of the second Congress, where again the emphasis was heavily prescriptive, the most crucial issue had been succinctly formulated. In declaring that the Negro-African writer was committed above all to the true expression of the reality of his people, which had, during the colonial period, been obscured, deformed, and denied, the "Résolution concernant la littérature" insisted, above all, on a very careful and particular definition of commitment.

Given the extent to which the discourses of the events of the 1950s were to influence the more properly literary-critical studies of the 1960s (examined in the next chapter), it is not surprising that the seminal study in the field, Lilyan Kesteloot's *Les Écrivains noirs de langue française: naissance d'une littérature* (interestingly published in Brussels in 1963), should have proposed "engagement" as a key term with both literary-historical and, more importantly, literary-critical ramifications. Kesteloot wrote, toward the end of her introduction: "We hope to demonstrate that black writers became truly original only after they had committed themselves."

Diop's position, at one extreme of the views expressed at the second Congress, continues as one of the two poles of the critical debate and is visible in Kesteloot's approach, for example. Senghor's perspective, based on his contention that "the spirit of the Negro-African civilization animates ... today's best Negro artists and writers," at the opposite extreme from Diop's, also survives as one of the major perspectives underlying critical discourse of the 1960s and later. Both Diop and Senghor use the term "engagement" in their formulations of the duty of the Negro-African writer or artist, but their meanings are very different. The ambiguity of the term, which continues to be exploited as a major concept, is equally visible in later debates.

NOTE

1. "Débat autour des conditions d'une poésie nationale chez les peuples noirs," *Présence Africaine*, *4* (1955), 36–62; *5* (1955–1956), 79–89; *6* (1956), 113–18; *Le Premier congrès international des écrivains et artistes noirs* (Paris-Sorbonne, 19–22 September 1956), *Présence Africaine*, *8–9–10* (1956); *Contributions au 1er congrès international des écrivains et artistes noirs*, *Présence Africaine*, *14–15* (1957); *Le Deuxième congrès des écrivains et artistes noirs*, vol. 1, *L'Unité des cultures négro-africaines*, *Présence Africaine*, *24–25* (1959); *Deuxième Congrès*, vol. 2, *Responsabilités des hommes de culture*, *Présence Africaine*, *27–28* (1959).

5

Seminal Studies:
Historiography and Criticism

The closing years of the 1950s witnessed a quickening and irreversible movement toward decolonization. Since 1958 and the adoption of the constitution of the Fifth Republic, partial independence had become possible within the French community for the West African states of Senegal, Ivory Coast, Chad, Gabon, and Congo (Brazzaville), and in 1960 Cameroun and Zaïre became republics. New cultural initiatives were also taken, the volume of material written by Africans increased all the time, and a far greater number of texts became overtly preoccupied with political concerns.

During the decade from 1959 to 1969, Negro-African literature in French established itself as a distinct academic discipline shaped by the usual range of publications: histories, bibliographies, anthologies, critical studies, studies of individual authors, and, toward the mid-1960s, by textbooks (for use both in schools and in higher education). The historiographical perspectives of these publications, their assumptions concerning the boundaries of the discipline itself, and their critical methods were greatly influenced by the wider contemporary sociocultural and political climate. They were also derived in part from earlier texts: those of African writers, delivered in particular at the conferences and congresses of the previous decade and published in *Présence Africaine*; the perspectives of various anthologies, those of Damas and Senghor in particular; and, above all, Sartre's brilliant essay, "Orphée noir."

Two relatively distinct approaches emerge from these texts. Although by no means mutually exclusive, they differ rather in their emphases. One is dominated by a cultural concern, emphasizing above all the racial dimension associated with Senghor's formulation of Negritude and exemplified in his writings. The other is dominated by a political concern, above all emphasizing the "engagement" associated with Negritude and given priority in Sartre's "Orphée noir." These two perspectives correspond to the latter's distinction between a Negro-African "littérature objective" and a "littérature subjective," also based on the dichotomy between the cultural (inextricably bound up with the racial), and the ideological and political:

> To this original simplicity of being there are two converging roads of access: one objective, the other subjective. . . . There exists in effect an objective Negritude which expresses itself in the customs, the arts, the songs, and the dances of the African populations. The poet as a spiritual exercise submits himself to the fascination of primitive rhythms, and allows his thought to run in the traditional forms of black poetry. [Allen's translation, pp. 31–32]

Césaire's poetry, on the other hand, characteristic of a "littérature subjective," is evidence of a different approach:

> It is necessary to plunge under the superficial crust of reality, of common sense, of reasonableness, in order to touch the bottom of the soul and to awaken the immemorial powers of desire. [p. 34]

Again referring to Césaire's poetry, Sartre writes:

> This dense mass of words, hurled into the air like rocks by a volcano, is the Negritude which arrays itself against Europe and colonization. [pp. 36–37]

The two expressions of Negritude identified by Sartre and described as "littérature objective" and "littérature subjective" also characterize the major *methodological* differences of approach that first became visible in the 1950s. These were given greater permanence and, more importantly, greater literary-critical significance in the seminal book-length studies of Negro-African literature and one major anthology published during the 1950s and 1960s: Janheinz Jahn's *Muntu* (1958), Lilyan Kesteloot's *Les Ecrivains noirs de langue française: naissance d'une littérature* (1963), Léonard Sainville's influential *Anthologie de la littérature négro-africaine: Tome 1, Romanciers et conteurs négro-africains* (1963), Edouard Eliet's *Panorama de la littérature négro-africaine (1921–1962)* (1965), Robert Pageard's *Littérature négro-africaine d'expression française* (1966), Lilyan Kesteloot's *Négritude et situation coloniale* (1968), and the British publication, *Protest and Conflict in African Literature* edited by Pieterse and Munro (1969) which was to shape the initial approaches to Negro-African literature in Britain (both in English and in French).[1]

It was these publications with their broad concerns which exerted a powerful influence on the shape of the literature, as an *autonomous* literature, establishing its independence and defining its ontology, drawing up its boundaries and, by extension, its affiliation to other literatures and disciplines. The criteria of *evaluation* proposed by these works, and their literary-critical apparatus, depend on and are insidiously influenced by the criteria of *definition* of the area, proposed by these general, seminal works, published during the decade from 1959 to 1969 and which are the subject of the present chapter.

The approach adopted by Janheinz Jahn's book, *Muntu* (first published in 1958), differs fundamentally from the other major studies of Negro-African literature of the period. Although he recognizes the politically committed "element" in Negro-African literature (and poetry in particular), the work focuses on the conceptual aspects of African philosophy which, expressed within African poetry and prose, define the literature's specificity. Having thus established its defining characteristics, he then proposes them as evaluative criteria. For it is these characteristics that guarantee the literature's authenticity, and "authenticity" is synonymous with artistic success. The cultural and racial are thus intimately bound up with literary-critical evaluative criteria. Thus, according to Sartre's distinction, it is the "objective" aspects of Negro-African literature which concern Jahn.

The first step in Jahn's methodology in *Muntu* can be described as a search for the ontology of African creative writing. This is undertaken through a reconstruction of Bantu philosophy, drawing on ancestral beliefs as set out in the work of various European and African ethnologists, including Father Placide Tempels' *La Philosophie Bantoue*, Marcel Griaule's *Dieu d'eau*, and Abbé Kagame's thesis *La Philosophie bantu-ruandaise de l'être*.[2] Jahn extrapolates a "Negro philosophy" from these works, valid not only for all the peoples of Africa but for members of the diaspora also, which survives, Jahn claims, in Haitian Voodoo rituals for example. Once the crucial concepts of his universal black philosophy are established, he then explores the work of various Negro-African writers, highlighting features of their work found within his philosophy.

The essential concepts that Jahn isolates are *muntu, Ntu,* and *nommo. Muntu* describes the notion that the dead continue to have influence in the world; they are part of the "force vitale."[3] *Ntu,* "the essential force," embraces all things as well as people; everything is interrelated. *Ntu* explains the absolute coherence of the world, a coherence that allows the African poet to commune with all things, both animate and inanimate. Most significant for Negro-African writing is the third concept proposed by Jahn, *nommo,* the "magic power of the word." In what Jahn describes as "African metaphysics," all transformation, creation, and procreation is made by the word. According to Jahn, the all-powerful aspect of the word pervades the work of numerous Negro-African writers. This he describes as a conviction that everything, including the poet himself, can be transformed by the *nommo* which pervades the revolutionary art of a Césaire just as much as the profound irony of Tutuola, for example (*Muntu,* p. 1). *Muntu, ntu,* and *nommo,* Jahn argues, form the conceptual basis of a universal black philosophy. From this point in his argument, he might have gone on simply to provide quotations from the work of black writers, which revealed this particular vision of the world. He takes his argument further, however, and argues that creative writing that does not display a way of thinking based on the conceptual touchstones he has identified is not authentically Negro-African.

A related argument considers the extent to which Negro-African writers have been annexed by Surrealism. There is a crucial difference between European Surrealist practice and what has been mistaken for an African Surrealism. The European Surrealist poet, Jahn argues, abandons himself to the power of words, which he hopes will take control of him in a state of almost subconscious trance. The African poet, on the other hand, remains master of the word which in turn gives him authority over the material world (*Muntu,* p. 156).

Thus, for Jahn, the defining characteristics of the field of study itself are not based on the author's color or race, nor on place of birth, nor the place in which he or she has lived. Similarly, Jahn rejects language as a literature's basic criterion of definition. The literatures of North America and South Africa, although they share a common language, are clearly distinct literatures, Jahn argues. Indeed the theoretical and philosophical consequences of employing a European language are, for Jahn, very limited. Language, for the neo-African writer, is simply a vehicle for the expression of Negro-African culture. This he justifies by stressing the neo-African writer's special relationship with language, bound up in the concept of *nommo,* described above. For it is the writer who gives language meaning; language is not a fixed code that the writer exploits. It is only by the act of "profération" that language acquires meaning. This brings to mind Saussure's opposition between "langue" and "parole." The Negro-African text is not the expression, or an act, of language; it does not bring a pre-existing meaning to life. The Negro-African text is better understood as "parole": language is given meaning by the poet's act:

> Every word which he pronounces is interpreted anew and the terms of his discourse, the chains of phonemes (lexemes and morphemes), thus receive this their specific meaning. [*Muntu,* p. 172]

This is because the image functions differently, Jahn argues, in Negro-African, as opposed to Western, poetry:

> In Western poetry, the image precedes the word. Images are "ideas" in the

Platonic sense, they are a preliminary donné. . . . But in African poetry, it is the word which precedes the image. Initially, there is a "thing" Kintu, which has nothing of the image, which is nothing other than the thing itself. But at the instant when that thing is named, evoked by Nommo, it undergoes a metamorphosis which transmutes it into an image. . . . Muntu . . . confers a symbolic value, a signification, a sense. [pp. 171–172]

Language, in the French sense of *langue*, is not, therefore, seen as a significant criterion for the definition of a literature. What is significant, Jahn argues, is cultural homogeneity: it is evidence of a common cultural heritage that distinguishes a body of texts and constitutes them into a coherent and autonomous literature. Thus, in literary terms, common stylistic features testify to a shared culture:

Literary works allow themselves to be categorized only according to their style; more precisely, according to an analysis of style; an analysis which allows each work its originality, but which allows it to be situated, starting from the basis of these ideal, literary, formal schemas of thought and expression. . . . Ernst Robert Curtius calls these schemas *topoi*. Only the identification of the *topos* (the general characteristics which constitute literary relationship, a literary "link") allows the categorization of works into groups which are significant for literary history; it is only after analyzing it that one can know to which literature this or that work belongs. [p. 16]

It is by this point in Jahn's method that the obvious parallels with Senghor's critical approach become clear. If Senghor's basic criterion is the extent to which a Negro-African text reveals its Negritude, Jahn is concerned above all with a text's "néo-africanité" as expressed by certain *topoi*. Both critics' approaches are open to the same criticisms: that their definitions of Negro-African culture are circumscribed and inadequate and that through underestimating the historical, political, and sociological differences between Africa and the various areas of the diaspora, not to mention the differences between various regions of Africa itself, they presuppose that Africa and the diaspora form a coherent cultural whole.

Nevertheless, Jahn's work (like Senghor's) was important in drawing attention to certain cultural specificities of Negro-African literature and laying less stress on language, in the French sense of *langage* rather than *langue*. By emphasizing the cultural distinctness of the literature, they helped prevent the absorption of African literature into French literature. Earlier, "indigenous literature" had been annexed by "les sciences coloniales"; "Negro-African" literature had by now been established as a sufficiently autonomous literature to be beyond easy annexation. Lilyan Kesteloot's pioneering work *Les Ecrivains noirs de langue française: nais-*

sance d'une littérature (1963) takes as its starting-point the *autonomy* of the literature and examines the conditions of its birth. Her work further fixed the literature as a distinct and independent subject. *Les Ecrivains noirs de langue française* is above all a history of the Negritude movement, and unlike Jahn (and Senghor) she bases her thesis not on the cultural but above all on the political.

Kesteloot's study has been of lasting influence in terms of the developing debate on Negro-African literature in French. Originally a doctoral thesis, the work was, significantly, carried out in the Department of Sociology of the Université libre de Bruxelles. Her work is generally regarded as the first analytical history of the Negritude movement, and, although inaccurate and in places incomplete, it remains the standard published history of the movement.[4]

Kesteloot bases the chronology of the movement on the appearance of successive periodicals. Thus the first four sections are devoted to *Légitime Défense, L'Etudiant Noir, Tropiques,* and *Présence Africaine.* The fifth section, "Situation actuelle des écrivains noirs," consists of interviews and analyses of them, composed along social-scientific, rather than traditionally literary-critical, lines. The perspective adopted by *Les Ecrivains noirs de langue française* implies that part of its purpose is to consecrate a new area, to recognize and publicize a new literary phenomenon, and one that is very much part of contemporary political developments. Thus the book opens with the following declaration:

> With the awakening of the African continent, demanding its freedom, it is time to recognize that black writers of the French language form a comprehensive and authentic literary movement. [p. 18]

Kesteloot then justifies her use of the term "literary movement":

> As early as 1948, "Black Orpheus," Jean-Paul Sartre's brilliant preface to L. S. Senghor's *Anthologie de la nouvelle poésie nègre et malgache de langue française* ... saluted the accession of the poets of "Negritude." Today, everything about this poetry, its abundance and quality, its diversity of style and form, its incontestable originality, prompts us to consider these neo-African authors as creators of an authentic literary school. It is obvious that an important phenomenon has occurred in creative writing in the French language, and that it must not be underestimated. [p. 7]

The introduction also discusses the wider context within which texts belonging to "Negro-African" literature should be considered. They should not be incorporated into French literature, because what unites them into a coherent body is that they "they express themselves ... in relation to colonized Negro societies" (p. 7). For Jahn the specificity of Negro-African literature depended on cultural homogeneity visible in a shared range of cultural *topoi*. This perspective conforms to Sartre's definition of one kind of Negro-African literature, a "littérature objective." Kesteloot, on the other hand, sees the specificity of Negro-African literature depending on a shared experience of oppression, together with its political consequences. Kesteloot thus concentrates on a Negro-African "littérature subjective" (according to Sartre's distinction).

A literary renaissance is, Kesteloot argues, a symptom of a wider renaissance:

> We may along with Aimé Césaire, look upon the appearance of literary works in the colonies as a symptom of their rebirth, and as proof that colonial peoples are capable of taking the initiative and re-examining their concept of a world thrown into confusion by colonization. [p. 8]

Furthermore, Kesteloot sees it as the responsibility of African artists and writers: "to bring order from this chaos" (p. 8). It is they who:

> catalyze the aspirations of the masses, helping them to regain their place in history, strengthening their national feeling—in other words preparing them for freedom. [p. 8]

The original subtitle of Kesteloot's study, "The Birth of a Literature," indicates that it is above all concerned with the history of the *birth* of a movement. In recording its birth, it stresses the historical context within which it was born, that of decolonization and the birth of new nationalisms. In historiographical terms, a further important element in her study is the way in which it draws up a particular canon of authors. The "fondateurs" cf the "literary renaissance" are Césaire, Senghor, and Damas; René Maran is included as an important "précurseur."

The literary-critical criteria that operate throughout Kesteloot's study are greatly influenced by the political context within which she considered the "movement" to have been born and the relationship between cultural and political renewal. The most obvious statement of the critical standards against which works have been measured comes in the conclusion. The article "Où va le roman" by the Haitian writer J.-S. Alexis, published in *Présence Africaine* (no. 13, 1957), is quoted by Kesteloot:

> In the present predicament ... the mission of our creators is to sing the beauty, tragedies, and struggles of our exploited peoples, re-examining the canons developed by Western cultures in relation to the cultural riches of our land. [p. 335]

Referring to Alexis' article, Kesteloot then continues:

> This formula seems to sum up perfectly the three fundamental aims of
> today's black literature: to express the drama and struggles of the black
> peoples—but by "singing" them, with a concern for the artistic element,
> which, measuring its distance from "Western canons," would rely on the
> "cultural riches" of Negro soil! [pp. 335–336]

Thus African literature must be conscious of contemporary popular political objectives and consciously artistic. Furthermore, it should be influenced not by works belonging to the Western canon, but by the Negro
cultural heritage. Kesteloot then goes on to argue that black writing is
necessarily politically committed writing:

> It is in this sense that the basic element of literature so far has been
> commitment. We know the word has lost value. Too often it has been an
> alibi for bad authors, both in France and elsewhere. Yet here it is compel-
> ling; further it regains its full dignity. [p. 336]

Here, the way in which Kesteloot confuses the circumstances of the literature's birth with its ontology becomes obvious. The sociopolitical context
in which the literature was born defines its nature:

> Commitment, where black writers are concerned, was the first prerequisite
> for the birth and flowering of this completely autonomous literary school.
> [p. 336]

Furthermore, having thus established the fundamental characteristics of the
literature's ontology (based on the circumstances of its birth), Kesteloot
then transmutes them into basic *evaluative* literary-critical criteria: "black
writers became truly original only after they had committed themselves"
(p. 11). The process of "engagement" also gives the Negro-African text a
"collective" dimension. The author no longer speaks only for himself: "It is
in this that he commits himself. It is not only himself that he expresses but
all Negro peoples in all parts of the world. He expresses an African soul"
(p. 11).

Although her approach stressed the sociopolitical context in which the
literature had been born and proposed political commitment as one of
the essential features of the new school, her analysis did not, of course,
wholly disregard the cultural and racial: the nature of the black writer's
commitment was inextricably bound up with *racial* factors:

> The present movement produces masterpieces in French only when the
> black writer, having discovered his own identity, gives free reign to his

sensibility and his vision of the world. He expresses an African soul which before had found *written* expression only in certain ethnological works such as those by Frobenius, Bauman, or Griaule. [p. 11]

Here Kesteloot includes the discovery of "authenticity" as a prerequisite for the accomplished work. Equally, the racial and liberationist elements of the new literature as an autonomous literature are stressed:

From the moment when they realized and accepted their "Negro" condition, black writers—stirred by an immense desire to express this condition and lead their peoples to freedom—were able to create a literature with its own characteristics whose ultimate appeal lies in the universality of its values. [p. 11]

Kesteloot's thesis was based on certain paradoxical methodological features and, like any pioneering work, contained inaccuracies and omissions. Her dating of *L'Etudiant Noir*, for example, was ludicrous. The most serious historical inaccuracy is her contention that the *prospect* of decolonization is crucial to an understanding of the work of Senghor, Césaire, and Damas. At the point when these three began to write, the process of decolonization was, of course, well under way in other parts of the world: in Iraq, Egypt, India, China, and French Indo-China, in particular. As far as other French colonies were concerned, outright active opposition existed in the form of Messali Hadj's "Etoile Nord-Africaine." The communists had also condemned colonialism, although their position later was more ambiguous. In addition, strikes were taking place in Senegal, and there was serious unrest in French Equatorial Africa. Kesteloot also fails to refer to other forces at work in France which were to influence Senghor, Césaire, and Damas: Lamine Senghor, Garan Kouyaté, and Emile Faure headed militant groups and published their anti-colonial periodicals, most importantly *La Race nègre*. In addition, French writers—most notably Gide and Londres—had published their condemnatory accounts of French colonialism.[5]

Factual inaccuracies, although influential in terms of methodology, can be (and have been) easily rectified. A more subtle and insidious element of Kesteloot's methodology which has remained curiously indelible is the process by which she established the canon—and the extent to which it has remained largely unchanged. René Maran, for example, remains outside the canon:

Having lived all his youth in France, in a boarding school, far from his parents and family, René Maran lost his Negro characteristics and acquired a French style, without effort, without self-alienation. His works are authentic and personal, and at the same time very French. They do not belong to Negro literature, although they influenced it. [pp. 106–107]

Here Kesteloot's argument displays similarities with those of Jahn and Senghor: one requirement is that the work reveal "l'âme nègre," or in Kesteloot's terms "le tempérament nègre." While Jahn explores at length the specificity of "néo-africanité" and Senghor goes to great lengths to describe what he means by "l'âme nègre," Kesteloot proceeds as though her terms were self-evident. Nor does she justify her assumption that Senghor, Césaire, and Damas are not "assimilés."

While Maran is regarded as a "précurseur du mouvement," Gilbert Gratiant, who in every way merits such a title, is not considered worthy of it. Here Kesteloot has no doubt been too strongly influenced by *Légitime Défense*'s perspective on Gratiant as an "assimilé." Kesteloot writes:

It is perfectly understandable that Gilbert Gratiant was no partisan of Negritude and laid claim to his French culture instead. [p. 25]

She does, however, point out that:

If Gratiant has one merit worth underscoring, it is to have acknowledged without shame the few drops of black blood that flow in his veins. He is one of the few before the Negritude generation who dared do this. [p. 26]

However, in his poetry—"Le Nègre," for example—there is a stronger concern to establish racial pride and to glorify the attributes of the Negro. Damas includes this poem, "Missions," from Gratiant's 1944 collection *Sans Mars ni Vénus,* in his anthology, *Poètes d'expression française.* Steins, in "Litérature engagée," his swingeing attack on Kesteloot's work, also cites Gratiant's poem "Magie Noire," from *Poèmes en faux vers* (Paris, 1931), and two other poems, "Noir" and "La part du nègre," from a roneo-typed collection of Gratiant's poems, distributed amongst his friends, as further evidence of Gratiant's significance as an early "neo-Negritude" writer.

Kesteloot's study can be regarded as seminal for a number of reasons. It was the first attempt to write a history of "Negro-African literature in French." Secondly, the work was written within the context of a European university, thereby consecrating the area, to some extent, as a legitimate field of academic study.[6] Most importantly, *Les Ecrivains noirs de langue française* established a particular literary-critical method based above all on historiographical and ideological criteria, criteria that had remained implicit in the work of earlier commentators—for example, in Sartre's difficult text "Orphée noir." Unlike Kesteloot's study, Sartre's essay, although analytical, did not seek to establish the criteria on which an academic study of the literature should be based. It exposed features of the literature which he found particularly interesting, especially from the point of view of a French writer. Kesteloot's work, on the other hand, set up different expectations and immediately became the seminal work in the field. Its inconsistencies and inaccuracies have, therefore, had an effect on the subsequent development of the discipline.

The year of publication of Kesteloot's book, 1963, was also the year in which Léonard Sainville published his well-known *Anthologie de la littérature négro-africaine: Tome 1, Romanciers et conteurs négro-africains*. Sainville's objective in publishing his anthology is made very clear:

> This book has been thought out and written from a very particular perspective, one adapted, above all, to meet the needs of current historical necessities. It aims to be a tool and means of propaganda in the hands of the rising generations. It hopes to be . . . the reference book of works which without equivocation express the struggle of Blacks against colonial or imperialist oppression. [p. 23]

For Sainville, historical factors have led Blacks worldwide to a common point. It is above all for this reason that it makes sense to discuss "la littérature négro-africaine":

> We tried to demonstrate a little earlier, that . . . a same cruel destiny made Blacks indistinguishable, whether those of Africa or their descendents on the American continent. Whether they had to endure the yoke of European colonization or that of imperialism . . . they came up against the same humiliations; together they must put up the same protest. At the moment it seems to us inadvisable to insist on the national differences which, here and there, underline differences and divide Blacks. [p. 23]

Sainville's emphasis is thus similar to Kesteloot's; both approaches interpret Negro-African literature as "subjective." Thus, the previous sixteen pages of introduction had been devoted to a résumé of historical events and their effect on the cultural life of the places concerned. The late flowering of the novel in Africa is explained by the stifling of the necessary socio-historical conditions: a sense of freedom, the triumph of individualism, the rejection of oppression by the aristocracy, economic development.

From the outset, Sainville's text is explicitly polemical and political:

> For centuries Western Europe has exploited, oppressed, colonized other people on the earth, despising, disfiguring, halting in their development, or simply denying—by declaring barbarous or inhuman—the cultures of other peoples. [p. 7]

The criteria of selection for the anthology are broad:

> Our choice is in no sense arbitrary. It has been determined both by the greater or lesser possibility of obtaining works we know to exist, and by

the criterion we believe to be constituted by the author's preoccupation not to whiten himself, but to take into consideration the existence, and the difficulties of countries where black men live. [p. 24]

The shape of the anthology is dictated by these concerns. Rather than arranging the texts in a straightforward chronological order, or by the author's country of birth, Sainville divides the texts into various subsections that only roughly correspond to historical periods, ranging from the beginnings of national consciousness to the present day. Within these sections, texts are arranged by country. The logic of the anthology further reinforced both Kesteloot's historiographical framework, attributing the "birth" of the literature to a particular historical moment, the awakenings of national consciousness. Sainville's anthology also further emphasized the ideological dimension of Negro-African literature and the potential of the literature as a contemporary political force. It was thus, once again, the ideological element of Negro-African literature which was proposed as the literature's outstanding feature. Perhaps surprisingly, when Edouard Eliet produced his *Panorama de la littérature négro-africaine (1921–1962)*, published by Présence Africaine in 1965, the first work on Negro-African literature in French which is intended to be read within a pedagogical context, the political was, again, proposed as paramount.

Eliet drew attention to the surprising absence of Francophone African literature within school syllabuses:[7]

It is in effect paradoxical that a poet like Senghor should be honoured with high distinctions by the Republic of Letters and yet none of his writings figure in school textbooks!

Currently Negro-African literature is attracting the attention of, and stimulating, international congresses. Tomorrow it will no doubt be included in Faculty programmes and it is already taught in Secondary schools in some African countries.

Our undertaking has come at the right moment to fill a gap and respond to a need. [p. 9]

In historical terms, Eliet concentrates on the years 1921 to 1962. In terms of theme, he focuses on Negro-African literature as a "littérature de combat." Furthermore, he is concerned to present works that he considers to be "des oeuvres caractéristiques." The corollary of this is that his study gives an impression of homogeneity, although he treats different genres—poetry, the novel, and essays—and considers the work of writers from disparate areas—Madagascar, Africa, and the West Indies.

The first chapter, "Etienne Léro et l'engagement poétique," based on the text of *Légitime Défense*, presents Léro as a "proto-Negritude" writer:

With Léro, West Indian poetry will undergo a metamorphosis for all
Blacks, by means of which all those who have understood, who have
admitted its message, will totally commit themselves to their individual
adventure. [p. 14]

The second chapter explores the concept of Negritude based on ideas expressed in the writings of Césaire, Fanon, Senghor, Sartre, Gratiant, and
Janheinz Jahn.

Although radically different, of course, Eliet presents the ideas of each
writer as though complementary, and he accepts the polemic of each. Quoting from Senghor, he writes:

Animism consists of an intuition of a surreal world where man is linked,
on the one hand to man . . . on the other to God by the mediation of
Ancestor-Spirits and half-gods. If the nature of Negritude is such, one
understands that Negro-African poets have used surrealism not as a tool,
but by assimilation. And what is most extraordinary is not that there
should be Negro-African surrealists, but that French could be "Negro-
African," that is to say: surrealists! [p. 17]

The introduction, the chapter on Léro, and that on Negritude, are followed
by three sections, the first devoted to the work of six poets, the second to
the work of Negro-African novelists, and the third devoted to Césaire and
Fanon as critics.[8] Derived very obviously from the ultimately fundamentally different approaches of Jahn in *Muntu* and Kesteloot in *Les Ecrivains
noirs de langue française*, Eliet's study further reinforces the political and
ideological dimension of Negro-African literature.

If Eliet's *Panorama* explained Negro-African literature in ideological
terms, Robert Pageard's study, *Littérature négro-africaine d'expression
française* (1966), differs only in degree, stressing the sociopolitical. As in
Kesteloot's study (and Eliet's), the circumstances of the literature's "birth"
are paramount. Pageard's introduction opens:

It is only at the beginning of the twentieth century that the social and
institutional conditions were brought together which permitted the birth of
a Negro-African literature in the French language. [p. 137]

One consequence of privileging the sociopolitical is that, as in Sainville's
anthology, the pragmatically functional aspects of the literature stand out.
Pageard writes, for example:

Negro-African literature . . . embraces all the problems which confront
every man, even if . . . it considers, as a priority, the difficulties which the
black man on his continent and beyond his continent comes up against. It
is thus that it is concerned:

1. to situate man in the universe and to evoke his potential (*Le regard du roi*, [etc.]);

2. to situate the black man within the rapid and uncertain evolution of modern humanity, to examine his means of attack and defence (poetic oeuvre of Senghor, [etc.]; works of history such as Ki-Zerbo [etc.]; poetic and novelistic work of Dadié [etc.]);

3. to study the psychology and external manner of behaviour of members of diverse categories or social classes of Africans, as well as the conflicts or threat of conflicts which can exist between these groups (theories of African socialism; novels such as *Karim* [etc.]);

4. to unveil and describe the harmonies and secret conflicts of the individual soul (*Un piège sans fin* de Bhêly-Quénum [etc.]);

The struggle against the colonial situation, which belongs to the second point outlined above, was, until 1960, the central theme or annex of numerous works. It has made way for a permanent and universal fight against all forms of racial discrimination and segregation. [pp. 163–164]

Within Pageard's methodology, the *literary* text is not privileged with special consideration; it is a written text like any other, whose *functional* characteristics, like those of any sociocultural phenomenon, are worthy of attention. The *linguistic* distinctiveness of the literary text is not, therefore, afforded great attention. Pageard argues:

Through the voices of francophone writers, Black Africa is thus participating in a vigorous and autonomous manner in the debates which will decide the orientation and, no doubt, the success or stalemate of territorial humanity, committed, not without precipitation and disorder, in an attempt to surmount its own nature.

In such a circumstance, what is said and what is done is worth more than the manner of saying and doing. That is why we do not attach prime importance to form. [p. 160]

Lilyan Kesteloot's *Négritude et situation coloniale* of 1968 focuses yet more narrowly on the literary text as a sociological document. Published in Yaoundé the year after Pageard's *Panorama*, the concern of this book is not to examine the genesis and development of the literary work within its sociopolitical context, but rather to recognize the *effect* of the literary work on contemporary historical circumstance:

works . . . react in their turn on reality, exert on it a certain pressure and can accelerate the development of social or political crises. [p. 5]

She is also concerned to judge the "realism" of the Negro-African text:

Have black writers deformed reality for the sake of their cause? Have they exaggerated the ills of their race or have they been faithful witnesses? [p. 21]

In this naive undertaking, Kesteloot attempts to draw on statistics to measure the "reality" drawn by the Negritude writers against "facts and figures" which, she claims, "speak as loudly as cries" (p. 21). The statistics are principally those of the United Nations and the archives of colonial companies. She also marshals information provided by ethnologists such as Georges Balandier. The conclusion to this initial section of *Négritude et situation coloniale* is unequivocal:

It seems, therefore, that black, West Indian or African writers have not in reality exaggerated the ills of their people! Often in fact, it seems to us, the literary formulation reduces the brutality of the statistics, the reports and the witnesses established by the colonizer himself. [p. 73]

In her final chapter, "What Do the Writers of Negritude Want?," Kesteloot interprets various tenets of Negritude and examines their sociological and practical significance. This takes the form of an *apologia* for Negritude considered as an ideological movement, and she explores in turn various criticisms commonly made. Beginning with the idea of a "retour aux sources," she explains that this in many cases involves a reevaluation of, rather than a return to, the past and traditional customs:

Black writers are not reactionaries, they do not extol the virtues of a return to traditional structures but to certain traditional values. [p. 80]

Kesteloot then examines the question of Negritude's "anti-racist racism," as Sartre termed it. She argues that the emphasis given to racial characteristics was an understandable reaction to having been exploited and humiliated as a result of belonging to a particular racial group:

For too long humiliated on account of his skin, it is precisely from the starting point of race that the black seeks to reconquer his contested humanity. [p. 80]

She then asks:

But this attitude can it be accused of racism? To affirm "that it is fine and good and legitimate to be Negro" is a proof of mental health: it is to prove that hierarchy and value are no longer being confused. It is, at the same time, to destroy, between men, an inequality which is without reason. [p. 81]

Kesteloot's purpose in her conclusion is, it would seem, above all to re-assure:

> If the cries of hatred have sometimes carried the Negritude writers to the extremes of a neo-racism, they have not failed, with a cool head, to rectify this attitude, in order not to slip into precisely those aberrations of which they accuse colonial Europe. [p. 84]

Kesteloot gives Césaire the last word: "What is Negritude, in essence, if it is not the aggressive proposition of fraternity?" (p. 84).

Kesteloot's *Négritude et situation coloniale* treats the literary text above all as a sociological document and one whose language is in no way distinctive. Implicit in her thesis is the literary text's witness to a certain sociopolitical reality and, concomitantly, the text's power to change that reality. Furthermore, her understanding of the manner in which the literary text has power to change reality is straightforward, not to say literal. For it is not the way in which reality is altered by a change in *consciousness* that she proposes, but a "real" chang—that is, one that can somehow be measured using the methods of the social sciences, such as statistical analysis.

Kesteloot's *Négritude et situation coloniale* exaggerated, to an extraordinary degree, a perspective on Negro-African literature which had dominated discussion of the field throughout the 1960s: a focus on the ideological reality witnessed by Negro-African literature. Furthermore, it obscured if not denied the *literary* qualities of African literature, attending to the text's "message" and its objective "truth," rather than the manner in which the message was conveyed.[9]

One critical work that was to expose in a small way the dangers and inadequacies of the approaches of the 1960s, and one that introduced a greater degree of self-consciousness into the discipline, was the British publication *Protest and Conflict in African Literature*, edited by Cosmo Pieterse and Donald Munro (1969). A collection of essays, the publication originated out of a series of talks and discussions at the Africa Centre in London. The purpose of the events was to "popularize the growing body of what is generically called African literature" (pp. ix–x). This collection of essays is one of the first English works to consider, in addition to Anglophone works, Negro-African literature in French. Of the nine texts that make up the book, three are devoted to Francophone writers: Gerald Moore's essay on "The Politics of Negritude," Clive Wake's "The Political and Cultural Revolution," and Jeanette Macaulay's "The Idea of Assimilation." The titles of these essays, like the title of the book, reveal their concern to situate the literature within its political context. In the introduction to the collection, the editors justify their commitment to the themes of "protest" and "conflict":

> There are clearly dangers in analyzing works of literature within the nar-
> row confines of a theme; none the less a representative selection of writers
> and their works was made to fit into the framework of the several forms of
> protest and conflict—mainly political and cultural—singled out for treat-
> ment. [p. x]

However, the three essays on Francophone literature differ considerably in
their treatment of literature. Moore uses various literary texts to illustrate
sociopolitical and racial attitudes. The way in which he quotes from
Césaire's *Discours sur le colonialisme*, followed by Senghor's poem "A
New York" (without concern for difference in genre), suggests that literary
language is not privileged above other discourses; it attempts to tell certain
truths about the world, truths that can equally well, it seems, be told in the
language of political tracts such as Césaire's *Discours*. Similarly, while
exploring the question of Africa's relationship with Europe, he quotes from
a poem by David Diop, and then asks:

> All right, what is the programme that underlines this kind of poetry? Is it
> African Socialism? No. Is it International Socialism? International Com-
> munism?

To ask these questions of a poem is to regard its language as cryptographic,
as coded.

Clive Wake's approach is very different. He is concerned to distinguish
very clearly between the political and the cultural. In fact, his essay is, in a
sense, a plea for this separation. He does, of course, recognize that "the
literary awakening of Africa is directly associated with the political awakening" (p. 44), but he also asks:

> Is African literature so absorbed in the present state of Africa that it forgets
> its future as literature? It brings us back to the very delicate problem of
> maintaining a balance between commitment and creation. Commitment
> can be creative, in the literary sense, but it can also destroy creation. In
> other words, is the African literature of the present and immediate past
> simply going to be the kind of literature that, in a few years, will be of
> interest only to the sociologist and historian, or the academic literary
> historian? [pp. 49–50]

Furthermore, Wake distinguishes between literature that is an expression
of self-awareness and literature that becomes part of culture. Thus he concludes:

> If we are to talk of a cultural revolution, we have to remember that culture
> is something which, revolution or no revolution, projects itself backwards

and forwards in time and that tradition is created by those writers who transcend the present. [p. 55]

The perspective of almost all the critical works of the 1960s focused on Negro-African literature as "self-awareness" and self-expression. Kesteloot's historiography, which explained the literature's relatively sudden birth in terms of "engagement," proceeding to incorporate this as a fundamental evaluative criterion, presented the Negro-African literary text as an act of political self-awareness. What was privileged among the multiple meanings of the amorphous concept of Negritude was not Negritude as a poetics, but Negritude as an ideological and racial attitude.

Sainville's anthology further exaggerated the ideological perspective proposed by Kesteloot, underlining "le combat des Noirs contre l'oppression coloniale ou impérialiste" (p. 23). Similarly, Eliet concentrated on "le thème de la littérature de combat" (p. 9), and Pageard, although he identifies a wider range of concerns, maintains that:

the struggle against the colonial situation . . . was, until 1960, the central theme or annex of numerous works. It made way for a permanent and universal struggle against all forms of racial discrimination and segregation. [p. 140]

The methodology of Kesteloot's *Négritude et situation coloniale* was, similarly, bound up with a particular conception of Negro-African literature which emphasized the degree to which it bore witness to a certain sociopolitical reality and its effect on that reality. Although one or two essays in *Protest and Conflict in African Literature* attempted to distinguish the concepts of the book's title from the specifically *literary*, the overall concerns of the essays it contained were, once again, ideological and sociopolitical.

Nevertheless, by the end of the 1960s the autonomy of Negro-African literature had been guaranteed by the works discussed above. Although now established as an autonomous literature, it was for political or ideological, sociological, anthropological, cultural, or racial reasons that it had been so established. The *literariness* of the literature, the poetics of its poetry, and the formal concerns of the Negro-African novel had all received remarkably little attention. It was not the literary features of Negro-African writing which had encouraged recognition of it as a distinct literature, but its *content*. As the need to draw attention to the ideological and political concerns of Negro-African literature became less pressing, so other aspects of the literature were explored and explained. During the 1970s the criticism of Negro-African literature became self-aware, and the contradictions, inconsistencies, and inaccuracies of earlier studies were revealed and attended to. Just as the number of literary texts had suddenly increased during the 1960s, so during the 1970s the criticism of Negro-African literature suddenly established itself as a self-conscious discipline. In 1969, a conference was held at the University of Abidjan, "Situation et perspectives de la littérature négro-africaine," and the *Actes du colloque* were published the following year as *Situation et perspectives*. This conference was symptomatic of a new self-awareness working within the secondary discipline.

NOTES

1. Other studies of a general kind published during the 1960s include: Thomas Melone (ed.), *De la négritude dans la littérature négro-africaine* (1962); V.-P. Bol and J. Allary, *Littérateurs et poètes noirs* (Léopoldville, 1964); Claude Wauthier, *L'Afrique des Africains: inventaire de la négritude* (1964); Roland Colin, *Littérature africaine d'hier et de demain* (1965); O. Dubois, *L'Afrique reconnue: panorama de la littérature négro-africaine* (1969); and Janheinz Jahn, *Manuel de la littérature néo-africaine* (1969).

Melone's *De la négritude* is a polemical study whose aim is succinctly expressed in its conclusion:

Senghor defined Negritude as "the crossroads of giving and receiving." He even compared Euroafrica—an osmosis of Negro and Western civilizations—to a concert where Europe would be the conductor and Africa, the tam-tam drummer. This modest study will have allowed the unmasking of the equivocation and mystification which obscure this double affirmation.

Historically we can affirm that there has never been, in the Negro-African adventure, "a sense of giving." [p. 129]

The historical account is made up of three sections in which the policy of cultural assimilation is discussed, as is the historical and existential consciousness of the Negro-African which it produces. Negritude is subsequently proposed primarily as the response to the historical events (and their psychological consequences) explored earlier in the study.

The second half of *De la négritude* proposes a range of definitions of Negritude and illustrates these by reference to various literary texts. Melone's range of definitions or descriptions of Negritude is broad:

Negritude, that thing which makes a Negro a Negro and not something else. [p. 17]

Negritude thus defines itself in a rough and ready manner, the message of a race. [p. 19]

Negritude does not imply, a priori, political action [p. 24]

Negritude thus presents itself first and foremost as the taking up of a position, at once a negation and affirmation. [p. 25]

Poetry of suffering, that is what is most important about the phenomenon of Negritude. [p. 25]

Camara Laye, Senghor, and Birago Diop illustrate Negritude defined as follows:

> Between the White and the Negro there is a distance and this distance, as the awareness of the relationship, is what Negritude is. [p. 86]

The early novelists, Camara Laye, Mongo Beti, and Ferdinand Oyono are discussed in terms of Negritude understood as "witness":

> Negritude . . . the expression of the Negro "situation," an expression which one can characterize in a word: it is a witness, a witness which seeks to be a revelation and a message: the revelation of the African reality, the message of the Negro people to other peoples of the world. [p. 87]

Negritude in the poetry of Senghor and Césaire is identified as "le langage de la conscience négro-africaine" (p. 128).

On the whole, Melone departs very little from the perspectives of Sartre's "Orphée noir," and he relies heavily on quotations from Sartre's essay at crucial points in his argument. Indeed, his concluding paragraphs are passages from "Orphée noir." Sartre's essay, published more than a decade earlier, was a considerable stimulus to the theoretical debate concerning Negro-African literature in French. Melone's work is, however, neither a tight academic study nor a highly original and exciting essay like Sartre's. Negritude is defined and explored in so many guises that Melone's position remains somewhat confused. One consequence of this is that later critics could not simply synthesize their views with Melone's or, alternatively, distinguish their polemic from his. *De la négritude* cannot, therefore, be considered a major text in the history of the criticism of Negro-African literature in French nor are the articulations of Negritude which it proposes major moments in the history of the term. An early African critic, however, Melone was an important reference for a number of years.

Littérateurs et poètes noirs by V.-P. Bol and J. Allary is divided into two parts. The first section, by Allary, is an unexceptional essay on Negro-African literature in French. The second section, by Bol, is a bibliographical essay that lists, in three parts, creative writing in French, English, and Portuguese and Spanish. A work that serves primarily as an introduction to the area, *Littérateurs et poètes noirs* has had little influence on the evolution of Francophone Negro-African literature.

In *L'Afrique des Africains: inventaire de la négritude*, Claude Wauthier examines Negro-African literature in its broad political and intellectual context. While earlier studies do not, of course, entirely overlook the political and intellectual, Wauthier argued that:

> none of these authors (Sartre, Damas, Jahn and Kesteloot) were concerned to place the literary movement which is Negritude, in the wider context of a cultural renewal which embraces ethnology, law, theology, history and folklore. Not that they ignored this context; but they only refer to it briefly. Their concern remains deliberately limited: to study African literature and not the larger whole constituted by an intellectual claim which has impregnated not only African poetry and the novel but also African research within different human sciences. [p. 16]

Although Wauthier is successful in providing a broad overview of his subject, his method is historical and descriptive rather than literary-critical. His principal thesis—

that African literature should be seen within the wider context of other disciplines—does not lead to an original understanding of the works of literature he discusses. Although Wauthier's study is well known and appears in the bibliographies of other more properly literary-critical works, *L'Afrique des Africains* has not entered the debate concerning the *methodology* of literary criticism. Nor did his study throw any new light on the complexities of Negritude.

Other general studies that failed to have any significant influence on the debate include: R. Colin, *Littérature africain d'hier et de demain* (Paris, 1965); O. Dubois, *L'Afrique reconnue: panorama de la littérature négro-africaine* (Paris, 1969); Janheinz Jahn's *Manuel de la littérature néo-africaine* (Paris, 1969), A. C. Brench, *The Novelist's Inheritance in Africa* (London and New York, 1967) and *Writing in French from Senegal to Cameroon* (London and New York, 1968); Mercer Cook and Stephen Henderson, *The Militant Black Writer in Africa and the United States* (Madison, 1969); Judith Gleason, *This Africa: Novels by West Africans in English and French* (Evanston, 1965); Gerald Moore, *African Literature and the Universities* (Ibadan, 1965); G. E. von Grunebaum, *French African Literature: Some Cultural Implications* (The Hague, 1964); G. Moore, *Seven African Writers* (Oxford, 1962).

2. Father Placide Tempels, *La Philosophie Bantoue*, 1948, French translation, Présence Africaine (Paris, 1949); Marcel Griaule, *Dieu d'eau: entretiens avec Ogotemmêli* (1948); Abbé Kagamé, *La Philosophie bantu-ruandaise de l'être*, Académie des Sciences de Belgique (Brussels, 1956).

3. Tempels had pointed to the "force vitale" as the essential feature of Bantu philosophy and Senghor later made it a cornerstone of his Negro ontology.

4. Subsequent theses that document more accurately the history of the Negritude movement and comparable movements include those by Martin Steins and Joseph Costissella: Martin Steins, "Les Antécédents et la genèse de la négritude senghorienne," unpublished Thèse d'Etat, Université de Paris III, 1981; Joseph Costissela, "Genèse et évolution de la négritude: des mouvements nègres à Paris (1919–1939) à Léopold Sédar Senghor (1928–1971)," unpublished Thèse d'Etat, Université de Paris IV, 1982.

5. Theses by Steins and Costissella; also M. Steins, "Littérature engagée," *Oeuvres et Critiques III* (2)/*IV* (1) (Autumn, 1979). Kesteloot did later acknowledge the importance of *La Revue du Monde Noir* in particular in the preface to the second edition of *Les Ecrivains noirs de langue française*.

6. Yet Kesteloot's study was undertaken within the Department of Sociology rather than within a literary discipline.

7. D. Blair has also briefly researched the French reception of African literature in "Etat et statut de la critique française de la littérature négro-africaine d'expression française," *Oeuvres et Critiques III* (2)/*IV* (1) (1979).

8. Although Frantz Fanon's criticisms of Negritude have introduced his works into literary-critical debate, the principal preoccupations of his texts do not fall within the area delineated by this study.

9. Other works with a similar methodology include: R. Chemain, *La Ville dans le roman africain* (1981); A. Chemain-Degrange, *Emancipation féminine et roman africain* (1980); G. Dago Lezou, *La Création romanesque devant les transformations actuelles en Côte-d'Ivoire* (1977); B. Fonlon, *La Poésie et le réveil de l'homme noir* (1978); D. Joualt, *Métamorphoses de l'après-indépendance dans le roman négro-africain d'expression française* (1982); B. Kabongo, *La Littérature pour quoi faire?*

(1975); I. Madubuike, *The Senegalese Novel: A Sociological Study of the Politics of Assimilation* (1980); P. Mérand, *La Vie quotidienne en Afrique noire à travers la littérature africaine d'expression française* (1977); S. L. Milbury-Steen, *European and African Stereotypes in Twentieth-Century Fiction* (1980); K. Milolo, *L'Image de la femme chez les romanciers noirs francophones* (1986); J. Sanon, *Images sociopolitiques dans le roman négro-africain* (1982); M. Schipper-de-Leeuw, *Le Blanc vu d'Afrique: le blanc et l'Occident au miroir du roman négro-africain de langue française des origines au Festival de Dakar (1920–1966)* (1973).

6

The Wider Debate

By the beginning of the 1970s, the study of "Negro-African literature in French" had become a well-established discipline. Secondary works, bibliographies, anthologies, critical introductions, general studies, studies of individual authors, and scholarly journals continued to appear, patrolling its frontiers, sorting, categorizing, exploring, explaining, and judging it. Critical and theoretical discourse became more systematic and more aware of its own contradictions and limitations. It also became more conscious of its prescriptive role in shaping the literature of the future and more overt about this aspect of its influence. Particular schools of criticism emerged positing different methods and purposes, as the eight studies examined later in the chapter demonstrate. Negritude continued to be exploited as a key term in four of the eight. *Sociologie du roman africain: réalisme, structure et détermination dans le roman moderne ouest-africain* (1970), by Sunday Anozie, which examines both the Francophone and Anglophone West African novel, avoids the term altogether. In Mohamadou Kane's study, *Roman africain et tradition* (1983), Negritude is defined as an ideological movement. Similarly, in endeavouring to rewrite the history of Negro-African literature in French, Ossito Midiohouan in his study *L'Idéologie dans la littérature négro-africaine d'expression française* (1986) identifies Negritude as an ideology associating it with a specific *locus* and time: Paris in the 1940s. Neither Kane nor Midiohouan allows Negritude to assume wider significance as a literary-critical trope or philosophical concept. Michel Hausser's important work, *Essai sur la poétique de la négritude* (1986) treats Negritude as a poetics and exploits the methods of contemporary linguistics, thus distinguishing his study from the other works chosen to represent the spread of approaches to Negro-African literature in French during the past two decades. Four other works have been selected: Stanislas Adotevi's *Négritude et Négrologues* (1972), Francis Anani Joppa's *L'Engagement des écrivains africains noirs de langue française: du témoignage au dépassement* (1982), Marcien Towa's *Poésie de la négritude* (1983), and Iyay Kimoni's *Destin de la littérature négro-africaine ou problématique d'une culture* (1975). Within these works Negritude—although not treated as an unproblematical term—plays a deceptive role in literary-critical and theoretical discussion. The eight works examined represent the range of approaches visible within the academic discipline. Numerous other publications have appeared since 1970, and a number of important conferences have taken place. These represent the wider context within which the academic discipline finds its place.

In all the countries of Francophone Africa, literature syllabuses had been drawn up for use at both school and university level. Publishers gradually committed themselves to specialist series, new publishing houses with an interest in the area also appeared, and specialist publishers continued to produce new series. For example, Présence Africaine introduced its scholarly *Critique Littéraire* collection in 1972 to complement the *Approches* series (dedicated to studies of individual authors and aimed principally at a pedagogical context), founded in 1962. Other specialist publishers in the field include C.L.E. (Centre de littérature évangélique), founded in 1963, and, most importantly, N.E.A (Nouvelles éditions africaines), founded in 1972.

Among French publishers specializing in the field, Les éditions Saint-Paul is important. Its *Comprendre* series now includes a dozen titles, mainly studies of individual authors. Similarly, Editions Fernand Nathan and Editions Hatier have published studies of major African and West Indian authors, the former appearing from 1964 onward, the latter since 1975. More relevant to the history of the criticism of Negro-African literature in French in general, however, and more concerned with the theoretical problems it generates, are the studies published by (in order of importance) l'Harmattan, Naaman, Silex, Le Seuil, P.U.F. (Presses Universitaires de France), and Gallimard. Many of the critical works produced by these publishers are university theses or adapted theses; most have appeared since 1970.

Centres for teaching and research in the field—in Africa, in France, elsewhere in Europe, and in America—have, increasingly in the past two decades, placed the subject within an institutional context. In 1962 C.E.L.R.I.A. (Centre de littérature romane d'inspiration africaine) was founded at the University of Kinshasa (formerly Léopoldville). The Centre is now based in Lubumbashi, and its work (which includes the publication of the journal *Lectures africaines*) is dominated by a sociological approach to literature. M. a M. Ngal, two of whose novels are considered in the conclusion, is a major contributor to *Lectures africaines*. Since 1970, a *Cahier de littérature et linguistique appliquée* has also been published by the University. At the University of Yaoundé, E.R.L.A.C. (Equipe de recherches en littérature africaine comparée) was founded in 1969 by Thomas Melone. The first work in a series of *Mélanges africains* has been published. It was also at Yaoundé that an important conference took place, *Le critique africain et son peuple comme producteurs de civilisation* in 1973 (proceedings published by Présence Africaine in 1977). Its conclusion was that African criticism should fulfil four requirements: it should attend to the scientific, the pedagogical, the political, and the aesthetic. The University of Abidjan has published *Annales de l'école des lettres et sciences humaines* since 1965 and, since 1979, a *Revue de littérature et d'esthétique négro-africaines*. Two important conferences have also taken place in Abidjan: *Situation et perspectives de la littérature négro-africaine* in 1969 (published in Abidjan in 1970) and, in the following year, *Le Théâtre négro-africain* (published in Paris in 1971). Since 1971 the University of Dakar has produced its *Annales*. Mohamadou Kane is arguably the most significant Senegalese literary critic in the field; his *Roman africain et tradition* is considered later. A number of important conferences have been organized by the University of Dakar: *Colloque sur la littérature africaine d'expression française* in 1963, *Fonction et signification de l'Art nègre dans la vie du peuple* in 1966 (the *Actes* published in 1967), and *Colloque sur la Négritude* in 1971 (the *Actes* published in 1972).

In France, the foundation of A.U.P.E.L.F. (Association des universités partiellement ou entièrement de langue française), in 1977, has been significant in terms of providing a central clearing house for information, for example. Noteworthy conferences that have taken place in France include *Négritude africaine, Négritude caraïbe*, held at the Université de Paris-Nord, in 1973, *La permanence et la mutation des mythes traditionnels africains dans les littératures modernes*, in Limoges in 1977, and, *Critique et réception des littératures négro-africaines*, at the Université de Paris III in 1978.[1] More recently, a *table ronde* organized by the Centre d'Etudes Francophones at the Université de Paris XIII in conjunction with the Centre International de Francophonie at the Université de Paris IV, addressed itself to the problems of *L'Oral et l'écrit, langues et littératures en contact* (1980); in the same year, a conference organized by C.E.R.C.L.E.F. (Centre d'études et de recherches sur les civilisations, langues et littératures d'expression française) at the Université de Paris XII looked at *Images de l'Afrique en Occident: la presse, les médias et la littérature*.[2]

Elsewhere outside Africa, important conferences have taken place in Sherbrooke, Quebec, on *Le Roman contemporain d'expression française* in 1970 (edited by Antoine Naaman and Louis Painchaud, 1971); in Vermont, on *Les littératures africaine et canadienne d'expression française: genèse et jeunesse* in 1971; and in Leiden, Holland, on *Text and Context:*

Methodological Explorations in the Field of African Literature in 1973 (published in 1977).[3]

Francophone African literature has, of course, always been part of the wider field of African literature (which includes both Anglophone and Lusophone writings), and thus the criticism of Francophone African literature has always been part of the broader debate surrounding the criticism of African literature in general. In English-speaking areas, interest in African writing naturally began with interest in texts in English, and it was only as the study of Anglophone African literature became established that Francophone texts gradually found their way into the debate. By the 1970s, English studies that included discussion of Francophone African writing were beginning to appear. For example, the collection of essays, based on talks and discussions at the Africa Centre in London, published in 1969, *Protest and Conflict in African Literature* (edited by Pieterse and Munro) includes articles on "The Politics of Negritude," "The Idea of Assimilation" with reference to Beti and Laye, and "The Political and Cultural Revolution," which includes discussion of three Francophone writers: Senghor, Kane, and Laye. Similarly, *Perspectives on African Literature*, a collection of essays edited by Christopher Heywood, includes a number that treat Francophone writing. Abiola Irele, in his collection of essays, *The African Experience in Literature and Ideology,* and Ulli Beier, in his work, *An Introduction to African Literature,* include articles devoted exclusively to Francophone literature. Within English criticism of African literature, Anglophone and Francophone African literatures are treated as distinct.

Studies limited to one particular genre, however, such as Eustace Palmer's *An Introduction to the African Novel* (1972) and *The Growth of the African Novel* (1979), and Simon Gikandi's *Reading the African Novel* (1987), treat texts written in both English and French. Nor do their authors consider necessary any lengthy theoretical discussion of the appropriateness of considering novels in the two languages within a single study. The "African novel" is treated as a stable critical concept, an established genre, which needs no elaborate theoretical justification. S. A. Gakwandi, in his study, *The Novel and Contemporary Experience in Africa,* however, makes brief mention of the question of the autonomy of the African novel:

> To talk of the African novel is to assume that it has its own distinctive characteristics which distinguish it from novels from other areas of the world written in the same language. [p. 4]

This is justifiable, he argues, because of what V. Le Vine states in his book, *Political Leadership in Africa* (1967). Gakwandi quotes from him:

> There is no lack of documentation for the proposition that the colonial period in Africa produced several trans-territorial political cultures that

survived the transition to independence and which continue to affect the internal and external politics of the ex-colonial state. [p. 4]

Robert Fraser, on the other hand, in the introduction to his study of *West African Poetry: A Critical History* (1986), reveals a degree of unease when he writes:

> My principal focus has been the procession of poets who have emerged in English-speaking Africa. . . . My third and eleventh chapters . . . provide an accompanying account of developments in French-speaking Africa, less a token gesture toward francophone poetry than as a much needed insight into one significant element in the pervading cultural milieu over the period I have elected to discuss. [p. 1]

Thus Fraser is not proposing "West African poetry" as a single autonomous field of study, but rather as an area, defined above all geographically, made up of distinct, yet related, elements, one of which is the "francophone element."

It will be clear from this brief look at various British publications of the late 1960s, 1970s, and 1980s that, although Anglophone criticism has incorporated Francophone African literature into its discussion of Anglophone African literature in various ways, the fundamental theoretical preoccupations of Francophone criticism of Francophone African literature have not entered the Anglophone literary-critical debate. There are a number of possible explanations for this. It may be that the less theoretically biased practices of English criticism (as opposed to French criticism) have rendered the English criticism of African literature less methodologically concerned than on the Francophone side. It may also be that as Francophone African literature has almost always been treated alongside Anglophone African literature (within Anglophone criticism), a distinct literary history is rarely proposed for the Francophone literature. Yet the literary history proposed for the Anglophone literature is not haunted by the vicissitudes of Negritude. Certain theoretical preoccupations have, as earlier chapters have demonstrated, underpinned the debate concerning the criticism of "Negro-African literature in French"—in particular, a dogged desire to prove the legitimacy of the area itself. Furthermore, the evaluative criteria proposed within the Francophone debate are intimately bound up with the criteria of definition of the area. This complex literary-historical and literary-critical alliance has not dominated the Anglophone debate, and this difference has encouraged the establishment of firm lines of demarcation that have militated against the integration of Anglophone criticism of Francophone African literature into the Francophone debate. Works by Ulli Beier, Abiola Irele, and Clive Wake—and Dorothy Blair's book, *African Literature in French: A History of Creative Writing in French from*

West and Equatorial Africa, devoted exclusively to Francophone African literature—have, however, constituted exceptions.

Interestingly, the nature of their contribution to the debate distinguishes them from Francophone criticism. This is most obvious in the way in which other criticism refers to them. In a study such as Hausser's *Essai sur la poétique de la négritude*, for example, which has one of the most complete bibliographies of any work in the area, work by Beier, Blair, and Wake is quoted to demonstrate *interpretative* concordance or disagreement. Other Francophone criticism, on the other hand, is usually referred to by Hausser to distinguish his own *methodological* approach, to highlight its specificity. Studies of individual Francophone African authors by British critics have, of course, been incorporated into the debate surrounding that author.

Even more trenchant differences between the American and French approaches to Francophone Negro-African literature have worked against the integration of American criticism into the French debate. In America, consideration of Francophone African literature generally takes place under the rubric of "Black Literature" or "Black Studies." Black American literature, Anglophone African and West Indian literature, and Francophone African and West Indian literature—and, indeed, South American literature in English, French, Spanish, and Portuguese—all fall under these rubrics. Furthermore, increasingly within the American academic institution, publications are appearing that cross the conventional dividing lines between disciplines. Christopher Miller's important book, *Blank Darkness: Africanist Discourse in French,* analyzes texts by, for example, Baudelaire, Rimbaud, Conrad, Sade, Céline, and Ouologuem and explores the relationship between their various discourses. The collection of essays, *Black Literature and Literary Theory*, edited by Henry Louis Gates, Jr, and published while he was Professor of English, comparative literature, and African studies at Cornell University, and even more his subsequent collection, *"Race," Writing and Difference*, span a number of traditionally distinct fields. Focusing on racial difference, the latter work addresses questions relevant to literary criticism, literary theory, black studies, Asian studies, comparative literature, women's studies, cultural sociology, and anthropology. As the back cover states: "It is a book whose insights can be brought to bear upon relationships that extend far beyond the confined boundaries of text." By addressing questions that are traditionally the concern of such a wide range of disciplines, however, there is a danger that the text is seen as marginal to them all. It may be for this reason that eclectic works such as Gates', despite their urgent theoretical interest, have not found their way into the French debate. Similarly, in a study such as Mercer Cook and Stephen Henderson's *The Militant Black Writer in Africa and the United States*, questions of fundamental significance to the Francophone debate are treated so peremptorily that they are simply wholeheartedly denied by Francophone criticism. Referring to Senghor's *Anthologie de la nouvelle poésie nègre et malgache de langue française*, Cook writes, "The poets included in this anthology display remarkable similarities in terms of tone, aspirations, *Negritude*," to which Hausser flatly remarks, "What needs to be emphasized, and forcefully, is on the contrary the obvious and fundamental incompatibilities of aspiration and tone" (p. 11).

In French-speaking areas, and in particular outside metropolitan France, African literature in French is frequently seen as part of Francophone literature. This does not necessarily mean that the integrity or autonomy of African literature in French is implicitly questioned, but rather that certain concerns of African literature can be made visible and understandable by a process of analogy with other literatures.

Whether or not as part of, or a branch of, other literatures, Negro-African literature in French is thus considered a significant discipline within and outside Africa, and it has given rise to centres of research and teaching worldwide. Outside Africa, interest is most concentrated in France, Canada, and the United States. The debate is thus an international one, although national concerns stand out within the secondary discourses of each country. Two particular traits are discernible in African criticism of the last two decades. First, the rewriting of literary history along national lines. Thus anthologies, histories, critical studies, and so on increasingly concern themselves less with "Negro-African," "African," "Sub-Saharan," or "West African" literature than with national literatures: Senegalese, Camerounian, and so forth. Second, there has been what might be described as a "retour aux sources critiques," an attempt to rediscover indigenous critical procedures—that is, methods that develop out of a traditional African context. The corollary of this is that European critical procedures are viewed with suspicion. For example, referring to the amorphous literature of "la nouvelle critique" in relation to African literature, Mohamadou Kane (1977) voices an opinion shared by a number of African literary critics:

> Criticism in Europe . . . is embarking on a too exclusively formalist approach which is divorced from the committed, collective and functional nature of African literature. . . . It looks to criticism for no other mission but that which makes it an objective and attentive servant of the work, concerned to detect and to link themes with structures, "writing to existence." Africa's political situation, our literary traditions, lead us to confer on criticism, as on the critic, particular missions. [pp. 258–259]

Kane's conviction that Africa's political position, combined with her literary traditions, render the "formalist" methods of "la nouvelle critique" inappropriate to African literature, is part of a broader and widely voiced concern about the "origins" and appropriateness of various critical approaches. In particular, many African critics are committed to "de-coloniz-ing" African literary criticism (Chinweizu was a pioneer in this respect). Critical perspectives—their values and preoccupations—must originate from within, and not outside, Africa. Thus in the preface to G. O. Midio-houan's study *L'Idéologie dans la littérature négro-africaine d'expression française* of 1986, he writes:

> The aim of this work is to present the history of Negro-African literature of French expression from an unknown perspective, unknown because different from the majority of works which are today authorities in the field.
>
> These last are, furthermore, the work of European critics who, what-ever is said, see Africa and Negro-African literature from their point of view *outside*. This primacy of European discourse which extends into African schools and universities is not without dangers and it is to be hoped that more and more Africans will affirm their presence in the field. [p. 7]

The criteria used to judge Negro-African literature must be appropriate to it, rather than "imported" from outside. The preface to J.-P. Makouta M'Boukou's book, *Introduction à l'étude du roman négro-africain de langue française: problèmes culturels et littéraires* (1980), is equally typi-cal of the perspective of many recent critical studies by Africans:

> If Negro-African writers have, during the course of the decades, done everything so as not to be assimilated by the West, but remain itself [Negro-African literature], while seeking, at the same time, true dialogue with other societies, it is today essential that criticism concerned with our texts not be assimilated by Western criticism, in order that the profound originality which truly distinguishes them might be brought to light and safeguarded.
>
> How easy it is, in fact, to be corrupted, and hence to deny oneself, when seeking to please one's judges! [p. 7]

What are considered to be "foreign" critical procedures are denounced. Speaking of "de nombreux jeunes Négro-Africains" and their reading of Western critics, Makouta continues:

> They discover not only insufficiencies but also errors of interpretation, exaggerations of judgement, which can all be accounted for in terms of the ignorance which these writers manifest with regard to the diverse contexts within which Negro-African literary works are born; these are geograph-ical, historical, sociological, ethnological, religious, politico-economic, and linguistic contexts. [p. 9]

African criticism of the 1970s and 1980s has been concerned, by and large, to "Africanize" its critical procedures. This has taken a number of forms, representative samples of which are examined in this chapter.

In France, on the other hand, critical practices have tended to be in line with general developments in criticism; the influence of "la nouvelle critique" stands out. The same is true of American criticism of Negro-African literature, although it now seems to have been annexed by comparative literature. The two collections of essays edited by Henry Louis Gates, Jr, *Black Literature and Literary Theory* (1984) and *"Race," Writing and Difference* (1986) exemplify this shift. While "national" trends do exist, the debate is sufficiently international to make any detailed discussion along exclusively national lines inappropriate. Similarly, a chronological approach to studies of the 1970s and 1980s fails to sort critical approaches into the particular "schools" within which they can best be understood. Describing and analyzing the "schools" of criticism of the last two decades brings to light the breadth of approaches to Negro-African literature during the 1970s and early 1980s.

The most obvious change in critical procedures over the last two decades is that their methods and practices become more varied and more explicit. The previously dominant methodology, characterized by a paradigmatic approach implicitly or explicitly associated with Negritude, gives way to more self-conscious and ostensibly "scientific" approaches thus recognizable as particular "schools" of criticism. Where Negritude remains at the centre of critical discourse, it is no longer used naively, as an unproblematical term. Critical works begin to fall into specific and distinct categories, sometimes owing allegiance to particular metropolitan schools or influences (structuralism, linguistic criticism, semiology, the writings of Althusser, and so on) and sometimes in direct opposition to them; thus titles appear such as Marcien Towa's *Poésie de la négritude: approche structuraliste* or Sunday Anozie's *Sociologie du roman africain,* which contrast with the very much more general and introductory works of the 1960s: Kesteloot's *Les Ecrivains noirs de langue française* or Robert Pageard's *Littérature négro-africaine d'expression française,* among many.

Eight studies will serve to illustrate the ambiguities, complexities, and paradoxes of the treatment of "Negro-African literature" in the 1970s and 1980s. As the bibliography of secondary discourses published during this period is large (and many works within it wholly unoriginal in terms of approach), these eight works, which characterize the major approaches of the period, form the focus of this chapter. They are: Stanislas Adotevi's, *Négritude et Négrologues* (1972); Marcien Towa's *Poésie de la négritude* (1983); Iyay Kimoni's *Destin de la littérature négro-africaine ou problématique d'une culture* (1975); Michel Hausser's study, *Essai sur la poétique de la négritude* (1986); Sunday Anozie's *Sociologie du roman africain* (1970); Guy Ossito Midiohouan's *L'Idéologie dans la littérature négro-africaine d'expression française* (1986); Francis Anani Joppa's *L'Engagement des écrivains africains noirs de langue française* (1982); and, finally, Mohamadou Kane's *Roman africain et tradition* (1982), which represents an attempt to resituate literary criticism within African tradition. Their respective titles suggest that their methodological differences can be accounted for in terms of what they foreground in the literary text: the ideological, political, sociological, or linguistic, for example. This impression is, however, misleading. The role attributed to Negritude, on the other hand (which is intimately bound up with the definition of the area under critical scrutiny), in the elaboration of the various critical discourses, either explicitly or implicitly, provides a more accurate assessment of their parallels and differences of approach.

The ubiquity of Negritude, in its numerous paradigmatic formulations, remains evident in all but a very few critical methods. In many studies Negritude continues to operate as the embodiment of a "standard" (in its multifarious forms) for Negro-African literature. Within other critical methods, however, it finds its way to the centre of discourse because of its alleged *inappropriateness* to literary critical debate.

Negritude had, of course, come under criticism from the moment it established itself as a significant concept. Even Sartre's "Orphée noir," which did so much to attract attention to Negro-African literature, pointed to problematical aspects of Negritude, in particular its "anti-racist racism." Sartre also viewed Negritude as a historical moment—that is, as part of a process that would inevitably come to an end, requiring something new. Other well-known critics of Negritude include Fanon, Mphahlele, Depestre, and Soyinka.[4] Yet despite considerable criticism, Negritude continued to be widely exploited within literary criticism as a relatively unproblematical term until the beginning of the 1970s.

Following the publication of Stanislas Adotevi's *Négritude et Négrologues*, in 1972, a more cautious approach to Negritude is visible. Adotevi's criticisms of Negritude in his notorious work are explicit and outspoken. It is less Negritude's literary manifestation than its political corollaries that are the subject of Adotevi's attack, however, but the work has also had considerable influence on the way in which Negritude is treated in literary studies.

Négritude et Négrologues attempts to "demystify" Negritude. Adotevi's perspective is that of the Marxist-Leninist, and he repeats the conviction that no "metaphorical construct" can make the black man's consciousness whole, a consciousness fragmented by the history of the white man. Unlike other critics of Negritude who regard the concept as inextricably bound up with the poetic genre and advocate other genres (in particular, the novel) as the way forward, Adotevi does not propose an alternative genre. Dignity and identity, Adotevi argues, can be regained only through the processes of economic and social revolution: "Commitment to the revolution in Africa was what mattered yesterday as today, and not to the polishing of verses" (p. 82); "it is a moral and political necessity to destroy definitively the very foundations of Negritude" (p. 122, footnote 1).

Adotevi's fierce polemic is contained within a flamboyant, baroque style. Two further quotations provide the key to his often satirical study: "Negritude is the *black* way of being *white*" (p. 207); "Negritude . . . fixes and coagulates . . . the most used theories about African traditions of which it pretends to be the literary reflection" (p. 113). The first premise is based on the notion that it is only as a result of difference (from the white man) that the black man is conscious of his blackness. The values of Negritude (those proposed by Senghor) are no more than the antithesis of white values. Adotevi is also suspicious of the influence of European ethnologists on the Negritude poets (Senghor in particular). Adotevi's second criticism (Negritude's reactionary dimension) points to what he considers to be the backward-looking traditionalism of Negritude. The promotion of a "retour aux sources" and too great an emphasis on African primitivism militate against the insertion of Africa into the modern world.

Adotevi's criticisms of Negritude are most appropriate to Senghor's formulation of Negritude. It is above all the latter's prose writings on African Socialism which most deeply concern Adotevi; Negritude as an "état poétique" (as Sartre presented it in "Orphée noir") is very little disturbed. What most concerns Adotevi is the reactionary political programs that he believes to be the logical corollary of the values of Negritude:

> We have to liquidate it [Negritude] because it is a compromise with im-
> perialism and neo-colonialism. . . . From now on our questions must be
> posed in terms of exploitation, so that blacks make the jump and arrive at
> an authentic socialism. . . . What is essential is that the black people get
> going.[5]

Adotevi's broadside left Negritude's literary manifestation little damaged.

However, *Négritude et Négrologues* publicized a number of difficulties associated with Negritude, most particularly inadequacies in its political formulation which had previously been generally ignored within the literary-critical debate. From 1972 onward, most literary critics writing about Negro-African literature take Adotevi's perspective into account in their studies and include his work in their bibliographies. Adotevi had wanted Negritude to disappear from contemporary discussion. Ironically, his contribution has simply been added to the large body of texts that complicate, confuse, and fuel the Negritude debate.

Similarly, Marcien Towa's *Poésie de la négritude: approche structuraliste*, published in 1983, has established itself as a major text within the

Negritude debate. As its title suggests, Negritude is foregrounded as a key term from the beginning. Towa's method derives from Lucien Goldmann's genetic structuralism and he begins by asserting the ideological dimension of Negritude: "For some years negritude has occupied a certain position among the ideological currents of our century" (p. 8). Negritude had been posited, implicitly, as the literary manifestation of an ideology in Adotevi's study. For Towa, Negritude, as a political program, has been misunderstood and deserves attention:

> the problem of Negritude correctly formulated presents a double aspect: firstly it is a matter of understanding, then and only then a matter of seeing and in what measure it can guide—or misdirect—action. [p. 8]

Yet, as Towa goes on to argue, "Negritude is linked to a literary current, or more precisely to a poetry, if not linked then even confused with it" (p. 8). Towa is thus interested, like Adotevi, in the political corollaries of Negritude (the extent to which it can provide a program for action), but he emphasizes that it must first be fully understood contextually. The particular context on which Towa focuses is that of Aimé Césaire's poetry. His intention is thus to explore the poetry of Césaire as it was he who coined the neologism and furthermore "explicitly and constantly elaborated its contents in his poems" (p. 8). Through the application of Goldmann's "structuralisme génétique," his aim is:

> to see whether between the internal structure of a work and the other global structures, there exist similarities or other significant relations. It is only by integrating the literary work into its social and historical context that it can be made intelligible, because the problems raised originate principally in society, in the relations between human groups. [pp. 9–10]

His approach is the logical consequence of his commitment to structuralism, because:

> structuralism considers that the true subject of historical action is the group and that a work is truly important only if it maintains a significant relationship with the group. It is therefore by confrontation, by the placing in parallel of the internal structure of the work with other vaster structures (religious, political, economic) that the work can be really understood. [p. 9]

Towa considers five areas, addressed in five sections. The first considers the function of art within society: "the influence of art on action is indirect, but real" (p. 17). In the second section of his study, entitled "Socio-historical Genesis of Negritude," Towa analyzes the "West Indian situation which we find at the beginning of the *Cahier d'un retour au pays natal*" (p. 30).

He considers the "social and human structure of the West Indies at the time of the birth of Negritude" (chapter 3), he draws up an "economic analysis of Martinican misery" (chapter 4), and he discusses the "ideological aspect of the Martinican situation towards 1932" (chapter 5); finally, he considers the "Parisian experience of black students" (chapter 6). He builds the third and fourth chapters around quotations from the *Cahier*.

Towa's approach reverses the usual hierarchy of "literary text" and "critical commentary." Where the second might be expected to weave its way around the first, in Towa's method the literary text explores and explains his commentary. Thus Césaire's text is used to strengthen and illustrate Towa's discourse. He quotes the following section from Césaire:

> At the end of the wee hours, this inert town and its beyond of lepers, of consumption, of famines, of fears squatting in the ravines, fears perched in the trees, fears dug in the ground, fears adrift in the sky, piles of fears and their fumaroles of anguish. [translation from Eshleman & Smith, 1983, p. 37]

Towa's text then continues: "'European or American tourists . . . are not really interested in these men and women they do not know them and they do not wish to know them'" (Towa, 1983, p. 33). Towa's discourse confers on Césaire's the status of "social commentary," which he uses to enrich his own description of the social realities of Fort-de-France. Thus Towa's discourse is "supported" by quotations from Césaire. The language of the "poetic" text is in no way privileged but, rather, treated as obscure prose. The fifth and sixth chapters of Towa's study are largely historical. The fifth concludes that:

> the revolutionary conscience of West Indian students leaving the islands before 1939 was feeble if not nonexistent, and that of Césaire must have been in its infancy. It was more in Paris that it took shape. [p. 46]

Towa depends, for his information, on the writings of the Negritude poets—Césaire's *Discours sur le colonialisme*, Damas' *Pigments*, Senghor's *Hosties noires*. He also relies heavily on Fanon's *Peau noire, masques blancs*.

Having discussed racial attitudes as experienced by the Negritude writers in Paris, Towa goes on to consider their reactions to this experience, as apparent in their poetry, which Towa describes as "leur mode essentiel d'expression," a record of the poet's experience. The poem constitutes "la réaction du poete à l'assimilationnisme" (p. 78), for example. Towa takes into account Damas's *Pigments* and the major works of Césaire and Senghor. This leads him, in the final section of his book, to address the question, "Qu'est-ce que la négritude?"

Towa begins by asking "Qu'est-ce qui fait qu'un Nègre est un Nègre"; his answer is: "ce n'est pas la race, mais la culture" (p. 246). And it is, needless to say, in Césaire's poetry that this is most clearly presented:

The central preoccupation . . . is the struggle for the complete liberation of the Negro, the complete taking in hand of his past, present and future destiny, the affirmation of the Negro as a historical subject, as a creator of history and culture. [p. 247]

Senghor is characterized, by contrast, as "the main popularizer of this [notion of Negritude]" (p. 266). Towa's principal concern is to demonstrate that "la poésie de Césaire est essentiellement et ouvertement politique" (p. 280) and that Senghor's typifies "la vieille négritude" of the "bon nègre" of Césaire's *Cahier*.

Towa's study consciously situates itself within a particular debate, the debate surrounding Negritude:

The most candid and the most well-developed attacks against Negritude come from the left. They are all carried out . . . according to the same schema. Firstly Negritude is reduced to "the black Essence," the black soul, then its racist and ineffectual character is demonstrated. [pp. 280–281]

Towa's defence of Negritude focuses on Césaire's Negritude. His is the "authentic revolutionary Negritude" in contrast to Senghor's.

Towa's method is based on a critical tautology. In the introductory pages of *Poésie de la négritude*, Césaire is referred to as:

the poet who created this neologism and who has explicitly and constantly elaborated *its contents* in his poems. [p. 8; my italics]

However, the coining of a neologism does not give the speaker a perpetual monopoly over its meaning. To refer to "the contents [of Negritude]" is to suggest that Negritude has some substance, some specific essence which Césaire has revealed in his poems. But as Towa himself points out, "Negritude is linked to a literary current, more precisely to a poetry, if it does not actually become confused with it" (p. 8). It is indeed this "confusion" which needs to be recognized; it cannot be explained away, because it stems from the multiplicity of meanings that Negritude has attracted to itself, within different contexts, at different times. What Towa fails to acknowledge is that Negritude does not have some existential substance independent of language which can, nevertheless, be "incorporated" in language; Negritude is, first and foremost, a poetics, but a poetics that offers political, social, and cultural corollaries. Towa, on the other hand, associates Negritude with some elements of Césaire's poetry (those which he too considers important), those associated with "the struggle for the complete liberation of the Negro," and then defines these as the characteristics of "authentic" Negritude. He then goes on to explore these characteristics of Césaire's poetry in depth, and as though his original definition of Negritude had been formulated independently of his knowledge of Césaire's poetry. The question that Towa's inadequate method begs is not "what is Negritude?," but "where is Negritude?" In other words, "within which discipline or discourse does Negritude reside?"

Adotevi had located "ideological Negritude" within Senghor's political discourse and its literary corollary principally within Senghor's poetry. Focusing mainly on the first—Negritude as a program for action—and finding it politically unsatisfactory, Adotevi proceeded to call for Negritude's demise. Towa, on the other hand, while also positing Negritude as an ideology with poetic parallels, focuses on the social and political commitment evident in the concerns of much of Césaire's poetic project. Equating Negritude with Césaire's social commitment and revolutionary poetics, most particularly that of the *Cahier*, Towa defends Negritude. Adotevi and Towa thus locate Negritude in the work of different writers: Adotevi associates it with all he finds unacceptable in Senghor's writings, while Towa associates it with all he admires in Césaire's writing.

Just as the critical methods, not to say machinations, of the studies by Adotevi and by Towa are made most visible by an examination of the guise assumed by Negritude within their discourses, and the role attributed to it within the literary histories that they propose, so, in Iyay Kimoni's study, the scrutiny of Negritude and its context reveals the study's hidden methods. Negritude enters the discourse of *Destin de la littérature négro-africaine ou problématique d'une culture* surreptitiously, as a corollary of the definition of the area under discussion: this is defined as "la littérature négro-africaine." A "littérature négro-africaine" cannot, however, exist independently of a "culture négro-africaine"; once the latter is proposed, the way is open for Negritude to enter the discussion. Kimoni's study is indeed committed to a perspective that must take account of Negritude, but it does this in a way that is very different from Towa's study. Kimoni takes both poetry and the novel into account and, from early on, makes barely disguised attacks on the poetry of Negritude:

When treating Negro-African literature . . . one finds oneself confronted by a literature of protest which rightly rails against the woes of the black peoples and demands for them dignity and justice. If the effort of protest against a social order deemed to be unjust—in this instance the colonial regime—attains its objective, it is difficult to think that the act of accusation will itself be sufficient to give the colonized back his dignity or rehabilitate him. [p. 9]

Kimoni doubts the power of "linguistic revolution," the power of metaphor, which lies at the heart of Sartre's analysis of the poetry of Negritude.
Kimoni's criticisms of Negritude become most overt when he treats its role
within literary criticism. For Kimoni, it is a function of literary commentary relying too heavily on the precepts of Negritude (as in Senghor's
criticism) which has resulted in the failure of criticism to bring to light
other themes and concerns of Negro-African literature; it has also led to
neglect of the novel.

    Kimoni begins from the premise that "Negritude criticism" (that is, criti-
cal methods based on the values of Negritude) has done Negro-African
literature a disservice. His criticisms of Negritude are not dissimilar to
other left-wing critics, but his object is not to posit the necessity of social
and economic revolution, in place of linguistic or metaphorical revolution,
but rather to draw attention to aspects of Negro-African literature which
cannot be identified in a myopic reading dominated by the concerns of
Negritude. Kimoni's criticisms of Negritude are implicit in his criticisms
of the limitations of Negro-African poetry. He has greater faith in
Francophone African novelists than poets, because "they undertake, on the
subject of Africa, not a metaphysical debate but rather a sociological one.
. . . Their love of Negritude is selective" (p. 10). His concern is to show:

> that it is possible to perceive, in this literary current, something more than
> aggression. While combatting colonialism, the literature poses the prob-
> lem of the future of African culture the transformation of which it already
> presages. [p. 10]

Where Marcien Towa's desire is to demonstrate the authentically revolutionary dimension of Negritude (in particular Césaire's Negritude as opposed to Senghor's), Kimoni is concerned rather to highlight the more
forward-looking (and in his view underestimated) cultural dimensions of
Negro-African literature, particularly the novel. Similarly, where other critics are suspicious of the role of European ethnologists in the enumeration of
so-called Negro attributes (emotion, intuitive reasoning, rhythm, aptitude
for dance, and so on), Kimoni looks to them as authorities:

> Ethnological discourse is indispensable for whose who want to know Af-
> rica through the literary culture. Ethnologists have in effect an idea of the
> Black and of his culture, which influenced and provoked that which is
> present in the literature. . . . The ethnologist's gaze is essential because it
> makes intelligible the discourse on African literature. It illuminates our
> subject. [pp. 11, 12]

His reservations concerning Negritude also include suspicion of its literary
historical role. In the first of the three sections of his study ("la présence

littéraire des Noirs"), Kimoni proposes a literary history of "Negro-African literature in French" antipathetic to its classic Kestelootian formulation (itself based on Sartre's analysis):

> Lilyan Kesteloot was able to study the transitory aspect of this movement, emphasizing the part played by the revolt of Surrealism and Marxism. We emphasize the stable character of the movement and associate it with all the phases which determined it from the inside to the point where we can talk of it in terms of the negro renaissance. [p. 13]

Kimoni's proposed method in the first part of his study is explained in his introduction:

> Our role is limited to an explanation of the reactions of Blacks starting from their taking up of a position in reviews and works of the imagination. We explain the reactions of Blacks by referring to history, to certain psychological explanations, relying on the *donnés* of cultural anthropology, and what we have seen in African society. [p. 13]

The second part of his study:

> aims to show that, on the one hand the attempt by Blacks to define themselves in opposition to the West is encouraged by researchers and European avant-garde artists, and on the other, that Negro-Africans endeavour to go beyond the attitude of European intellectuals of the 'twenties and 'thirties. [p. 14]

It is only in the third part of his study that the literary text comes into the foreground:

> The third part reveals how Africans view their culture in concrete terms. This is the work of Negro-African novelists. They bring us into the presence of the people themselves. [p. 15]

For Kimoni, poetry and the novel have distinct, specific, and clearly defined roles within Negro-African literature. It is in the third part of his study that this emerges, and proves to be at the heart of his thesis:

> With the appearance of the novel, African literature passes in effect from the abstract stage where the antagonism of two ideologies dominated, Negritude and the politics of assimilation, to a concrete phase where realist description was going to show the sense of mutation of traditional society and that of colonial society itself. [p. 172]

It is Kimoni's conviction that the image of African culture conveyed by the novel differs fundamentally from that conveyed by poetry (p. 172). Further-more, poetry is concerned with a theoretical formulation, whereas the novel displays "the new *concrete* modifications which Negro-Africans make to their traditions" (my italics). Thus the third part of Kimoni's study explores various themes of the African novel: "the weakening of values" (pp. 178–189), "confrontation" (pp. 190–208), "metamorphoses" (pp. 209–229). Under these headings, Kimoni's text focuses on particular subthemes—for example, "the administration," "the missions," "the city." Reference to particular novels is generally made by means of footnotes. For example, he writes:

> The creation of Europe, the city is the point of contact between the West and Africa. It is the symbol of the social and economic transformation of the black continent. . . . The city appears in turn as a commercial centre and a lucrative market, made possible by the exploitation of industrial sites, factories and shops. [p. 187]

The associated footnote simply reads, "Cf. Eza Boto, *Ville cruelle*; et Fer-dinand Oyono, *Chemin d'Europe*."

In his conclusion, Kimoni considers the role of literature in terms of Africa's future development:

> Will literature succeed in inculcating among the African populations the sense of cultural difference and really to promote among them a taste for progress? [p. 231]

Kimoni thinks not. His conclusion opens, however, more optimistically:

> The study of African literature and the analysis of its preoccupations reveals that beyond colonialism there is, among Negro-African writers, an attempt to affirm the originality of African culture on the one hand, and a desire to push Africa into the path of progress, on the other. Literature appears at once as the cement of the cultural conscience and, at the same time, as an instrument in the service of the economic and social develop-ment of the black continent. [p. 231]

Kimoni sees the novel as a more appropriate genre for the construction of a modern Africa. Negro-African poetry in French, on the other hand, belongs to a period in which Negritude and the politics of assimilation dominate (p. 172). Kimoni's criticisms of Negritude are therefore implicit in his criti-cisms of poetry, as a genre, as opposed to the novel. *Destin de la littérature négro-africaine* treats literature as a sociological phenomenon and Negri-tude as a "socio-poetical" occurrence belonging to a particular and limited historical period.

Adotevi's *Négritude et Négrologue*, Towa's *Poésie de la négritude*, and Kimoni's *Destin de la littérature négro-africain* are all underpinned by ideological concerns. They are preoccupied by the apparently tangible relationship between literature and political and sociological reality. The most extreme statement of this comes in Towa's declaration of his commitment to structuralism (p. 9), quoted earlier. The precise nature of the ideological presuppositions inherent in these three studies is apparent not so much in their stated intentions but through an examination of the way in which Negritude is defined and seen to function, within each study. This is also the case in Francis Anani Joppa's, *L'Engagement des écrivains africains noirs de langue française: du témoignage au dépassement* (1982).

Joppa's stated approach is threefold:

> To define the notion of commitment in Negro-African literature of French expression, to scrutinize the artistic expression of this notion and to see the extent to which the content of this literature reflects the political, social and cultural realities of black Africa. [p. 7]

Joppa is interested in the textual manifestation of "engagement": "it is much less a matter of the theoretical analysis of the notion of commitment than of its artistic expression" (p. 7). Thus, he explores "the manner in which Negro-African writers treat reality," and he is interested, therefore, in the analysis of both the literary and the social (p. 8). In terms of the structure of his work, Joppa rejects a chronological approach, on the grounds that thematic similarities between early and later works make it less useful to treat novels of a particular period as a group. The nationality of the author is also considered an unhelpful, if not misleading, means of classification:

> The nationality of the authors does not seem to play a sufficiently important role in the choice and treatment of themes to merit a worthwhile distinction between the works of one country and another. . . . The works reflect fundamental realities common to all the countries which are treated in this study. [p. 11]

While Joppa allows that there exist "plusieurs cultures africaines" (p. 11), he argues that:

> Most Negro-African writers, if not all, seek and demonstrate behind the diversity of cultures and realities, the profound unity of situations and of *Negro-African civilization*. [p. 11; my italics]

Having proposed the notion of a "civilisation négro-africaine," it becomes clear that Joppa's presentation of Negro-African literature is fundamentally influenced by the literary discourse and historiography associated with Negritude, Senghorian Negritude, in particular. The "universality" of "la civilisation négro-africaine" is, according to Joppa's own formulation, less a *donnée* than a construct assembled in response to colonialism. The search for cultural authenticity was prompted by "colonialist lies." Thus, Joppa argues, "the efforts of writers to rehabilitate African values is, logically, part of the same perspective as that of colonialism" (p. 12).

Joppa sees the efforts of the first Negro-African writers as belonging within the same perspective as that of colonialism. Adotevi had declared that Negritude was "a compromise with imperialism and neo-colonialism." Their perspectives are thus similar, although Joppa sees the ideological stance of the early Negro-African writers as historically unavoidable, whereas for Adotevi they are culpable for their ideological myopia.

In the first chapter of Joppa's study, he provides quotations from interviews, lectures, and essays, offering various definitions of what it means for the Negro-African writer to be "committed," ranging from dominantly political expressions to more culturally based formulations. An example of the former is provided by Charles Nokan:

> The writer, an integral part of the people, must express the difficulties, the pains, the joys of this last, its fight for the improvement of its condition. The African artist has to fight against cultural imperialism, colonialism, neo-colonialism and their black agents. He is obliged to defend the national culture, to enrich it, to make it revolutionary, to dedicate his works to the struggle of all the exploited for a better life. [p. 17]

Sekou Touré, on the other hand, argues: "The least of our original artistic manifestations is equivalent to an active participation in the life of our people" (p. 21).

Joppa's method is to reveal various dominant themes of Negro-African literature in French, most particularly the novel, and the extent to which these are the corollaries of "commitment." He considers, for example, "les rapports colonial-indigène," juxtaposing a quotation from Césaire's *Discours sur le colonialisme*: "Between the colonizer and the colonized, there is only room for chore, intimidation, pressure, the police, taxes, theft, rape" (p. 30). Joppa also quotes Oyono: "One never encounters the hand of the White in the same dish of food" (p. 30).

The second section of Joppa's study is entitled "L'Affirmation" and under this heading themes characterized as "les valeurs négro-africaines" (chapter 4) and "l'authenticité africaine" (chapter 5) are considered. In his introduction Joppa had stated that "all criticism implies the utilization of a system of references" (p. 13). Here, predictably, it is the constructs of Senghorian Negritude to which Joppa refers. Having briefly outlined "Negro-African values," Joppa illustrates these by reference to various novels and poems. Here, however, his method is not merely descriptive: the espousal of "les valeurs négro-africains" is an essential part of the Negro-African writer's "commitment." He quotes approvingly from Senghor:

> There is no civilization without a literature which expresses and illustrates its values. . . . And without written literature, no civilization will go beyond simple ethnographic curiosity. [p. 159]

Joppa continues:

> The creation of authentic works and the exaltation of Negro-African values are two inseparable aspects of the Negro-African writer's commitment. [p. 159]

Authenticity and the extolling of Negro-African values are thus indissolubly linked in Joppa's presentation of "engagement." Gradually, Senghor's classic criteria of Negritude work their way into Joppa's discourse. The latter continues:

> These two aspects [the creation of authentic works and the extolling of Negro-African values] are better understood dialectically because they inform each other. The values which the Negro-African writer sets out to extol already constitute . . . his writer's prereflexive *cogito* and confer particular qualities on his work. [p. 160]

From here the logical progression is toward the equating of "l'authenticité" and "l'africanité":

> By celebrating the values which belong to the African, the writer is only really revealing . . . the "juice and sap of Negritude" on which his work is nourished. Thus by exploring the major aspects of these values, by elucidating the traditional climate in which these writers operate, we hope, at once, to bring out the most important aspects of the authenticity, the africanity, of this literature. [p. 160]

Joppa thus arrives at a point where he can treat "l'authenticité" and "l'africanité" as synonymous. Toward the end of the chapter, Joppa's discourse becomes more polemical as he considers various criticisms of Negritude (pp. 197–207): that it is reactionary in its glorification of the past, that it is overly concerned with race, that its conception of culture is static rather than dynamic. Joppa defends Negritude against these attacks on the grounds that historical circumstance justifies certain traits from which, as time passes, Negro-African literature can free itself (p. 199).

The third section of *L'Engagement des écrivains africains noirs* is divided into two chapters, "La Révolte" (chapter 6) and "L'Universel" (chapter 7). Again Joppa's frame of reference is that of Negritude. Drawing attention to "Negro humanism," Joppa argues that "Negritude ... is a moment of the universal conscience" (p. 292). Joppa's discourse foregrounds the sociological in literature. The literary text is treated as a sociological document in which, for example, ideological perspectives can be read. *L'Engagement des écrivains africains noirs de langue française: du témoignage au dépassement* provides an example of a secondary discourse ostensibly committed to one line of discussion (the nature and manifestation of "engagement" in literature), gradually ousted by the myriad constructs of Negritude. Nor is this simply a descriptive process. The criteria of Negritude operate as evaluative criteria from the point at which "authenticity" and "l'africanité" are equated.

Michel Hausser's *Essai sur la poétique de la négritude* (1986) differs fundamentally from the four studies discussed earlier in this chapter. Negritude continues to be exploited as a key term, but whereas in the other studies Negritude functions surreptitiously in shifting guises, Michel Hausser's sets out to locate Negritude in a fixed context. *Essai sur la poétique de la négritude* exploits the methods of linguistics to determine Negritude's "vie textuelle." The subject of Michel Hausser's study is, broadly speaking, the work of "les écrivains noirs de langue française" (p. 4). He distinguishes this literature from exotic literature and certain works by "non-French writers of French literature" (Beckett and Ionesco, for example), on the grounds that their "work finds itself *ipso facto* integrated into our literature, without its origins being examined" (p. 4). But, Hausser continues:

> This is not the case with black writers of French expression from the moment they refuse (if they refuse) the cultural norms of the society whose language they use. Their revolt against the norms, even if they are similar to certain "autochthonous" revolts, like that, recently, of the surrealists, obeys neither the same principles nor the same intentions. [p. 4]

In his introduction, Hausser juxtaposes the corpus of texts written by "les écrivains noirs de langue française" with "des littératures africaines francophones" (in the plural; p. 5) and "les écrivains noirs" (p. 5) and refers to them as constituting (in the sense in which "l'histoire littéraire l'entend"), "une école nouvelle" (p. 5). The "fonction historique qu'en attendent ses promoteurs" (p. 5) is also mentioned:

> They have not ceased to proclaim that they were expressing the needs, desires, thoughts, the being, not only of their people but of a whole race. [pp. 5–6]

However, Hausser does not employ a variety of terms to circumscribe his area of study without acknowledging the "contradictions" and "ambiguïté" of the field which account for the appropriateness of such a variety of terms.

Hausser distinguishes his essay from other works that "in a general way ... privilege three types of orientation: historical, sociological, thematic" (p. 7), such as those discussed earlier in the chapter. He does not point out, however, that it is not their concern to foreground the historical, sociological, or thematic that distinguishes these works from his own, but their very different exploitation of Negritude. Hausser argues, "they bear witness more to an ideological need, that of the author and of the 'class' to which he belongs" (p. 7). What concerns Hausser most, however, is that other studies:

> tend ... to neglect the textual reality, one is almost tempted to say: the textual life. Or the texts become ... transparent ... documents whose nature varies according to the intentions of the researcher, sociological for one, political for another, etc., or problems inherent in all texts are deemed resolved: problems of writing, communication, signification. [p. 8]

This is largely the case, but the studies discussed earlier also take into account questions that fall outside the scope of Hausser's discussion. These are mainly historiographical and theoretical problems concerning the history and theory of "Negro-African literature" as an independent and autonomous literature. As will become clear a little later, Hausser sidesteps these difficulties by attributing considerable significance, within his method, to what might be described as the "biblio-historical." For the "working definition" that Hausser uses is based simply on the contents of Senghor's *Anthologie*.

Hausser begins by considering the concept of the "texte littéraire" which he defines (after H. Meschonnic) as a:

> space which is materially created by an utterance of linguistic form, whose function is to produce a network of *directed* significations. [p. 8; Hausser's emphasis]

His study is then described as follows: "It is a reflection on textual functioning applied to a specific 'literature'" (p. 9). Defining a relatively objective method of studying "le fonctionnement textuel" on the one hand, and justifying the limits of his field of study (constituting "une littérature spécifique"), on the other, occupies the remaining pages of his introduction.

The theoretical suppositions in the definition of "une littérature spécifique" are complex: historical and historiographical factors are paramount. One definition would embrace "(all) works written in French by black writers," but "a global treatment," Hausser argues, "is ... utopic. It might be possible but not defensible. For historical and textual reasons" (p. 9). Here it becomes clear that Hausser's method will be to undertake a textual study of a "littérature spécifique." The definition of this autonomous "littérature spécifique" is one of the first problems of Hausser's method.

In terms of literary history—that is, texts concerned with the history of the (at this stage in his argument, amorphous) body of texts variously termed "littérature nègre," "littérature négro-africaine," etc.—Hausser cites, first and foremost, Lilyan Kesteloot's *Les Ecrivains noirs de langue française: naissance d'une littérature.* Hausser stresses Kesteloot's emphasis on "A [UNE] literature":

> in spite of differences of generation and style, writers like Senghor and Césaire, Beti and Oyono, to limit ourselves to the best known authors, are, in the end, interchangeable. This unitary vision is not . . . without foundation. [p. 10]

Since 1960, however, and the gradual accession to independence of previously colonized African countries, the notion of a single Francophone African literature is no longer tenable:

> Briefly, the history, geography, and politics forbid the consideration, from the perspective of this study, of all black literary production. One is led to choose a field whose unity is clearly definable. [p. 10]

Hausser limits himself to Negro-African poetry, as "consecrated" by Senghor's *Anthologie de la nouvelle poésie nègre et malgache.* According to Hausser, "It is this which consecrates the birth, the contents and the extension of that which henceforth is known by the name *Negritude,* a vague and complex notion" (p. 11). While Hausser emphasizes "the obvious and profound incompatibilities of aspiration and tone" of the poets of Senghor's anthology, he is nevertheless clear that "it bears witness all the same . . . to the reality of Negritude" (p. 11). Negritude is thus defined not as a concept, psychology, or ideology, manifest in a particular body of texts, but as the body of texts itself. Furthermore, for the purposes of his analysis, this body of texts will be considered as a single text:

> If one accepts the recognition of a "system" in the whole oeuvre of a poet, what prohibits the discussion, similarly, of a system in relation to the works of a plurality of poets who feel solidarity? To consider them, then, as the work of a subject called, for example, Negritude? [p. 18]

Negritude becomes "the writing subject."

Hausser's study takes into account recent developments in linguistics. Ideological concerns are also kept within the discussion as:

The Negritude-text is envisaged not as a historical or poetic subject, that is to say as a place where an ideology is made and unmade, by means of communication. [p. 22]

Basing his method on Chomsky, Ricoeur, Benveniste, Greimas, Jakobson and Todorov, in particular, Hausser divides his study into three sections. Establishing the *locus* from which Negritude speaks and its means of communication are the concerns of the first part of the study:

The subject Negritude, proposed . . . as an ability in a situation, is a certain experience of the world and of language which is expressed in a situation and in precise historical and geographical conditions which, therefore, impose a certain type of communication. [p. 26]

The second section considers the guise assumed by Negritude in its relationship with the world:

Reality is not apprehensible independent of the text, it has a correlative relationship with it. The real thus conceived, the referent will be read, on the one hand alongside the subject, on the other alongside the object. [p. 26]

The first two chapters are devoted to an examination of these. The third part places the text within the context of language:

In its capacity as a literary subject, Negritude possesses a complex literary experience. This transpires in a semiotic reading of the text. Elsewhere Negritude is confronted by two types of language, one French and the other Negro, and it [Negritude] releases (semiotically) from the text, a particular conception of language. [p. 26]

The three major factors conditioning Negritude seen as a "compétence"— "jeu dans la situation historique contemporaine," "jeu dans le monde réel," and "jeu dans le langage" (p. 26)—are examined in the three sections of the study. Nor does Hausser consider a purely semantic study sufficient:

It seemed indispensable . . . to penetrate into the semiotic universe. Only three ways in . . . will be considered, those precisely which the theory of Negritude privileges: phonetic redundancy, rhythms and images. [p. 27]

The complexity and eclecticism of Hausser's methodological approach are in part the corollary of the elusiveness of his object of study: Negritude. Recognizing its amorphous nature, Hausser looks to literary history (Senghor's *Anthologie*) for a coherent body of texts on which to operate his linguistic study. Hausser's *Essai sur la poétique de la négritude* testifies, once again, to the instability of Negro-African literature in French that offers neither national and linguistic nor geographic coherence as a field of study.

Concern about the political corollaries of this instability are not visible in Hausser's study, and it is, of course, in part precisely this concern for the ideological parallels of these literary-critical and theoretical problems which accounts for the methodological inconsistencies and subjectivities of the studies discussed earlier in the chapter. Hausser, on the other hand, locates Negritude within a particular textual or "biblio-historical" context fixed in the past, thereby making possible a more coherent, although self-contained, study.

Three further works provide examples of approaches to Negro-African literature in French during the relevant period. In two of them, *Sociologie du roman africain* by Sunday Anozie and *Roman africain et tradition*, by Mohamadou Kane, Negritude no longer operates as a major trope in the discussion.

In *L'Idéologie dans la littérature négro-africaine d'expression française,* it is Midiohouan's explicit purpose to rewrite the literary history of Negro-African literature in French, attributing a considerably less significant role to Negritude than in former studies.

Published in 1986, his book focuses on the ideological. Although it defines its field of investigation as "la littérature négro-africaine," with its attendant associations with the Negritude polemic, his study avoids being drawn into the Negritude debate by constant reference to the historiographical. By foregrounding the ideological, with its political and nationalistic concerns, Midiohouan recognizes that, initially, Negro-African literature belonged within a colonial, pre- (and usually pro-) nationalistic context. The concept of a "Negro-African" literature makes sense only from outside Africa, from a vantage point that can simultaneously view black literatures from a number of areas. In the early years, that vantage point was of course Paris, *locus* of the Negritude debate. However, Midiohouan also seeks to emphasize the African perspective. In particular, he points to "le roman colonial négro-africain" as the other important root from which Negro-African literature grew. Many studies, most obviously Lilyan Kesteloot's seminal work, fail to attribute much importance to the works of René Maran, Bakary Diallo, Félix Couchoro, Ousmane Socé Diop, and Paul Hazoumé, for example. What Midiohouan emphasizes is that although these works are clearly influenced by colonial perspectives in terms of their ideologies, they testify to a desire to explore Africa's past. Of Paul Hazoumé's *Doguicimi*, Midiohouan writes:

Doguicimi reveals in its author a profound knowledge of the history, habits and institutions in the Kingdom of Dahomey in the nineteenth century and gives us a panorama of daily life under the reign of Guézo.

But Paul Hazoumé approaches this society as an ethnologist, that is to say with colonialist presuppositions, by acknowledging *a priori* the superiority of Western civilization. [p. 77]

Unlike many earlier studies, Midiohouan's perspective takes into account the ambiguities of his area of study and relates this to attendant methodological problems:

The study of Negro-African literature poses the problem of the definition of a field of investigation with precise boundaries. This fact is linked to the ambiguity of the literary phenomenon, to the conditions of emergence and evolution of the production of Blacks (either Africans or of African origin), but also to the relatively recent character of literature in the European languages. [p. 13]

This study opens with a brief "Essai de titrologie" which considers the four criteria operative within different definitions of the field of investigation: racial, geographical, cultural (taken as a whole, and considered in relation to one particular characteristic), and linguistic. Rather than opting for a particular criterion or set of criteria, Midiohouan concludes:

This rapid tour . . . of the problematics of designation leads us to the conclusion that Negro-African literature is *difficult* to define; and here is an essential element of its definition, the property of being difficult to define. [p. 22]

Despite recognizing the ambiguity and difficulty associated with the definition of his field of study, Midiohouan's purpose is specific: to demonstrate that what he regards as the "dominant historiography" is based on a misconception: the role of "engagement" in the literature's genesis (p. 10). In rewriting the history of Negro-African literature in French, Midiohouan seeks to demonstrate, first, that "engagement" was not the only phenomenon responsible for the emergence of the literature and, furthermore, that a number of writers associated with its emergence were not "engagés" in the way later histories have suggested:

In the Negro-African intellectual world certain writers known today as "committed" were rather suspected, not without reason, in the eyes of their brothers, and . . . militant unanimity is no more than a myth proposed above all by criticism. [p. 11]

Midiohouan's first chapter explores problems of definition. Chapter two considers factors of literary production, 1900–1960, briefly examining education in Africa (French and Belgian), "the editorial infrastructure," and "the cultural context." Chapters three, four, and five cover the three major periods of Negro-African literature: from 1920 to 1945, from 1945 to 1960, and from 1960 onward. The first is characterized as a period of genesis, "le genèse: entre l'ambiguïté et la compromission'; the second is described as moving "du compromis à la révolte," and the third simply as "la littérature négro-africaine depuis les indépendances."

According to Midiohouan's thesis, the genesis and evolution of Negro-African literature can be correctly identified by a careful study of the ideological framework within which works of Negro-African literature were written. The institutional context provided by "la littérature coloniale" is thus emphasized in addition to the context in which Negritude was born, in Paris in the 1930s. Similarly, Midiohouan emphasizes the theatrical activities (and their traditional African elements) of the Ecole William Ponty, also in the 1930s. Negro-African literature, Midiohouan argues, is inextricably bound up with the sociopolitical context in which it is written. That context was, initially, the context of colonial literature. Since 1960, it has been the context of political independence. The preliminary association with colonial literature meant that African writers were influenced by the colonialist ideology:

> If, before the Second World War, writers supported the *civilizing mission* of France, debated tradition and modernism, the dialogue between Africa and the West while at the same time affirming—as the colonial ideology advocated—the primacy of the cultural over the political, it was because the context in which they lived did not permit them to think of the political future of Africa outside the colonial context. [p. 214]

Similarly, after the Second World War, there remained a "culturalist" vein, represented by Senghor, in particular. But, at the same time, a new generation of writers emerged who in poetry, but more particularly the novel, were committed to the denunciation of the colonial order and affirmed their desire to make literature a weapon in the fight for the liberation of Africa. Nor does Midiohouan deny the relationship between sociopolitical context and the concerns of literature after independence: "This narrow relationship . . . is also visible after independence, under the triple sign of continuity, renewal and diversification" (p. 215); continuity, in terms of themes that were present during the colonial period, which have been modified; renewal, in terms of Africa's contemporary problems, particularly in the novel; diversification, in terms of complex and rich creative possibilities.

Midiohouan's concerns are, initially, historiographical. The dominant historiography, he argues, remains that which foregrounds Negritude. As ideological concerns underpin this historiography (it argues that the birth of Negro-African literature coincides with political "engagement" by the Negritude poets), his study seeks to reinstate other ideologies that have, equally, been associated with Negro-African literature, in particular the colonial ideology. This leads him to conclude that rather than appearing suddenly at a particular historical moment, Negro-African literature emerged gradually, slowly freeing itself from a colonial ideology and asserting an ideology appropriate to an independent Africa. Thus Negritude as an ideology, and one intimately associated with a historiography, is put into perspective by Midiohouan's study.

Although written at a very particular moment in terms of literary-critical mood, Sunday Anozie's *Sociologie du roman africain: réalisme, structure et détermination dans le roman moderne ouest-africain* (1970) made a distinct contribution to the criticism of "Negro-African literature" or the "African novel," in particular. The collection in which the work was published, *Tiers monde et développement*, and the work's subtitle, give clear indications of the perspective of the study. Abandoning Negritude and the myriad critical approaches it generates, Anozie relies on the writings of Barthes, Lukacs, Balandier, Bastide, and Sartre to emphasize the role of the novelist within the changing political and social context of West Africa. The principal sociological texts on which he bases his study are Georges Balandier's *Sociologie actuelle de l'Afrique noire* (1963) and Roger Bastide's *Sociologie et Psychanalyse* (1950).

As it is the sociological that is paramount in Anozie's study, it is not confined to the work of Francophone novelists, but takes into account Anglophone novelists also:

> Novels written in West Africa, in English or French, are here considered as forming a totality or as integrated into the same literary space. [p. 8]

Anozie admits that such an "espace littéraire" is neither "coherent nor complete" but nevertheless holds that the corpus displays "fairly distinct properties . . . susceptible to an objective and careful analysis, that is to say a sociological one" (p. 8).

The two principal criteria for the inclusion of works within his study are temporal (he is concerned with the two decades between 1947 and 1967), and geographic (his study is based on the novels of West Africa). Having thus delimited his field of investigation, he proposes to "describe some aspects of the thematic system or structure of the West African novel" (p. 8). He continues:

> In other words our aim consists in extracting from this novel a body of characteristics and interdependent themes, . . . choosing for this "types of subject" (heroes or protagonists) and the nature of the conflict (the diverse incidences of tradition and modernism) which drive these novels. [p. 9]

Anozie defends his inclusion of both Francophone and Anglophone writers on the grounds that the justification for approaching them separately gives too much weight to the historical event of colonialism:

> The weakness [of this method] is a function of its presentation of too short and too static a view of the social reality of West Africa. [p. 8]

He also seeks to justify his concern to base his analysis on "thematic structure-patterns."

As Anozie's study unfolds, his thesis begins to emerge, despite his often elliptical style and misleading title. This does not concern the "sociology of the African novel," which would involve a study in which different types of novel were examined in relation to historical forces. It is, rather, a psychological study of novels' heroes located not in precise political or social situations but within a vague cultural setting. Anozie's conclusion is optimistic: the hero of the West African novel is becoming increasingly "messianic"; that is, he is becoming more and more the model of a success-ful social pioneer, combining both vision and social commitment.

Anozie's study distinguishes itself from other studies of the 1970s and 1980s for a number of reasons. First, it avoids Negritude in any guise. Second, it proposes the "West African novel" as a coherent field of study, and examines both Francophone and Anglophone novels. Third, it relies on the methods of another discipline, sociology, to a much greater extent than other studies. While his study reveals obvious shortcomings, it neverthe-less served to open up the methodological possibilities in the area. Like Midiohouan's study and Mohamadou Kane's, he also focused on the Afri-can context of African writing, rather than on the "pôle européen."

Midiohouan's study is concerned to emphasize the "pôle africain" as well as the "pôle européen" in the genesis of the literature. This is connected with the most important recent developments in the criticism of Negro-African literature, which is to emphasize the "Africanness" of African literature and to reveal its roots within African culture, African languages, and African constructs. Mohamadou Kane's *Roman africain et tradition* (1982) studies the African novel from the point of view of Afri-can tradition:

> This work has been centred around a particularly significant element of the content which allows, without losing sight of form, the identification of the power lines of the novel, to underline the unity, to retrace the story and to proceed to a synthesis of its characteristic elements and problems.
>
> No theme can better serve this end than those of tradition. [p. 15]

A study of traditions, Kane continues:

> allows the identification of certain disparities in Central West African

novels. In one case the accent is on the central role of animism in traditional culture, in the other the emphasis is on the social structures and
beliefs which echo tradition. [p. 22]

In addition, an investigation of traditions makes it possible to:

situate, to determine and explain, at the heart of current debates on African
cultures, the influence of the movements of Negritude and nationalism in
the African novel. The theme of traditions leads to the crucial problem of
the future of African cultures confronted by modernism. [p. 23]

Kane defines his use of "tradition" on the basis of the definition provided
by *A Dictionary of the Social Sciences*:

The tradition rests on the principle of "transmission" from one generation
to another, of tastes, beliefs and values. It functions like an ideology which
determines the specificity of the group. It assures the continuity, stability
and venerability. Tradition, which is a sociological reality, must not be
confused with traditionalism, which is the individual's relationship with
this last. [p. 23]

The first and second sections of Kane's study ("Tradition et identité";
"Tradition et progrès") cover the periods before and after the Second
World War. The third and final section of his study, devoted to the African
novel from 1960 onward and entitled "Traditions et perspectives," considers the question of:

The future of traditions in a world which seems to have opted for progress,
materialism, uniformity in the manner and ways of thinking, with a technical and technological bias. [p. 30]

Although Kane's overt intention is to locate a theme that will reveal the
breadth and depth of the African novel and thus provide access to its study
as a whole, his method has important historiographical ramifications also.
As he writes in his conclusion:

The birth, like the progress of the African novel, came via the
revalorization of traditions. It is significant that the emergence of this
genre is situated precisely at the end of an era, marked, in the painting of
ways and customs, landscapes and peoples of Africa, by extravagance,
fantasy, the recourse to stereotypical myths. [pp. 486–487]

Here, Kane's historiography comes close to Midiohouan's. In both cases,
African literature is seen to emerge out of colonial literature, gradually
freeing itself from the concerns of the colonial novel, whether these are

described as a group as the concerns of "colonial ideology" (in Midio-houan's case), or individually considered as "the taste for the picturesque, the unusual, the primitive" (in Kane's case). Similarly, the traits of the African novel identified by Kane, in particular recourse to tradition, could also be described as the assertion of an ideology appropriate to Africa. Furthermore, the definition of tradition that Kane uses includes an ideological dimension: "It [tradition] functions as an *ideology* which determines the specificity of the group" (p. 23; my italics). Midiohouan may use the concept of an ideology in a very much more (modern) political sense, but nevertheless, in historiographical terms, their perspectives produce a similar understanding. Kane's analysis, however, leads to a closer scrutiny of the texts themselves, whereas Midiohouan's approach tends toward an abstract discussion of the nature of the political commitment of various African writers.

Of particular significance, in terms of the history of the criticism of Negro-African literature, is the creation of a historiography—in both Midiohouan's and Kane's studies (as in Anozie's study examined earlier)—that is not dominated by Negritude. Nor does Negritude play a pivotal role in their accounts of the history of Negro-African literature. This they achieve by avoiding a "pan-negrist" perspective, on the one hand, and by emphasizing the relationship between colonial literature (and the colonial novel in particular) and the emergent African literature, on the other. Their perspectives—which foreground the ideological, in one instance, and tradition, in the other—are representative of the dominant traits in the contemporary treatment of Negro-African literature. For it is the "Africanization" of literary history and literary criticism that dominates current trends. In a sense, with the exception of Hausser's study, the studies examined earlier—Adotevi's *Négritude et Négrologue*, Towa's *Poésie de la négritude*, Kimoni's *Destin de la littérature négro-africaine*, Joppa's *L'Engagement des ecrivains africains noirs*—are moving in that direction. The discipline had to free itself from the all-pervasiveness of Negritude, in both historiographical and evaluative literary-critical terms, and these earlier studies work through this process. The discipline is now free to explore, for example, the inherently critical features of the oral tradition. As an oral text is transmitted from one teller to the next, the changes that are made are part of a critical process. It is this kind of critical phenomenon which will, more and more, concern African literary criticism, shifting the focus of debate toward the specifically African features of both oral and written literatures.

It is not exclusively within literary-critical and literary historical debate, however, that the problems and paradoxes of "Negro-African literature in French" are being explored. The concerns that are foregrounded in critical discourse have found direct expression within the African novel itself, most strikingly, in M. a M. Ngal's two novels, *Giambatista Viko ou le vol du discours africain* (1975) and *L'Errance* (1979). These works belong within the debate concerning the transposition of material from the oral to written (European) text. This area, and Ngal's novels, are considered here in the Conclusion. As always, it is literature and not criticism which has the last word. Critical problems and paradoxes become the generative tropes of the nascent literature.

NOTES

1. *Les Littératures d'expression française. Négritude Africaine, Négritude Caraïbe*, Centre d'Etudes Francophones de l'Université Paris Nord, Editions de la Francité, 1973; "Mythe et littérature africaine," *L'Afrique littéraire et artistique*, *54–55* (1979–80); "Critique et réception des littératures négro-africaines," *L'Afrique littéraire et artistique, 50* (1978).

2. *L'Oral et l'écrit*, "Itinéraires et contacts de cultures," 1, Editions l'Harmattan, 1982; "Images de l'Afrique en Occident: la presse, les médias et la littérature", *L'Afrique littéraire et artistique, 58* (1981).

3. *Le Roman contemporain d'expression française*, ed. Antoine Naaman and Louis Painchaud, Faculté des Arts, Université de Sherbrooke, Québec, Canada, 1971; see also *Littératures ultramarines de langue française, genèse et jeunesse*, Sherbrooke, Editions Naaman, 1974; *Text and Context. Methodological Explorations in the Field of African Literature. African Perspectives, 1* (1977).

4. The most significant texts that criticize Negritude are, in chronological order: G. d'Arbousier, "Une dangereuse mystification: la théorie de la négritude, *La Nouvelle Critique*, 7 (June 1949), 34–47; F. Fanon, *Peau noire, masques blancs* (1952); J.-S. Alexis, "Du Réalisme merveilleux des Haïtiens," *Présence Africaine*, *8–9–10* (1956), 245–271; A. Franklin, "La négritude: réalité ou mystification? Réflexions sur 'Orphée noir'," *Présence Africaine, 14* (1953), 287–301; F. Fanon, *Les damnés de la terre* (1961); E. Mphalele, *The African Image* (1962); R. Ménil, "Une doctrine réactionnaire: la négritude," *L'Action, 1* (1963), 37–50; R. Depestre, "J. Price-Mars et le mythe de l'Orphée noir ou les aventures de la négritude," *L'Homme et la société, 7* (1968), 171–181; F. Boulaga, "Le Bantou problématique," *P.A., 66* (1968), 4–40; D. Boukman, "La Négritude en question," *Jeune Afrique, 531* (9 March 1971), 59–61; H. Aguessy, "La Phase de la négritude," *Présence Africaine, 80* (1971), 33–48; S. Adotevi, *Négritude et Négrologues* (1972); T. Nata, "Négritude et négritudes" and M. Condé, "Pourquoi la négritude? Négritude ou révolution," in *Négritude africaine, négritude caraïbe* (1973), 146–150 and 150–154; W. Soyinka, *Myth, Literature and the African World* (1976); M. Towa, *Poésie de la négritude* (1983).

5. Interview by Depestre, Benedetti, and Timossi, *L'Afrique littéraire et artistique*, 7 (1969), 28.

Conclusion

For such a broad, ill-defined, heterogeneous, multinational, and multi-generic subject as "Negro-African literature in French" it would be absurd to expect to find any great degree of coherence in its literary history or criticism. Thus the lines of argument followed by this study do not lead to a single conclusion. Certain analytic routes do emerge, however, which a number of critics have traveled; once a particular way has been marked out, it is difficult for those arriving subsequently not to be drawn onto the previously sign-posted path. Such is the case with the analytical route left behind by Negritude. The most striking observation that can be made is the extent to which Sartre's formulations of Negritude in his complex text "Orphée noir" have directed the progress of all subsequent secondary discourse.

The shifting boundaries of the literature known by so many appellations ("négrophile," exotic, colonial, Francophone Negro-African, neo-African, African, and so on) have demanded sensitive, flexible, and original critical approaches. Criteria of definition have often been too intimately bound up with criteria of evaluation, to the point where the validity of the critical judgement has rested solely on criteria previously proposed for the definition of the text under critical scrutiny. This was most obviously the case with colonial literature, where the criteria proposed for the definition of the area were then used as a yardstick against which the early texts by Africans were measured. If the text failed to conform to these criteria of definition, the text was deemed unsuccessful.

While African texts were rapidly subsumed under "colonial literature," in the Caribbean national literatures were defined relatively early, in turn affecting literary-critical attitudes. The critical discourses surrounding Francophone West Indian and most particularly Haitian texts were to influence debates among Blacks in Paris. Similarly, black American perspectives on literature were to open up debates surrounding the aims and scope of a pan-Negrist literature.

Senghor's *Anthologie de la nouvelle poésie nègre et malgache*, prefaced by Sartre's complex, paradoxical, and elliptically argued "Orphée noir," represented both the canonization of the field of "Negro-African literature in French," and the founding of its basic critical discourse. Sartre's text testified to the critical complexity of the literature and provided a critical vocabulary for secondary discourses. Negritude was at the centre of this critical vocabulary, and Sartre exploited its critically generative features to the full, sanctioning its flexibility as a critical trope. The paradoxes of a non-French literature in French were picked up in the Debates and Congresses of the 1950s, in which issues of nationalism dominated discussion. The relative importance of race and class, explored by Sartre, was taken up later as a major subject of debate. While Sartre stressed Negritude's historicity as a literary doxy belonging to a particular historical moment, Sartre's exploitation of the term within secondary discourse guaranteed its survival as a literary-critical trope. At the same time Sartre emphasized Negritude's ideological significance, assuring it a place within political, as well as cultural, debate.

As the final chapter of the book demonstrates, Negritude continued to operate surreptitiously as an influential critical trope in studies of the 1970s and even early 1980s. This can be accounted for in a number of ways. First, while African literatures use European languages there will always be a "colonial legacy" present within the very language of the literature. This opposition between a non-French identity, culture, and civilization (features of an African literature) and the French language, lies at the centre of Sartre's analysis in "Orphée noir." It is only where African literatures are written in African languages that the theoretical concerns associated with Sartrean Negritude are no longer relevant to critical debate. Second, African literature is still relatively new and therefore still preoccupied by its ontology in a way that no established literature is likely to be. The "Africanness" of African literature is still a controversial question in contemporary debate and the concept of Negritude is, of course, in one guise, about the nature of "Africanness." Thus Negritude again finds its way into discussion.

While Negritude constantly reemerges as a central trope in literary-critical discourse, there have been periods when other key terms focused discussion. The immediate prospect of independence, for example, thrust concepts of nationalism and "engagement" into the centre of debate. Again, "engagement" was exploited in numerous guises, ranging from commitment to revolutionary Marxist objectives, to what amounted to little more than a commitment to an abstract conception of "artistic integrity."

Lilyan Kesteloot's study *Les Écrivains noirs de langue française*, the significance of which can be attributed principally to its seminal nature, focused on "engagement" as both a literary-historical concept (it was the act of "engagement," she argued, that brought about the birth of the literature) and a literary-critical one. For Kesteloot, it was a commitment to racial and cultural authenticity and to political independence which was involved. Other major studies of the 1960s gave more or less weight to these facets of "engagement" in their analyses of Negro-African literature in French, with Jahn at the racial and culturalist extreme and Sainville at the ideological extreme.

These same elements in the criticism of Negro-African literature in French emerge with greater definition from the mass of critical texts produced since 1970. Differences between more recent secondary discourses, it emerged, were differences dependent on what was foregrounded in readings of Negro-African literature in French: Negritude (as a cultural movement or an ideology), the sociological, the ideological, or African tradition. These differences are further marked by their affiliation to various European schools of criticism associated with Marxism, structuralism, and the exploitation of the resources of linguistics.

More recently, discussion of the Africanization of African criticism has been intense. Some critics have advocated the elaboration of an African esthetics based exclusively on material from the oral tradition, for example, and the resources and critical procedures inherent in the evolution of oral discourses are attracting considerable attention.

A further more recent development is the appearance of texts that in some way question the distinction between the "fictional" and the "critical" text. There is no doubt that critical discourse has had a profound influence on the evolution of African literature, but it may increasingly be the case that texts that do not advertise themselves as "secondary discourses" but rather as "fictional texts" contribute in important ways to literary-critical debate, as has been the case in recent French writing. The African critic and writer, M. a M. Ngal, in two seminal novels, *Giambatista Viko ou le viol du discours africain* (1975) and *L'Errance* (1979), explores the relative significance, for the assimilated or partly assimilated African, of African and European imaginative discourse, philosophy, and religion. This takes the fictional form in *Giambatista Viko* of a narrative that recounts the experiences of an African intellectual who, in the hope of achieving literary success, writes a novel based on material from the oral tradition. African elders judge the undertaking to be a sacrilege, a prostitution of oral material, and the protagonist is compelled to undergo initiation in various sanctuaries in order to be cured of his "alienation."

Giambatista Viko will serve as a striking warning to writers and critics who might regard the oral tradition simply as a resource to be exploited. The relationship between African discourses in African languages and European languages and structures is immensely complex. Any symbiosis, although ultimately of extreme literary and literary-critical significance, cannot be successfully brought about without enormous subtlety and sensitivity to the full significance of both traditions—and their many variants.

The texts examined in this book themselves constitute a tradition, loosely defined. Although allied to and intersected by other traditions (critical and theoretical texts concerned, for example, with African literature in general or "Third World literature"), it displays a degree of autonomy, less visible since the mid-1980s. A literary-critical tradition builds up its own momentum as a result of the interdependence of critical texts. This momentum or self-generative nature can carry debate along exciting and unexpected routes; it can also force it into cul-de-sacs. To find its way back, the route along which it has travelled has to be mapped. One of the aims of this study has been to sketch the outlines of that map in order that others can judge the direct and interesting ways along which criticism can travel—and identify the blind-alleys and circular routes of debate.

Bibliography

Unless otherwise indicated, place of publication was Paris. The only abbreviation used is: *P.A.* (*Présence Africaine*).

Abanda Ndengue, Jean-Marie, *De la Négritude au Négrisme* (Yaoundé, 1970).

Achille, L. T., "Les 'Negro Spirituals' et l'expansion de la culture noire," *P.A.*, *8–9–10* (1956), 227–237.

Achiriga, Jingiri, J., *La Révolte des romanciers noirs de langue française*; Preface by Georges Ngal (Ottawa, 1973).

Actes du Colloque sur la littérature africaine d'expression française, Dakar, 26–29 March 1963 (Dakar, 1965).

Actes du Colloque: Fonction et signification de l'Art nègre dans la vie du peuple, Dakar, 30 March–8 August 1966 (1967).

Actes du Colloque sur le théâtre négro-africain, Abidjan, 1970 (1971).

Actes du Colloque sur la négritude, Dakar, 12–18 April 1971, under the auspices of l'Union Progressiste Sénégalais (1972).

Actes du Colloque de Yaoundé: le critique africain et son peuple comme producteur de civilisation, 16–20 April, Société africaine de culture, 1973 (1977).

Actes du colloque sur la critique et récéption des littératures négro-africaines, Université de Paris III, 10–11 March 1978, *L'Afrique littéraire et artistique*, *50* (1978).

Adotevi, Stanislas, *Négritude et Négrologues* (1972).

African Literature Today: Focus on Criticism, edited by E. D. Jones (London, 1975).

L'Afrique littéraire, 77, "Fiction et autobiographie" (1985).

Aguessy, Honorat, "La phase de la négritude," *P.A.*, *80* (1971), 33–48.

Alexis, Jacques-Stephen, "Du Réalisme merveilleux des Haïtiens," *P.A.*, *8–9–10* (1956), 245–271.

Alexis, Jacques-Stephen, "Ou va le roman," *P.A.*, *13* (1957).

Allen, Samuel W., *The American Negro Writer and His Roots* (New York, 1960).

Amadi-Tshiwala, Regina, "Critical Bearings in African Literature," *P.A.*, *115* (3) (1980), 148–155.

Amuta, Chidi, *The Theory of African Literature* (London and New Jersey, 1989).

Anadou, David, *Le Fils du fétiche*, later edition (1971).

Anon, "*Batouala*, par René Maran," *Nouvelle Revue Française* (January–June 1922) 103–106.

Anozie, Sunday Ogbonna, *Sociologie du roman africain: réalisme, structure et détermination dans le roman moderne ouest-africain* (1970).

Anozie, Sunday Ogbonna, *Structural Models and African Poetics: Towards a Pragmatic Theory of Literature* (London, 1981).

Antoine, Régis, "La Relation Exotique," *Revue des Sciences Humaines*, *37* (147) (July–September 1972).

Antoine, Régis, *Les Ecrivains français et les Antilles: des premiers pères blancs aux surréalistes noirs* (1978).

Aragon, Louis, "D'une poésie nationale et de quelques exemples." *Les Lettres Françaises* (2 December 1953).

Aragon, Louis, *Journal d'une poésie nationale* (1954).

Arbousier, Gabriel d', "Une dangereuse mystification: la théorie de la négritude," *La Nouvelle Critique*, *7* (June 1949), 34–37.

Arnold, A. James, *Modernism and Negritude: The Poetry and Poetics of Aimé Césaire* (Harvard, 1981).

Ashcroft, B., Griffiths, G., & Tiffin, H., *The Empire Writes Back: Theory and Practice in Post-Colonial Literatures* (New York and London, 1989).

Azim, F., *The Colonial Rise of the Novel* (London and New York, 1993).

Bâ, A. Hampaté, "Culture Peuhle," *P.A.*, *8–9–10* (1956), 85–97.

Badibanga, *L'Eléphant qui marche sur les oeufs*; Preface by Jean-Richard Bloch (Brussels, 1931).

Balandier, Georges, "Le Noir est un homme," *P.A.*, *1* (1947), 31–43.

Balandier, Georges, "La Littérature noire de langue française," *P.A.*, *8–9* (1950), 393–402.

Balandier, Georges, *Sociologie actuelle de l'Afrique noir* (1963).

Bastide, Roger, "Variations sur la négritude," *P.A.*, *36* (1961), 7–17.

Bastide, Roger, *Sociologie et psychanalyse* (1950).

Banham, Martin, & Clive Wake, *African Theatre Today* (London, 1976).

Beier, Ulli (ed.), *An Introduction to African Literature: An Anthology of Critical Writing*, 2nd edition (London and New York, 1979).

Beti, Mongo, *Ville cruelle* (1954).

Blair, Dorothy, S., *African Literature in French: A History of Creative Writing in French from West and Equatorial Africa* (London and New York, 1976).

Blair, Dorothy S., "Etat et statut de la critique française de la littérature négro-africaine d'expression française," *Oeuvres et Critiques, III* (2)/*IV* (1) (Autumn 1979).

Blerald, Alain, *Négritude et politique aux Antilles* (1981).

Bois, W. E. B. du, *The Souls of Black Folk* (Chicago, 1903).

Bol, V. P., & J. Allary, *Littérateurs et poètes noirs* (Léopoldville, 1964).

Boukman, Daniel, "La Négritude en question," *Jeune Afrique, 531* (9 March 1971), 59–61.

Boulaga, F., "Le Bantou problématique," *P.A.*, *66* (1968), 4–40.

Brench, A. C., *The Novelists' Inheritance in Africa* (London and New York, 1967).

Brench, A. C., *Writing in French from Senegal to Cameroon* (London and New York, 1967).

Brindeau, Serge, et al., *La Poésie contemporaine de langue française depuis 1945* (1973).

Cellard, Jacques, "Négritude et francité," *Le Monde, 1* (6 April 1976), 29.

Cendrars, Blaise, *Anthologie nègre* (1947).

Césaire, Aimé, "Nègreries: Jeunesse noire et assimilation," *L'Etudiant Noir* (1935), 2.

Césaire, Aimé, "Introduction à la poésie nègre americaine," *Tropiques, 2* (1941).

Césaire, Aimé, "Poésie et connaissance," *Tropiques, 12* (1945), 157–170.

Césaire, Aimé, *Cahier d'un retour au pays natal* (1947); Preface by A Breton.

Césaire, Aimé, Préface to René Depestre, *Végétations de clarté* (1951).

Césaire, Aimé, *Discours sur le colonialisme* (1955).

Césaire, Aimé, "Réponse à Depestre, poète haïtien: éléments d'un art poétique," *P.A.*, *1–2* (1955), 113–15.

Césaire, Aimé, "Sur la poésie nationale," *P.A.*, *4* (1955), 39–41.

Césaire, Aimé, "L'homme de culture et ses responsabilités," *P.A.*, *8–9–10* (1956), 116–122.

Césaire, Aimé, "Culture et colonisation," *P.A.*, *8–9–10* (1956), 190–205.

Césaire, Aimé, "Liminaire," *Monde noir d'expression francaise, P.A.*, *57* (1966), 3–10.

Césaire, Suzanne, "Misère d'une poésie: John Antoine-Nau," *Tropiques, 4* (1941), 48–50; reprinted by J.-M. Place (Paris, 1978).

Chemain, Arlette, "Quelle critique adopter pour la littérature africaine?," *Recherche, pédagogie et culture, 35–36* (1978), 33–38.

Chemain, Roger, *La Ville dans le roman africain* (1981).

Chemain, Roger, *L'Imaginaire dans le roman africain* (1986).

Chemain Roger, & Arlette Chemain-Degrange, *Panorama critique de la littérature congolaise contemporaine* (1979).

Chemain-Degrange, Arlette, *Emancipation féminine et roman africain* (Dakar, 1980).

Cherchari, Amer, *Réception de la littérature africaine d'expression française jusqu'en 1970: essai de bibliographie* (1982).

Chevrier, Jacques, *Littérature nègre: Afrique, Antilles, Madagascar*, 3rd edition (1979).

Chinweizu, & Onwuchekwa Jemie, *The West and the Rest of Us* (New York, 1975).

Chinweizu, O. Jemie, & Ihechukwu Madubuike, *Toward the Decolonization of African Literature*, Vol.1, *African Fiction and Poetry and Their Critics* (Enugu, Nigeria, 1980).

Clavreuil, Gérard, *Erotisme et littératures* (1987).

Clifford, James, & George E. Marcus (eds.), *Writing Culture: The Poetics and Politics of Ethnography* (Berkeley, 1986).

Cohen, William B., *The French Encounter with Africans* (Bloomington, 1980).

Colin, R., *Contes noirs de l'Ouest Africain* (1957); Preface by L. S. Senghor.

Colin, R., *Littérature africaine d'hier et de demain* (1965).

Collins, Marie, *Black Poets in French* (New York, 1972).

Colloque sur littérature et esthétique négro-africaines (Abidjan-Dakar, 1979).

Condée, Maryse, "Pourquoi la négritude? Négritude ou révolution," *Négritude africaine, négritude caraïbe* (1973), 150–54.

Condée, Maryse, "Négritude césairienne, négritude senghorienne," *Revue de littérature comparée*, 48 (1974), 409–419.

Congres international des écrivains et artistes noirs I, P.A., 8–9–10 (June–November 1956).

Congres international des écrivains et artistes noirs II, Tome I, "L'Unité des cultures négro-africaines," *P.A.*, 24–25 (February–May 1959); Tome II, "Responsabilités des hommes de culture," *P.A.*, 27–28 (August–November 1959).

Cook, Mercer, & Stephen E. Henderson, *The Militant Black Writer in Africa and the United States* (Madison, 1969).

Cornevin, Robert, *Le Théâtre en Afrique noire et à Madagascar* (1970).

Cornevin, Robert, *Littératures d'Afrique noire de langue française* (1976).

Costissella, Joseph, "Genèse et évolution de la négritude: des mouvements nègres à Paris (1919–1939) à Léopold Sédar Senghor (1928–1971)" (unpublished Thèse d'état, Université de Paris IV, 1982).

Critique et réception des littératures négro-africaines, Université des Paris III, March 1978, published in *L'Afrique littéraire et artistique*, 50 (4), (1978).

Crosta, Suzanne, et al., *Perspectives théoriques sur les littératures africaines et caraibéennes* (Toronto, 1987).

Dabla, S., *Nouvelles écritures africaines* (1986).

Dailly, Cristophe, & Barthélémy Kotchy, *Propos sur la littérature négro-africaine* (Abidjan, 1984).

Dago Lezou, Gérard, *La création romanesque devant les transformations actuelles en Côte-d'Ivoire* (Abdijan-Dakar, 1977).

Damas, Léon Gontran, *Pigments* (1937).

Damas, Léon Gontran, *Poètes d'expression française 1900–1945* (1947).

Dash, J. Michael, "Marvellous Realism: The Way out of Negritude," *Black Images*, *3* (1) (1974), 80–95.

Dash, J. Michael, *Literature and Ideology in Haiti 1915–1961* (London, 1981).

Delobsom, A. A. Dim, *L'Empire de Mogho-Naba: Coutumes des Mossi de la Haute-Volta*; Preface by Robert Randau (1932).

Depestre, René, "Lettre à Ch. Dobzynski," *Les Lettres Françaises* (16 June 1955).

Depestre, René, "Réponse à Aimé Césaire: Introduction à un art poétique haïtien," *P.A.*, *4* (1955), 42–62.

Depestre, René, "J. Price-Mars et le mythe de l'Orphée noir ou les aventures de la négritude," *L'Homme et la société*, *7* (1968), 171–181.

Depestre, René, *Bonjour et adieu à la négritude*, 1980.

Desalmand, Paul, *Vingt-cinq romans clés de la littérature négro-africain* (1981).

Desportes, Georges, "Points de vue sur la poésie nationale," *P.A.*, *11* (1956–57), 88–99.

Dhombres, Dominique, "Négritude, latinité et modernité," *Le Monde* (6–7 April 1975), 7.

Diallo, Bakary, *Force-Bonté*; Preface by Jean-Richard Bloch (1926).

Diop, Alioune, "Niam n'goura ou les raisons d'être de *Présence Africaine*," *P.A.*, *1* (1947), 7–14.

Diop, Alioune, "Séance d'ouverture," *P.A.*, *8–9–10* (1956), 9–18.

Diop, David, "Contribution au débat sur la poésie nationale," *P.A.*, *6* (1956), 113–115.

Diop, Papa Samba, *La Critique littéraire négro-africaine d'expression française: situation et perspectives* (unpublished thèse de 3e cycle, Université de Paris Val-de-Marne, 1980–81).

Dogbe, Yves-Emmanuel, *Négritude, culture et civilisation: essai sur la finalité des faits sociaux* (Le Mée sur Seine, 1980).

Dorsinville, Max, *Solidarités* (Montreal, 1988).

Dubois, O., *L'Afrique reconnue: panorama de la littérature négro-africaine* (1969).

Durand, Oswald, *Rires et Pleurs I*, extracts reprinted in Louis Morpeau, *Anthologie d'un siècle de poésie haïtienne 1817–1925* (1925); Kraus reprint (Nendeln, 1970).

Egejuru, Phanuel A., *Black Writers, White Audience: A Critical Approach to African Literature* (Hicksville, NY, 1978).

Egejuru, Phanuel A., *Towards African Literary Independence: A Dialogue with Contemporary African Writers* (Westview, CT, 1980).

Egundu, Romanus N., *Modern African Poetry and the African Predicament* (London, 1978).

El Kholti, Mohamed, Léopold Sédar Senghor, et al. (eds.), *Les plus beaux écrits de l'Union Française et du Maghreb* (1947).

Eliet, Edouard, *Panorama de la littérature négro-africaine (1921–1962)* (1965).

Emeto, Julie, "Critique littéraire: l'approche sociologique est-elle efficace?," *Présence Francophone*, *17* (1978), 31–43.

Erickson, John, D., *Nommo: African Fiction in French South of the Sahara* (York, SC, 1979).

Eshleman, Clayton, & Annette Smith, *Aimé Césaire: The Collected Poetry, a Bilingual Edition* (Berkeley, Los Angeles, London, 1983).

Etiemble, "Aimé Césaire et *Tropiques*," *L'Arche*, *1* (4) (1944), 137–142.

Fabre, M. J., "*La Revue Indigène* et le Mouvement Nouveau Noir," *Revue de Littérature Comparée*, *1* (1977), 30–39.

Fanon, Frantz, *Peau noire, masques blancs* (1952).

Fanon, Frantz, *Les damnés de la terre* (1961).

Fanoudh-Siefer, Léon, *Le Mythe du nègre et de l'Afrique noire dans la littérature française de 1800 à la 2e Guerre Mondiale* (1968).

Fayolle, Roger, "*Batouala* et l'acceuil de la critique," *Actes du colloque sur la critique et la réception de la littérature africaine d'expression française* (1978), 23–29.

Fayolle, Roger, "Quelle critique africaine?," *P.A.*, *123* (1982), 103–110.

Finn, Julio, *Voices of Negritude: With an Anthology of Negritude Poems Translated from the French, Portuguese and Spanish* (London, 1988).

Finnegan, Ruth, *Oral Literature in Africa* (Oxford, 1970).

Fonlon, Bernard, *La Poésie et le réveil de l'homme noir* (Kinshasa, 1978).

Franklin, Albert, "La Négritude: réalité ou mystification? Réflexions sur 'Orphée noir'," *P.A.*, *14* (1953), 287–303.

Fraser, Robert, *West African Poetry: A Critical History* (Cambridge, 1986).

Gakwandi, Shatto Arthur, *The Novel and Contemporary Experience in Africa* (London, 1977).

Garret, Naomi M., *The Renaissance of Haitian Poetry* (1963).

Garrot, Daniel, *Léopold Sédar Senghor: critique littéraire* (Dakar, 1978).

Gassama, Makhily, *Kuma: interrogation sur la littérature nègre de langue française* (Dakar-Abdijan, 1978).

Gates Jr., Henry Louis (ed.), *Black Literature and Literary Theory* (New York and London, 1984).

Gates Jr., Henry Louis (ed.), *"Race," Writing and Difference* (Chicago and London, 1986).

Gates Jr., Henry Louis, *The Signifying Monkey: A Theory of Afro-American Literature* (New York and Oxford, 1988).

Geno, Thomas T., & Roy Julow (eds.), *Littératures ultramarines de langue française: négro-africain, antillaise, québécoise, franco-americaine, comparée: genèse et jeunesse* (Sherbrooke, 1974).

Gerard, Albert, *Essais d'histoire littéraire africaine* (1984).

Gerard, Albert, *Etudes de la littérature africaine francophone* (Dakar-Abdijan, 1977).

Gerard, Albert, "La Francophonie dans les lettres africaines," *Revue de littérature comparée, 48* (1974), 371–386.

Gikandi, Simon, *Reading the African Novel* (London, 1987).

Gleason, Judith, *This Africa: Novels by West Africans in English and French*, (Evanston. IL, 1965).

Glissant, Edouard, *Le Discours antillais* (1981).

Glissant, Edouard, "Note sur une 'poésie nationale' chez les peuples noirs," *Les Lettres Nouvelles, 4* (1) (1956), 391–397.

Gore, Jeanne-Lydie (ed.), *Négritude africaine, Négritude caraïbe* (1973).

Gourdeau, Jean-Pierre, *La littérature négro-africaine d'expression française* (1973).

Gratiant, Gilbert, "D'une poésie martiniquaise dite nationale," *P.A.*, *5* (1955–56), 84–89.

Griaule, Marcel, *Dieu d'eau: entretiens avec Ogotemmêli* (1948).

Guibert, Armand, "Les Poètes de la négritude: thèmes et techniques," *Actes du colloque sur la littérature africaine d'expression française* (1965), 219–226.

Guibert, Armand, *Léopold Sédar Senghor* (1962).

Gurnah, A. (ed.), *Essays on African Writing: A Re-evaluation* (Oxford, 1993).

Hargreaves, Alec G., *The Colonial Experience in French Fiction: A Study of Pierre Loti, Ernest Psichari and Pierre Mille* (London, 1981).

Hausser, Michel, *Essai sur la poétique de la négritude*, 2 vols. (1986).

Hausser, Michel, "Lecture idéologique et orientation textuelle," *Oeuvres et critiques, III* (2)/*IV* (1) (1979).

Hausser, Michel, *Pour une poétique de la négritude I* (1988), publication in book-form of volume one of the thesis, previously published in typescript.

Hazoumé, Paul, *Doguicimi*; Preface by Georges Hardy (1937).

Heywood, Christopher (ed.), *Perspectives on African Literature* (London, 1971).

Hoffmann, Léon-François, "French Negro Poetry," *Yale French Studies*, 21 (1958), 60–71.

Hughes, Langston, & Christiane Reygnault, *Anthologie africaine et malgache* (1962).

Hymans, Jacques Louis, *L. S. Senghor: An Intellectual Biography* (Edinburgh, 1971).

Images de l'Afrique en Occident: la presse, les médias et la littérature, Centre d'études et de recherches sur les civilisations, langues et littératures d'expression française, Université de Paris Val-de-Marne, 20–21 April 1980, *L'Afrique littéraire et artistique, 58* (1) (1981).

Irele, Abiola, *The African Experience in Literature and Ideology* (London, 1981).

Irele, Abiola, *Lectures Africaines: A Prose Anthology* (London, 1969).

Jadot, Jean-Marie, *Les Ecrivains africains du Congo Belge et du Ruanda-Urundi: une histoire, un bilan, des problèmes* (Brussels, 1959).

Jahn, Janheinz, *Manuel de la littérature néo-africaine du XVIe à nos jours de l'Afrique à l'Amerique* (1969).

Jahn, Janheinz, *Muntu: l'homme africain et la culture néo-africaine*, first published in German in Düsseldorf, 1958 (published in French, 1961).

Joachim, Paul, *Oraison pour une renaissance* (1983).

Jones, Edward, *Voices of Negritude: The Expression of Black Experience in the Poetry of Senghor, Césaire and Damas* (Valley Forge, 1971).

Joppa, Francis Anani, *L'Engagement des écrivains africains noirs de langue française: du témoignage au dépassement* (Sherbrooke, 1982).

Joualt, Didier, *Métamorphoses de l'après-indépendance dans la roman négro-africaine d'expression française* (unpublished Thèse de 3e cycle, Université de Paris XII, 1982).

Joubert, Jean-Louis, Jacques Lecarme, Elaine Tabone, & Bruno Vercier, *Les Littératures francophones depuis 1945* (1986).

Jourda, Pierre, *L'Exotisme dans la littérature française depuis Chateaubriand: Tome II, du Romantisme à 1939* (1956).

Kabongo, Bujitu, *La Littérature pour quoi faire?* (Kinshasa, 1975).

Kadima-Nzuji, Mukala, *La littérature zaïroise de langue française* (1984).

Kagamé, Abbé, *La Philosphie bantu-ruandaise de l'être* (Brussels, 1956).

Kane, Mohamadou, "Sur la critique de la littérature africaine moderne," *Le Critique africain et son peuple comme producteur de la civilisation* (1977), 257–275.

Kane, Mohamadou, *Roman africain et tradition* (1982).

Kayo, Patrice, *Panorama de la littérature camerounaise* (Baffousam, Cameroon, 1978).

Kesteloot, Lilyan, *Les Ecrivains noirs de langue française: naissance d'une littérature*, first published 1963 (6th edition, Brussels, 1977). Translated by Ellen Conroy Kennedy as *Black Writers in French: A Literary History of Negritude* (Washington, DC, 1991); quotations are from this edition.

Kesteloot, Lilyan, *Anthologie négro-africain: panorama critique des prosateurs, poètes et dramaturges noirs du XXe siècle*, first published 1967 (3rd edition, Verviers, 1981).

Kesteloot, Lilyan, *Négritude et situation coloniale* (Yaoundé, 1968).

Khatibi, A. (ed.), *Du Bilinguisme* (1985).

Kimoni, Iyay, *Destin de la littérature négro-africaine ou problématique d'une culture*, Postface by Kalanda Mabika (Kinshasa/Sherbrooke, 1975; 2nd edition, 1985).

King, Bruce, & Kolawole Ogungbesan (eds.), *A Celebration of Black and African Writing* (Ibadan, 1975).

Knight, Vere W., "Négritude and the isms," *Black Images*, *3* (1) (1974), 3–20.

Klima, Vladimir, Frantisek Ruzicka, & Petr Zima, *Black Africa: Literature and Language* (Prague, 1976).

Kom, A. (ed.), *Littératures africaines* (1987).

Kotchy, Barthélémy, "Perspectives sur la littérature négro-africaine: présentation générale," in *Situation et perspectives de la littérature négro-africaine* (1970), 85–86.

Lacharriere, J. Ladreit de, *"Batouala,"* *L'Afrique Française* (1922), 36–37.

Larson, Charles R., *Panorama du roman africain*; Introduction by Edris Makward (1975).

Larson, Charles R., *The Novel in the Third World* (Washington, DC, 1976).

Lebel, A. Roland, *L'Afrique occidentale dans la littérature française depuis 1870* (1925).

Lebel, A. Roland, *Etudes de littérature coloniale* (1928).

Lebel, A. Roland, *Le Livre du pays noir* (1928).

Lebel, A. Roland, "Poètes de l'Afrique noire," *Outre-mer, 1* (1929).

Lebel, A. Roland, *Histoire de la littérature coloniale en France* (1931).

Leblond, Marius-Ary, *Anthologie coloniale* (1946).

Lecherbonnier, Bernard, *Initiation à la littérature négro-africaine* (1977).

Leiner, Jacqueline, *Imaginaire-Langage-Identité culturelle-Négritude* (Tübingen, 1980).

Leiner, Jacqueline, *Six conférences sur la littérature africaine de langue française* (1981).

Léry, Jean de, *Histoire d'un voyage fait en la terre de Brésil* (1578), new edition with Introduction and Notes by Paul Gaffard (1880), Volume II.

Leusse, Hubert de, *Afrique occidentale: heurts et malheurs d'une rencontre: les romanciers du pays noir* (1971).

Le Vine, Victor, *Political Leadership in Africa* (Stanford, 1967).

Lezou, Gérard Dago, *La création romanesque devant les transformations actuelles en Côte-d'Ivoire* (Dakar, 1977).

Lindfors, Bernth, Ian Munro, Richard Priebe, & Reinhard Sander (eds.), *Palaver: Interviews with Five African writers in Texas* (Austin, TX, 1972).

Lindfors, Bernth, & Ulla Schild (eds.), *Neo-African Literature and Culture: Essays in Memory of Janheinz Jahn* (Wiesbaden, 1976).

Littérature africaine d'expression française (Dakar, 26–29 March 1963), Université de Dakar, "Langues et Littératures," *14*.

Littérature africaine et antillaise, double issue of *Oeuvres et Critiques, III* (2)/*IV* (1) (1979).

Littératures d'expression française: Négritude Africaine, Négritude Caraïbe, Centre d'Études Francophones, Université de Paris XIII, 26–27 January 1973.

Littératures ultramarines de langue française: Genèse et jeunesse, Actes du colloque de l'Université de Vermont, 1971 (Ottawa, 1974).

Lomami-Tshibamba, *Ngando*; Preface by G. Périer (Brussels, 1948).

Lubin, Maurice A., *L'Afrique dans la poésie haïtienne* (Port-au-Prince, 1965).

MacKay, Claude, *Banjo: A Story Without a Plot* (New York, 1929).

Madjri, Dovi J., *Sociologie de la littérature togolaise* (Lomé, 1975).

Madubuike, Ihechkwu, *The Senegalese Novel: A Sociological Study of the Impact of the Politics of Assimilation* (Washington, DC, 1980).

Makouta-Mboukou, Jean-Pierre, *Introduction à la littérature noire* (Yaoundé, 1970).

Makouta-Mboukou, Jean-Pierre, *Introduction à l'étude du roman négro-africain de langue française: problèmes culturels et littéraires* (Abidjan, 1980).

Makouta-Mboukou, J.-P. , *Spiritualités et cultures dans la prose romanesque et la poésie négro-africaines* (Abidjan, 1983).

Maran, René, *Batouala: veritable roman nègre* (1921).

Masolo, D. A., *African Philosophy in Search of Identity* (Indiana and Edinburgh, 1994).

Mateso, Locha, *La Littérature africaine et sa critique* (1986).

Matieu, Martine (ed.), *Le Roman Colonial* (1987).

Mbwil a Mpaang, Ngal, *Tendances actuelles de la littérature africaine d'expression française* (Kinshasa, 1973).

Melone, Thomas (ed.), *De la Négritude dans la littérature négro-africaine* (1962).

Melone, Thomas , "Le Thème de la négritude et ses problèmes littéraires," *Actes du colloque sur la négritude*, 103–119, and *P.A.*, *48* (1963), 133–150.

Melone, Thomas , "La Critique littéraire et les problèmes du langage: point de vue d'un Africain," *P.A.*, *73* (1970), 3–19.

Melone, Thomas , et al., *Mélanges africains* (Yaoundé, 1973).

Menil, René, "Naissance de notre art," *Tropiques*, *1* (1941).

Menil, René, "Une doctrine réactionnaire: la négritude," *L'Action*, *1* (1963).

Mérand, Patrick, *La Vie quotidienne en Afrique noire à travers la littérature africaine d'expression française* (1977).

Mérand, Patrick, & S. Dabla, *Guide de littérature africaine* (1979).

Michel, Jean-Claude, *Les Ecrivains noirs et le surréalisme* (Sherbrooke, 1982).

Midiohouan, Guy Ossito, *Contribution à l'étude de l'accueil et de la réception critique de littérature négro-africaine en France (1908–1948)* (unpublished Thèse de 3e cycle, Université de Paris III, 1979).

Midiohouan, Guy Ossito, *L'Idéologie dans la littérature négro-africaine d'expression française* (1986).

Milbury-Steen, Sarah L., *European and African Stereotypes in Twentieth-Century Fiction* (London, 1980).

Miller, Christopher L., *Blank Darkness: Africanist Discourse in French* (Chicago and London, 1985).

Milolo, Kembe, *L'Image de la femme chez les romanciers noirs francophones* (Fribourg, 1986).

Mohome, Paulus M., "Négritude: Evaluation and Elaboration," *P.A.*, *68* (1968), 122–140.

Montaigne, "Des Cannibales," *Essais*, later edition (Paris, 1962).

Moore, Gerald, *Seven African Writers* (Oxford, 1962).

Moore, Gerald, (ed.), *African Literature and the Universities* (Ibadan, 1965).

Moore, Gerald, "The Politics of Negritude," in C. Pieterse & D. Munro, *Protest and Conflict in African Literature* (London, 1969), 26–42.

Moore, Gerald, *Twelve African Writers* (London, 1980).

Morand, Paul, *Anthologie de la poésie haïtienne indigène* (Port-au-Prince, 1928).

Morpeau, Louis, *Anthologie d'un siècle de poésie haïtienne 1819–1925* (1925); Kraus reprint (Nendeln, 1970).

Mouralis, Bernard, *Individu et collectivité dans le roman négro-africain d'expression française*, Annales de l'Université d'Abidjan (Abidjan, 1969).

Mouralis, Bernard, *Les Contre-littératures* (1975).

Mouralis, Bernard, *Littérature et développement: essai sur le statut, la fonction et la représentation de la littérature négro-africaine d'expression française* (1984).

Mphalele, E., *The African Image* (London, 1962).

Mpondo, Simon, "Provisional Notes on Literature and Criticism in Africa," *P.A.*, *78* (1971), 118–142.

Naaman, Antoine, & Louis Painchaud (eds.), *Le Roman contemporain d'expression française* (Sherbrooke, 1971).

Naigiziki, J. S., *Escapade ruandaise* (Brussels, 1950)

Nantet, Jacques, *Panorama de la littérature noire d'expression française* (1972).

Nardal, Paulette, "Eveil de la conscience de race," *La Revue du Monde Noir, 6* (1932).

Nata, Théophile, "Négritude et négritudes," in *Négritude africaine, négritude caraïbe* (1973), 146–150.

Naville, Pierre, "Présence Africaine," *P.A.* (1947), 44–46.

N'diaye, Papa Gueye, *Manuel de littérature africaine* (1978).

Negritude: traditions et développement, sous la direction de Guy Michaud, Brussels, 1978, Université de Paris X, Centres d'études des civilisations, Laboratoire d'Ethnopsychologie, Colloque du printemps, 1976 et printemps 1977 sur le thème "Identité collective et relations interculturelles."

Nenekhaly-Camara, Condotto, "Conscience nationale et poésie négro-africaine d'expression française," *La Pensée, 103* (1962), 7–17.

Ngal, Mbwil a Mpaang, *Tendances actuelles de la littérature africaine d'expression française* (Kinshasa, 1973).

Ngal, Mbwil a Mpaang, *Giambatista Viko ou le viol du discours africain* (Lubumbashi, 1975).

Ngal, Mbwil a Mpaang, "La Critique de la littérature négro-africaine," *Revue de langues vivantes* (Kinshasa, January 1979), 4–12.

Ngal, Mbwil a Mpaang, *L'Errance* (Yaoundé, 1979).

Ngal, Mbwil a Mpaang, "Réception de l'oeuvre de Césaire en Zaïre," *Oeuvres et critiques, III* (2)/*IV* (1) (1979), 119–123.

Ngandu Nkashama, P. , *Comprendre la littérature africaine écrite* (1981).

Ngandu Nkashama, P., *Littératures africaines* (1984).

Ngara, Emmanuel, *Stylistic Criticism of the African Novel* (London, 1982).

Nona, E., "La Faune précolombienne des Antilles françaises," *Tropiques, 10* (1944), 42–52.

Nordmann-Seiler, Almut, *La Littérature néo-africaine* (1976).

Obenga, *Sur les chemins des hommes* (1984).

Ogunba, Oyin, & Abiola Irele (eds.), *Theatre in Africa* (Ibadan, 1978).

Ogunbesan, Kolawole (ed.), *New West African Literature* (London, 1979).

L'Oral et l'écrit, langues et littératures en contact, Centre d'études franco-phones, Université de Paris XIII, 25–26 April 1980, *Itinéraires* (1982).

Pageard, Robert, *Littérature négro-afrcaine d'expression française: le mouvement contemporain dans l'Afrique noire*, first published 1966 (4th edition, 1979).

Palmer, Eustace, *An Introduction to the African Novel* (London, 1972).

Palmer, Eustace, *The Growth of the African Novel* (London, 1979).

Paricsy, Pal (ed.), *Etude sur la littérature africaine contemporaine* (Budapest, 1971).

Peters, Jonathan, *A Dance of Masks, Senghor, Achebe, Soyinka* (Washington, DC, 1978).

Pierre-Louis, U., "Le roman français dans une impasse: perspectives comparées du roman d'Haïti, des peuples noirs et de l'Amérique Latine," *P.A.*, *27–28* (1959), 57–68.

Pieterse, Cosmo, & Donald Munro (eds.), *Protest and Conflict in African Literature* (London, 1969).

Preto-Rhodas, Richard A., *Negritude as a Theme in the Poetry of the Portuguese-Speaking World* (Florida, 1970).

Price-Mars, J., *Ainsi parla l'oncle* (Compiégne, 1928).

Price-Mars, J., "Séance d'ouverture," *P.A.*, *8–9–10* (1956), 7–8.

"Prix Coloniaux," *Outre-Mer*, *1* (1929).

Quillateau, Claude, *Bernard Binlin Dadié, l'homme et l'oeuvre* (1967).

Rancourt, *Poètes et poèmes* (1981).

Randau, Robert, *Diato* (1923).

Reboullet, André, & Michel Tetu (eds.), *Guide culturel: civilisations et littératures d'expression française* (1977).

Revue du Monde Noir (1931–32); Kraus reprint (Nendeln, 1971).

Rial, Jacques, *Littérature camerounaise de langue française* (Lausanne, 1972).

Ricard, Alain, *Théâtre et nationalisme: Wole Soyinka et LeRoi Jones* (1972).

Riffaterre, Michael, *Essai de stylistique structurale* (1971).

Le Roman Colonial, presented by Martine Mathieu, 1987.

Rombault, Marc, *La poésie négro-africaine d'expression française* (1976).

Roscoe, Adrian, *Mother Is Gold: A Study in West African Literature* (London and New York, 1971).

Rouch, Alain, & Gérard Clavreuil, *Littératures nationales d'écriture française: Afrique noire, Caraïbes, Océan Indien, histoire littéraire et anthologie* (1986).

Roumain, J., "Après-midi," *La Trouée*, *3* (1927), 1; reprinted in C. St-Louis & M. A. Lubin, *Panorama de la poésie haïtienne* (Port-au-Prince, 1950); Kraus reprint (Nendeln, 1970), pp. 393–394.

Sadji, Abdoulaye, *Nini, mulâtresse de Sénégal* (1954, reissue 1955).

Said, E., *Culture and Imperialism* (London, 1993).

Sainville, Léonard, "Le Roman et ses responsabilités," *P.A.*, *27–28* (1959), 31–48.

Sainville, Léonard, *Anthologie de la littérature négro-africaine: Tome 1, Romanciers et conteurs négro-africains* (1963).

Sanon, J. Bernadin, *Images socio-politiques dans le roman négro-africain* (Sherbrooke, 1982).

Sartre, Jean-Paul, "Orphée noir," Introduction to L.S.Senghor, *Anthologie de la nouvelle poésie nègre et malgache de langue française* (1948), IX–XLIV; also in *Situations III* (1949), 229–286; translations by S. W. Allen (1976).

Schipper-De-Leeuw, Mineke, *Le Blanc vu d'Afrique: le Blanc et l'Occident au miroir du roman négro-africain de langue française des origines au Festival de Dakar (1920–1966)* (Yaoundé, 1973).

Schipper-De-Leeuw, Mineke, *Text and Context: methodological explorations in the field of African literature* (Leiden, 1976).

Senghor, Léopold Sédar, *Hosties noires* (1948).

Senghor, Léopold Sédar (ed.), *Anthologie de la nouvelle poésie nègre et malgache de langue française*; Preface by Jean-Paul Sartre, "Orphée noir," first published, 1948 (second edition, 1969); quotations from "Orphée noir" are from S. W. Allen's translation (1976).

Senghor, Léopold Sédar, "L'Esprit de la civilisation ou les lois de la culture négro-africaine," *P.A.*, *8–9–10* (1956), 51–65, reprinted under the title, "L'Esthétique négro-africaine," in *Liberté II* (202–217).

Senghor, Léopold Sédar, "Suite du débat autour des conditions sur la poésie nationale chez les peuples noirs: réponse," *P.A.*, *5* (1955–1956), 79–83.

Senghor, Léopold Sédar, "De la Négritude: psychologie du Négro-africain," *Diogène*, *37* (1962), 3–16.

Senghor, Léopold Sédar, *Liberté I: négritude et humanisme* (1964).

Senghor, Léopold Sédar, "Sur la poésie: l'émotion nègre et le verbe," *Afrika*, *7* (2) (1966), 42–47.

Senghor, Léopold Sédar, *Les Fondements de l'Africanité ou négritude et arabité* (1967).

Senghor, Léopold Sédar, "Qu'est-ce que la négritude?," *Etudes françaises* (Montreal), *3* (1) (1967), 3–20.

Senghor, Léopold Sédar, *Liberté II: nation et voie africaine du socialisme* (1971).

Senghor, Léopold Sédar, "Problématique de la négritude," *Colloque sur la négritude*, 13–28; also in *P.A.*, *78* (1971), 3–26; and in *Liberté III*, 268–289.

Senghor, Léopold Sédar, *La Parole chez Paul Claudel et chez les négro-africains* (Dakar, 1973).

Senghor, Léopold Sédar, *Liberté III: négritude et civilisation de l'universel* (1977).

Senghor, Léopold Sédar, *La Poésie de l'action* (1980).

Serequeberhan, T., *The Hermeneutics of African Philosophy: Horizon and Discourse* (New York and London, 1994).

Serpos, Noureini Tidjani, *Aspects de la critique africaine* (1987).

Situations et perspectives de la littérature négro-africaine, Colloque de l'Université d'Abidjan, 16–25 April 1969, *Annales de l'Université d'Abidjan*, Série D (Abidjan, 1970).

Snyder, Emile, "The Problems of 'Negritude' in Modern French Poetry," *Comparative Literary Studies*, University of Maryland (1963), 101–114.

Soyinka, Wole, "L'Ecrivain dans l'Afrique contemporaine," *L'Afrique actuelle*, *19* (1967), 2–4.

Soyinka, W., *Myth, Literature and the African World* (London and New York, 1976).

Spivak, G. C., *The Post-Colonial Critic: Interviews, Strategies, Dialogues*, edited by Sarah Harasym (New York and London, 1990).

Statutes of the Académie des Sciences Coloniales (1922).

Steins, Martin, "Littérature engagée," *Oeuvres et Critiques, III* (2)/*IV* (1) (Autumn 1979), 181–195.

Steins, Martin, "Les Antécédents et la genèse de la négritude senghorienne" (unpublished Thèse d'Etat, Université de Paris III, 1981).

Sthele, H., "Les Dénominations génériques des végétaux aux Antilles françaises: histoire et légendes qui s'y attachent," *Tropiques, 10* (1944), 53–87.

Tempels, Placide, *La Philosophie Bantoue*, first published 1948 (French translation, 1949).

Text and Context: Methodological Explorations in the Field of African Literature (Leiden, 20–24 September 1976), special issue of *African Perspectives, 1* (1977).

Le Théâtre négro-africain, Abidjan, 15–20 April 1970 (1971).

Tollerson, Marie S., *Mythology and Cosmology in the Narratives of Bernard Dadié and Birago Diop* (Washington, DC, 1981).

Tougas, Gérard, *Les Ecrivains d'expression française* (1973).

Towa, Marcien, *Léopold Sédar Senghor: négritude ou servitude?* (Yaoundé, 1971).

Towa, Marcien, "Poésie de la négritude: approche structuraliste" (thèse de 3e cycle, Ecole Pratique de Hautes Etudes, 1969; subsequently published, Paris, 1983).

Traore, Bakary, *Le Théâtre négro-africain et ses fonctions sociales* (1958).

Tshiwala, Amadi, "Critical bearings in African Literature," *P.A., 115* (1980), 148–155.

Tshonga, Onyumbe, "La Critique littéraire dans la revue *Présence Africaine* de 1947 à 1975" (unpublished Thèse de 3e cycle, Université de Bordeaux III, 1979).

Umezinwa, Wilberforce, *La Réligion dans la littérature africaine: étude sur Mongo Beti, Benjamin Matip, et Ferdinand Oyono* (Kinshasa, 1975).

Viatte, Auguste, *Histoire comparée des littératures francophones* (1980).

Von Grunebaum, G. E., *French African Literature: Some Cultural Implications* (The Hague, 1964).

Wade, A. Mustapha, "Débat autour des conditions d'une poésie nationale chez les peuples noirs: autour d'une poésie nationale," *P.A.*, *11* (1956–1957), 84–87.

Wake, Clive, "The Political and Cultural Revolution," in C. Pieterse & D. Munro, *Protest and Conflict in African Literature* (1969), 43–55.

Wake, Clive, "The Personal and the Public: African Poetry in French," *Review of National Literatures*, *2* (2) (1971), 104–123.

Wall, C. A. (ed.), *Changing Our Own Words: Essays on Criticism, Theory, and Writing by Black Women* (London, 1990).

Warner, Keith, *Voix française du monde noir* (1984).

Wauthier, Claude, *L'Afrique des africains: inventaire de la négritude*, first published 1964 (3rd edition, 1977).

Wauthier, Claude, *The Literature and Thought of Modern Africa*, first published 1966 (2nd edition, London, 1978).

Williams, P., & Chrisman, L. (eds.), *Colonial Discourse and Post-Colonial Theory: A Reader* (New York, 1994).

Wright, Edgar, "African Literature: Problems of Criticism," *Journal of Commonwealth Literature*, *2* (1966), 103–112.

Wright, Edgar (ed.), *The Critical Evaluation of African Literature* (London, 1973).

Yale French Studies, "Post-Colonial Conditions: Exiles, Migrations, and Nomadisms," *83* (1 & 2) (1993).

Yoder, Carroll, *White Shadows: A Dialectical View of the French African Novel* (Washington, DC, 1980).

Zadi Zaorou B., "La parole poétique dans la poésie africaine: domaine de l'Afrique de l'Ouest francophone" (unpublished thèse d'Etat, Université de Strasbourg II, 1981).

Zuccarelli, Guy, "Un Portrait du Docteur Price-Mars," *La Revue du Monde Noir*, *3* (1932); Kraus reprint (Nendeln, 1971), 22–25.

Index

About the Author

BELINDA ELIZABETH JACK is Lecturer in French at Christ Church, University of Oxford. She has been appointed British Academy Post-doctoral Fellow at the European Humanities Research Centre in Oxford. She is the author of *An Introduction to Francophone Literatures*.

ISBN 0-313-29511-5

90000>

EAN

9 780313 295119

HARDCOVER BAR CODE